P9-DGR-286

CO
RE

THE CONSCIOUSNESS REFORMATION

Robert Wuthnow

UNIVERSITY OF CALIFORNIA PRESS
Berkeley   Los Angeles   London

University of California Press
Berkeley and Los Angeles, California

University of California Press, Ltd.
London, England

Copyright © 1976 by
The Regents of the University of California

ISBN 0-520-03138-5
Library of Congress Catalog Card Number: 75-27937
Printed in the United States of America

CONTENTS

In Memory of
VICTOR ROBERT WUTHNOW
(1905–1965)

PREFACE

For some years, a gradual, largely imperceptible, yet overwhelmingly profound cultural shift has been taking place in American society. This shift has wrought changes in our basic conceptions of ourselves and in the meanings we ascribe to our worlds. Although there are perhaps many ways in which to describe this shift, its fundamental components can be readily identified: an ever declining willingness to attribute the ultimate governance of life to the supernatural; a correlative decline in the rugged individualistic ethos that flourished so prominently throughout the nineteenth century and that even today has far from disappeared; a dramatic increase in the prevalence of scientific understandings of life and perhaps most significantly of social scientific understandings which emphasize the importance of social, economic, and cultural forces in human affairs; and more recently, and therefore as yet less profound, an increase in the popularity of what might be called mystical or experiential understandings of reality which rely more on intuitive insights into the nature and meaning of life than on logical or philosophical explanations.

Societies are organized with reference to systems of ultimate meaning such as those just described. Conceptions of the forces ultimately and eternally governing reality serve either to undergird or to undermine systems of political authority, methods of distributing scarce economic resources, styles of family life, and standards of moral conduct in relation to one's self and to one's neighbor. When these conceptions change, changes in the concrete patterns of societies often follow. Our interest in the present volume is to examine the effects that the current cultural shift away from theism and individualism and toward science and mysticism is having in both the private and public realms of society. We are concerned chiefly with documenting the great extent to which the public's willingness to support or participate in various efforts to change life styles and social arrangements, on the one hand, and its tendency

vii

to resist such changes, on the other, is influenced by its location with respect to the alternative conceptions of reality that are now competing for ascendancy. Although much of our discussion is concerned with describing these influences in a strictly contemporary setting, we also present historical evidence which situates the cultural shifts at issue in a broader perspective and which allows some educated speculations to be made about the future.

The problem on which this study focuses is clearly of contemporary importance both to those who are engaged in the struggle to bring about improved social conditions and to those who are simply interested in trying to understand more fully the changes going on around them. But the problem of specifying the relations between alternative cultural meaning systems and the concrete conditions of social life is also one that has stimulated scholars throughout history and that is likely to continue to do so in the future. Therefore, we have attempted in the pages that follow to focus not only on recent social and cultural events but to present a general theoretical discussion of the nature of cultural meaning systems and to illustrate a method of studying such meaning systems empirically which hopefully will be of broader application than to the contemporary period alone.

The research reported here was initially inspired by a desire to make sense of the waves of protest and unrest that swept the nation's campuses during the late 1960s and early 70s. Although much research was already being conducted on the so-called counter-culture at that time, little systematic attention had been devoted to the deeper cultural meanings—the symbols, the assumptions, the values, in short, the "consciousness"—of those involved in the counter-culture. Hence, with the generous assistance of a grant from the Institute for Religion and Social Change to Professors Charles Y. Glock and Robert N. Bellah at the University of California, Berkeley, a four-year research project commenced in early 1971 to examine the symbolic (and especially the "religious") dimensions of the counter-culture. The study called for a series of in-depth inquiries into the nature of specific religious, quasi-religious, and political movements associated with the counter-culture, the results of which have been published in a separate volume entitled _The New Religious Consciousness,_ Charles Y. Glock and Robert N. Bellah, editors, and a more general cultural assessment using historical and survey research methods.

As the study got under way, it became evident that the student protests of the sixties were only the visible tip of a much more general cultural development which had been emerging for several decades and which seemed likely to continue long after the highly vocal fervor of the counter-culture itself had dissipated. It also became clear as the study progressed that the broader cultural shift with which we were concerned could scarcely be examined in anything but a preliminary way by a single study such as ours. Convinced both of the profound historical importance of the current cultural shift and of the unique opportunity afforded by the counter-culture and the broader social unrest surrounding it for examining the general relations between alternative forms of consciousness and social change, we have nevertheless ventured to publish the conclusions of our inquiries, tentative though they necessarily must be.

In the course of writing this book I have incurred many debts which can never be fully repaid. Without the generosity of the Institute for Religion and Social Change and the gracious encouragement of its directors, John Phillip and Daniel Dever, this study would likely have never been initiated. Its completion was also greatly facilitated by an international conference on new religious consciousness organized and hosted by the institute in Honolulu in 1974.

Robert Bellah and Charles Glock administered the larger research project of which the present study was a part and tirelessly read working papers, chaired seminars, rewrote survey questions, edited manuscripts, pointed out theoretical oversights and logical inconsistencies, and more than once rescued those of us who were fledgling researchers from the hands of failure and despair. Their ideas are omnipresent in the pages that follow in a way that footnotes can never fully reflect. To them also must be given credit for bringing together the research team, known eventually as the Berkeley Religious Consciousness Group, which, through countless hours of informal association and discussion, contributed immeasurably to the present study: Randy Alfred, Barbara Hargrove, Donald Heinz, Gregory Johnson, Karen Landsman, Ralph Lane, Linda Pritchard, Harlan Stelmach, Donald Stone, Alan Tobey, James Wolfe.

A considerable debt to the staff of the Survey Research Center at the University of California, Berkeley, for conducting the field research, the results of which form the backbone of the present report, must also be acknowledged. William Nicholls drew the sample and administered the entire field operation. Charlotte

Coleman supervised the interviewing staff. Heidi Nebel cleaned the raw data and readied it for computer analysis. Karen Muhonen assisted ably as both secretary and programmer. Tom Piazza performed most of the actual computer processing.

Early drafts of the manuscript were typed by Karen Muhonen and by Emily Harris. The final manuscript was typed by Janet Mesik and proofread by Robbie Crane, Sandy Goers, and Renette Saunders.

All or parts of the manuscript were read by Robert Bellah, Charles Glock, Steven Hart, Donald Heinz, Tom Piazza, Donald Stone, Guy E. Swanson, and Claude Welch. Their comments stimulated many much-needed revisions. I am also especially grateful to Joseph Breznau, Otis Dudley Duncan, Richard Kalish, Charles McCoy, Zwi Werblosky, and Bryan Wilson for valuable comments and criticisms.

Finally, I owe a deep debt of gratitude to the women in my life— my wife, Sally, my daughters, Robyn and Brooke, and my mother, Kathryn—who agonized, consoled, rejoiced, suffered, and celebrated with me in the private travail without which no books would ever be written.

R.W.

INTRODUCTION

Every age has known social unrest, turmoil, and change, but our time has provided an exceptionally well-furnished laboratory in which to observe the processes of social conflict and transformation. The late 1960s and early 70s will long be remembered for the extensive variety of social experiments they produced not only in politics but in family styles and living arrangements, religion, education, dress, and leisure activities. This so-called counter-culture for a time consumed the imaginations and energies of a whole cohort of young people. Communes once again flourished in sufficient numbers to arouse more attention from scholars than they had for over a century. For the first time in American history Eastern religious movements were popular enough to command widespread investigation. Political groups like SDS (Students for a Democratic Society) and the SLA (Symbionese Liberation Army) earned reputations capable of making them objects of debate and analysis for years to come. Besides these more visible manifestations of social unrest, gradual changes have also occured in standards of sexual conduct, in attitudes toward racial and sexual minorities, in religious commitment, in political opinions, and in other indicators of public response toward basic social institutions, many of which have continued to show change even as the more visible forms of counter-cultural activity have subsided. In combination, these various manifestations of social unrest and experimentation add up to a major historical development in American society having profound practical and theoretical implications.

The purpose of this book is to formulate and test insofar as possible a theory explaining the recent upsurge of experimentation with alternative life styles and social arrangements and the broader climate of support that has surrounded this experimentation. The theory presented stresses the role of longer-range cultural shifts which have created a "new consciousness" in which experimentation with social alternatives tends to be regarded as more meaningful and legitimate than it has in the past. This emphasis is in contrast with previous

1

analyses of the counter-culture, and of protest more generally, which have largely neglected the influence of broader cultural tendencies, focusing instead on "objective" social causes such as strains within the economic or educational systems or opportunities formed by sustained economic affluence.[1] Hence, the larger purpose of the present study is to offer a theoretical and conceptual discussion of symbolic cultural constructions which may have applications for understanding instances of social unrest and transformation more generally.

In choosing to focus on the ways in which people subjectively understand their lives rather than on objective social conditions, we are siding with a perspective on human behavior that assumes that people seldom act solely on the basis of objective social circumstances, but rather according to the meanings they attribute to their circumstances. This perspective is, of course, in keeping with a long tradition of social theory including both the Weberian and symbolic interactionist positions. We also accept as given the assumption that people adopt relatively comprehensive or transcendent, but nonetheless identifiable, understandings of life which inform their attitudes and actions under a wide variety of conditions. Accordingly, our concern is not so much with the immediate, transitory meanings that develop in particular social situations, but with the overarching symbolic

1. Among the more general treatments of the rise of contemporary social experiments, see Kenneth Keniston, *The Uncommitted: Alienated Youth in American Society* (New York: Dell Publishing Company, 1965), *Young Radicals: Notes on Committed Youth* (New York: Harcourt, Brace & World, 1968), *Youth and Dissent: The Rise of a New Opposition* (New York: Harcourt Brace Jovanovich, 1971); Theodore Roszak, *The Making of a Counter Culture: Reflections on the Technocratic Society and Its Youthful Opposition* (Garden City, N.Y.: Doubleday & Company, 1969), *Where the Wasteland Ends: Politics and Transcendence in Postindustrial Society* (Garden City, N.Y.: Doubleday & Company, 1972); Charles A. Reich, *The Greening of America* (New York: Bantam Books, 1970); Lewis S. Feuer, *The Conflict of Generations* (New York: Basic Books, 1969); Philip Slater, *The Pursuit of Loneliness: American Culture at the Breaking Point* (Boston: Beacon Press, 1970); Erik H. Erikson (ed.), *The Challenge of Youth* (New York: Doubleday & Company, 1965), especially chapters by Bruno Bettelheim, Talcott Parsons, and Reuel Denney; Seymour Martin Lipset, *Rebellion in the University* (Boston: Little, Brown & Company, 1972); Harvey Cox, *The Feast of Fools* (New York: Harper & Row, 1969); Gibson Winter, *Being Free: Reflections on America's Cultural Revolution* (New York: The Macmillan Company, 1970); and William Braden, *The Age of Aquarius: Technology and the Cultural Revolution* (New York: Pocket Books, 1971).

frames of reference, which we shall refer to as *meaning systems,* by which people come to grips with the broader meaning and purpose of their lives. In particular, we are concerned with discovering whether or not there may be some change taking place in the transcendent systems of symbolic meaning inherent in American culture, some change that has been conducive to the origin and development of social experiments and that may continue to nourish social experimentation in the future.

The possibility of some general shift in American world views is not an unfamiliar theme among observers of the culture. Many students of American religion have argued that Christianity is slowly withering away, to be replaced by some variety of personalistic, humanistic, or scientific world view. Other students of religion have seen a trend away from hard and fast doctrines toward a more experiential and mythic approach to the questions of meaning and purpose in life.[2] Observers of the more general culture have for a long time claimed that people are becoming less individualistic in their thinking and more collectivistic or other-directed. Other scholars have tried to show that so-called modern, scientific world views have begun to recede relative to world views that are somehow more primitive and mystical.

The present study is focused on four meaning systems, each of which supplies a distinct understanding of the meaning and purpose of life and each of which appears to be dominant among a fairly sizable segment of the American people. Each of these broad systems of meaning seems to be either conducive to or antagonistic to social experimentation. Each has also been thought by some social observers to be either gaining or losing prominence in American culture. These meaning systems are distinguished from one another by what they identify as the *primary force governing life.*

The first meaning system, which will be called the *theistic* mode, lies at the center of America's major religious traditions. It is an understanding of life that identifies God as the agent who governs

2. Two discussions of macroscopic change in religious orientations to which the present study is especially indebted are Charles Y. Glock, "Images of 'God,' Images of Man, and the Organization of Social Life," in Charles Y. Glock (ed.), *Religion in Sociological Perspective: Essays in the Empirical Study of Religion* (Belmont, Calif.: Wadsworth Publishing Company, 1973); and Robert N. Bellah, "Religious Evolution," in *Beyond Belief: Essays on Religion in a Post-Traditional World* (New York: Harper & Row, 1970), pp. 20–50.

life. God is assumed to have a purpose for each person's life. He watches over and cares for each person, hears his prayers, and guides him in his daily decisions. Through knowing God, trusting in him, and following his will, one finds meaning and happiness. God is also assumed to be the creator of the universe and the one who directs the course of history. He has established laws, found in the Bible, which men should obey both in their private lives and in the affairs of state.

The second meaning system is what has become known as rugged American *individualism*. Rather than God being the agent who governs life, the individual is in charge of his own destiny. He is free to choose his own goals in life. He sets his own course; there is no predetermined path he must follow. Success or failure is attributed to the characteristics of the person himself. In the classic American version of individualism these characteristics tend to include such virtues as hard work, willpower, determination, thrift, honesty, and the avoidance of such vices as laziness, drunkenness, and deceit. The most basic of these is willpower, for a person is totally free to follow good or to choose evil. The person with a strong will who cultivates these various characteristics is assured of happiness and good fortune.

The third meaning system has found its clearest expression in modern *social science*. Like individualism, it stresses the role of man in human affairs rather than God. But unlike individualism, it understands life to be governed chiefly by social forces rather than individuals. Family background, social status, income, the society a person resides in, the nature of the political system he lives under, influence him more than anything else. An individual does not simply choose his own goals, he is socialized into them. In one culture he is likely to believe in one set of goals; in another culture, in a different set. One's happiness and good fortune are not entirely within his control; they vary according to the kind of chances the society has given him.

The fourth meaning system is most akin to *mysticism*. Unlike the other three meaning systems which presume to understand the meaning of life and the forces that govern life, it holds that such things cannot be understood; they can only be grasped intuitively from the experiences one has, particularly from the mystical or ecstatic experiences one has. In such experiences the blinders of normal perception are stripped away and one ''sees'' that life makes sense, one feels that it hangs together. But the mystic does not rely solely on sheer feelings. He too has a philosophy about the forces governing life, just as the proponents of the other forms of consciousness do. The forces that influence his life most are his own intense experiences. In such experiences he can alter time and space. He can experience God. He can escape the social and cultural forces that impinge upon him. He can create reality itself.

These meaning systems are not necessarily mutually exclusive. Since virtually all Americans have been exposed at one time or another to each of them, it is entirely probable for some people to espouse more than one at the same time. Nevertheless, each clearly offers different interpretations of the influences that people feel impinging upon their lives.

In focusing on these meaning systems and their relations to contemporary social unrest and experimentation we do not mean to discount the importance of more objective social factors. To the extent that a shift in consciousness can be discerned, this shift undoubtedly has its roots in other changes that have taken place in social, political, and economic structures. But our primary concern is not with these structural changes. It is instead with the character of the four meaning systems we have briefly introduced and with their *independent* role in helping to legitimate, or else in helping to legitimate opposition to, contemporary forms of social experimentation.

DESIGN OF THE STUDY

In deciding how best to examine the nature of the relation between trends in different meaning systems and contemporary social experimentation, one option would have been to study the members of specific groups or movements that have actually spearheaded this experimentation. The larger research project of which the present study is a part, in fact, included some studies of such groups. It was recognized, however, that these studies by themselves would be limited in two respects. First, an understanding of why people engage in social experimentation obviously requires some understanding of the people who don't. A study focused only on new groups would reveal little about the differences between their participants and people pursuing more ordinary styles of life. Second, much of what has aroused attention in recent years as social experimentation is not embodied in any specific group or movement or, if it is, this embodiment represents only the iceberg tip of a larger but less visible form of experimentation. The few groups who advocate eating organic foods clearly do not subsume the wider but less organized degree of interest in organic foods that exists in the society. The relatively small numbers of people who engage in demonstrations or who join revolutionary political groups should not be dissociated from the larger number of people who value radical political change or the even larger group who are deeply disenchanted with existing political structures. Other forms of social experimentation may be even more difficult to pin down to any specific group or even to any specific form of personal activity. Much of the commentary on the so-called counter-culture among youth in the late sixties described it chiefly as a new set of values, such as valuing the inner self, valuing body awareness, valuing more intimate relations with others. Still other forms of social experimentation consist mostly of an attitudinal willingness to vote for or support in other ways various social policies; for example, legalizing marijuana, granting more freedom to homosexuals, changing the tax system, limiting the power of the police. A study focused on the members of specific social movements would obviously fail to tap these more subtle forms of social experimentation.

For these reasons, a study of a more general sample of people was decided upon. For purposes of describing the extent of various social experiments, the best focus for this study would obviously have been a sample of the national population. For analytic purposes, however, this was not the best option. First, because of the greater costs of conducting a national survey instead of a survey of some local population, a national survey, given a fixed budget, would have meant being able to obtain considerably less information from each person in the study. Since no standard, efficient way has been developed to measure different meaning systems, it was necessary to obtain a fairly large body of information from each person interviewed. Second, many of the attitudes, values, and life styles with which this study is concerned have not yet become widespread in the American population generally. Because of the possibility that they may become more widespread, however, it seemed fruitful to study them where they were already most fully developed; that is, where enough people were experimenting with new things and where the relations between these things and other social and cultural factors had become crystallized enough that a detailed analysis could be pursued.

The population that satisfied all of these conditions was the San Francisco Bay Area. Not only was it convenient to the University of California, Berkeley, from where the study was administered, making it efficient for both survey methods and the ethnographic methods called for by the larger project, it was and is a focal point for much cultural ferment and social change. It was here that much of the so-called new culture among youth was born and continues to be nourished. Consequently the Bay Area provides a natural laboratory for the study of social experimentation. It affords an opportunity to view a variety of novel social and cultural experiments while they are still in an early stage of development and before they perhaps become more widely diffused throughout American culture.

The data upon which this inquiry is based were collected from a sample of 1,000 randomly selected persons living in the San Francisco-Oakland Standard Metropolitan Statistical Area (Alameda, Contra Costa, Marin, San Francisco, and San Mateo counties).[3]

The sample was designed to yield a larger sample of youth (age 16 to 30) relative to their numbers in the general population than of "mature" respondents (age 31 and over), since one of the interests

3. The sample was chosen by first selecting 116 census tracts, representing 116 geographic areas each relatively homogeneous in ethnic composition, type of housing, and economic level. The probability of each tract being chosen was proportionate to the numbers of household residents age 16 and over as reported by the 1970 U.S. Census. (As is standard practice, residents living in institutions such as prisons, mental hospitals, convalescent homes, and military reservations, or in other group quarters—totaling 2.6 percent of the San Francisco Standard Metropolitan Statistical Area—were excluded from the sample.) From these 116 tracts, 4 in outlying districts, all predominantly rural, over 50 miles from the center of the metropolitan area, and comprising less than 0.5 percent of the total SMSA population, were excluded to make the sample more reflective of the metropolitan community and to reduce travel costs in interviewing. In the remaining 112 tracts, 2 blocks in each were chosen (probability proportionate to the numbers of housing units reported in the 1970 Census) and a full list of the housing units on these 224 blocks was prepared by visits to each block. From these blocks a sample of 1,800 housing units was randomly selected. In addition, a sample of 10 dormitory rooms was selected to represent the number of persons living in such quarters. Next, interviewers were sent to these 1,810 units, where they listed each household member and then selected respondents, using a "Respondent Selection Label" that randomly indicated which person or persons to interview depending on the number of persons in each household.

BRIDWELL LIBRARY
SOUTHERN METHODIST UNIVERSITY
DALLAS, TEXAS 75275

of the study is to examine generational differences in understandings of life, values, and attitudes. Consequently, in each household with at least one person age 16 to 30 an interview was either completed or attempted, while among the households with persons age 31 and over, half were randomly excluded.[4] In parts of the subsequent analysis where it is desired that data be representative of the general population, a weighting factor is merely assigned which gives each person over age 30 approximately double the weight of each person under 30.[5]

Interviews lasting approximately one hour and fifteen minutes and conducted by professional interviewers were done with each person in the sample. Each interview consisted of over 350 questions covering assumptions about meaning in life, religious beliefs, per-

4. Of the original 1,810 households drawn, 649 contained someone age 16 through 30, 1,286 someone over 30 (316 households contained persons both under and over age 30), 79 households were vacant, and the composition of the remaining 113 households was undetermined either because of people chronically not at home (up to a dozen calls were made at many of these homes) or refusals to cooperate. Of the 649 households with youths, interviews were completed in 565, a response rate of 87 percent, and of the 1,286 households with mature respondents, 674 were randomly excluded, leaving 612 households, of which interviews were completed in 435 or 71 percent. Response rates for youths and mature respondents in 12 geographic areas represented by the 112 census tracts are presented in Appendix C as is a comparison of the demographic characteristics of respondents interviewed with those of the larger Bay Area population.

5. The weight assigned to people age 16 through 30 is .5805 and to people over age 30 is 1.5448. These weights were derived as follows: of the 649 screened households found to contain at least one youth, the number of youths in the household was reported on the screening form for 647. These households contained a total of 1,025 youths. Adjusting for the two households not screened gives 1,025 x 649/647 = 1,028. Of the 612 not randomly excluded households with at least one person over 30, 596 were screened, containing a total of 976 such persons. Adjusting for the nonscreened households gives 976 x 612/596 = 1,002. But there were 1,286 households with people over 30, counting those randomly excluded. Adjusting for random exclusions gives 1,002 x 1,286/612 = 2,106. Thus, the estimated proportion of youths is 1,028/(1,028 + 2,106) or 32.8 percent, virtually the same proportion as that given by the 1970 census for the Bay Area (32.6 percent). And the proportion of older people is 67.2 percent (children under age 16 are not included in these computations). A representative sample of 1,000 Bay Area residents, therefore, would contain 328 youths and 672 older people. But since the sample actually contains 565 youths and 435 older people, the number of youths needs to be multiplied by .5805 to equal 328 and the number of older people needs to be multiplied by 1.5448 to equal 672.

sonal experiences, values and aspirations, political opinions, life style, and background. The questions were developed and refined through preliminary interviews with over a hundred persons not included in the sample. A copy of the interview guide is included in Appendix D.[6]

No attempt will be made, it should be noted, to generalize the specific Bay Area findings to American society at large. Their purpose is more to illuminate the *analytic* relations between highly general meaning systems and more specific kinds of values, attitudes, and involvements. Many of these relations may not be too different in the Bay Area from other large metropolitan centers (a comparison of the Bay Area with other cities and a discussion of the conditions making it a seedbed for cultural innovation is presented in Appendix A). Still, the initial motivation in choosing this area was that it is in some respects probably more pronounced on many of the social experiments to be examined and it will, therefore, be regarded as relatively unique in comparison with other areas.

What data such as these, collected at only one point in time, do not do, of course, is to afford a way to assess propositions about *trends* in different meaning systems. A series of studies conducted periodically would obviously be needed to document the presence or absence of such trends. Given the impossibility of doing this for past time periods and the substantial delay that would be required if future developments had to be covered, the present research design appears to be the most preferable interim strategy. It affords a chance, first, to determine whether or not highly general meaning systems can even be tapped with standard survey procedures; second, to discover if there are, in fact, relations between these meaning systems and more specific manifestations of social experimentation; and third, to find out if these meaning systems are located in the

6. The interviews were conducted between March 15 and August 15, 1973, by a team of 45 professional interviewers from the Survey Research Center. The largest share of interviews was completed by the first of June, with the remaining time devoted to following upon persons not at home or reluctant to be interviewed. To encourage cooperation, a letter of introduction explaining the nature of the study was mailed to each household prior to the interviewer's initial call. In addition, during the final month of the field work, interviewers sought names of respondents remaining to be contacted from neighbors and from telephone directories and attempted to contact them either by telephone or by mail to make appointments for interviews.

society in a way that is consistent or inconsistent with the idea that a cultural shift is taking place. In addition to the Bay Area data, moreover, there is a substantial amount of evidence available from historical sources. Although relatively unsystematic, this evidence provides a rich source of suggestive material on trends that helps to put the Bay Area data in perspective.

CHAPTER 1

The Scope of
Social Experimentation

Before the question of *why* the counter-culture of the sixties and early seventies took place can be addressed, the question of *what* took place must be answered. What was the counter-culture? What kinds of social experiments took place? How many people actually experimented with such things as drugs, communal living, radical politics? How many others came to be supportive of these experiments? Has the counter-culture ended? Was it superficial? Or did it result in important changes in attitudes and values?

The counter-culture was certainly more than the images most publicized by the press: the killings at Kent State, the demonstrations at the Democratic National Convention in Chicago, People's Park, Woodstock, Timothy Leary, the flower children of the Haight-Ashbury. And yet, the more common ways in which it touched people's lives is a story that has remained untold. How many people, for example, had brief encounters with drugs? How many experienced a heightened sense of political alienation? How many came to be tolerant of homosexuality or communal marriages? On the other hand, how many people simply felt disgust? How many experienced a heightened fear of radicalism? A new desire for strong police power?

Much of the Bay Area study was devoted to finding answers to such questions, at least insofar as they applied to the Bay Area where much of the counter-culture reached its height. The expectation in studying the Bay Area was that if large numbers of people there had been involved in the counter-culture, it would be more feasible to discover why the counter-culture had taken place. If only small numbers had been involved, this would also be of interest since it

11

would indicate that even fewer had probably been involved elsewhere. By themselves, the Bay Area data afford no generalizations about the nation at large or even about trends over time in the counter-culture. Fortunately, other data are available that help illuminate these more general questions. These data, much of them from national polls, are often less comprehensive than would be desired. Yet they do touch on a variety of the social experiments that were a part of the counter-culture and often provide comparisons over time as well.

The reader who seeks a definitive answer as to the true significance of the counter-culture will undoubtedly be disappointed by this evidence. Even the most able students of the counter-culture have come to little agreement about its significance. The interpretations range from those which regard it as a sweeping and soon-to-be universal revolution in values to those which pass it off as an overly publicized escapade by a handful of boisterous young people. The data to be reviewed here will not resolve these differences. Many of the differences lie more in the interpreter's perspective than in his knowledge of the evidence. If an attempt is to be made to explain part of the reason why the counter-culture took place, though, the necessary starting point is an examination of just what it was that occurred.

It is well known that the counter-culture involved experiments not only in politics or sexual behavior but in other areas of life as well. It will facilitate the present discussion if these various areas are kept distinct for the time being. Doing so will allow an appraisal to be made both of the range of the different experiments that took place and of the magnitude of experimentation that took place within each area. Experiments in five areas will be considered: in politics, economic policies, religion, family and sexual styles, and leisure styles. The aim in each area will be to see what the magnitude of experimentation with nonconventional alternatives was and how this magnitude changed over time.

POLITICAL EXPERIMENTATION

The political experiments that occupied most observers' attention during the late sixties and early seventies were those that sought either to establish some new form of government or to modify the present form of government through relatively nonconventional means. Thus, formally organized groups such as Students for a Democratic Society (SDS), the Weather People, the Black Panthers, the Symbionese Liberation Army (SLA), and the numerous socialistic alliances were of considerably greater interest than, say, the Young Republicans, chiefly because of their devotion to such alternative political systems as anarchism, socialism, and Maoism. The number of different political philosophies that came to be espoused was itself remarkable. Those that became best known ranged from the not-so-nonconventional "participatory democracy" ideals set forth in the SDS's Port Huron statement, to the hard-line socialism of the Progressive Labor Party, the grass-roots populism of the Black Panthers and various segments of the New American Movement (NAM), the anarchistic tendencies of the Weather Underground, and the Maoist-Stalinist confluence of the SLA. But, apart from the particular political ideals they espoused, these groups were also of interest simply because of the nonconventional means they chose to bring about political change. In place of the usual electoral methods, a variety of alternative political tactics were tried, including sit-ins, campus confrontations, massive demonstrations, political kidnappings, mock guerrilla warfare, and strategic bombings. None of these were without precedent, yet all were beyond the pale of generally accepted political strategies. Moreover, these tactics were not limited just to members of formally organized movements, but came to be used more or less spontaneously by others as well.

No systematic attempts have been made to estimate how many people actually became involved in alternative political experiments during the sixties and early seventies. Some, such as the SLA and the Weather People, were clearly limited to a small but highly visible "lunatic fringe," while others, such as SDS, came to be relatively widespread. But just how widespread has defied even the most careful observers. Many of those who engaged in political experimentation during this time, furthermore, never became involved in specific movements but merely formed a loose coterie of occasional activists, taking part in protests or demonstrations or other events as the opportunity arose.

Some estimates of the size of this larger group of experimenters have been made, although the results are not entirely consistent. For instance, a nationwide poll of college students in 1970 found that fully 60 percent claimed to have taken part in a demonstration.[1] At about the same time, however, a study of senior men at the University of California, Berkeley, which had been widely touted for its radical activity, found only 55 percent claiming to have been in demonstrations.[2] No samples of the general U.S. population were asked this question, but the results would obviously have been smaller. In the Bay Area, again probably more 'radicalized' than most parts of the country, only 17 percent claim to have taken part in a demonstration.[3] The numbers vary considerably, however, depending on the nature of the question asked. Thus, a 1972 Bay Area survey found that only 5 percent had taken part in a protest that turned violent and only 6 percent had participated in a sit-in.[4]

Taking part in a demonstration is obviously no sure sign of commitment to nonconventional political forms. But the figures for the numbers who engaged in sit-ins or violent demonstrations do seem to correspond rather well with the numbers who identify themselves as political experimenters *ideologically*. Table 1 summarizes questions from several surveys which asked people in one way or another how closely they identified with radical political causes. The results are remarkably the same, in spite of the fact that two of the surveys are of general Bay Area samples, one is a nationwide sample of college

1. Figures from Harris surveys cited in Seymour Martin Lipset, *Rebellion in the University* (Boston: Little, Brown & Company, 1972), p. 45.
2. Survey conducted as part of a longitudinal study of "Changing Life Styles and Values Among University Males" by the Institute for Research in Social Behavior in Berkeley under the supervision of Dean Manheimer, Glen Mellinger, and Robert Somers and supported by a grant from the National Institute of Mental Health (MH-21425). The figures for 1971 are from a random sample of approximately 1,000 senior males at the University of California, Berkeley, who were interviewed in March 1971. The response rate for this study was 90 percent. The figures for 1973 are from the second wave of a study initially conducted among freshmen males in 1971. The 1973 figures are only for those in the sample who are still enrolled at Berkeley. This study was conducted by mail in the fall of 1973. Of the initial 90 percent who took part in the first wave of this study, approximately 80 percent also cooperated in the second wave, making an actual response rate of approximately 72 percent.
3. All percentages reported in this chapter from the Bay Area sample are weighted to make them representative of the Bay Area population age 16 and over.
4. Survey conducted by the "Model Social Indicators Project" under the supervision of J. Merrill Shanks, director of the Survey Research Center. Questions cited in this section are from the subproject on political alienation directed by Herbert McClosky. This survey confirmed the 1973 finding that 17 percent had taken part in a "peaceful protest rally or march." It also found that 20 percent had taken part in a boycott.

Table 1. **RADICAL POLITICAL EXPERIMENTATION***

Ever took part in demonstrations or marches, not just watched (Bay Area, 1973)	17%
Have taken part in a protest that turned violent (Bay Area, 1972)	5%
Have participated in a sit-in (Bay Area, 1972)	6%
Personally, I'm in favor of what [an avowed revolutionary] is trying to do, even if (he) she does break a few laws (Bay Area, 1973)	4%
Political position: radical (Bay Area, 1973)	4%
Breaking the law is often necessary to get the government to act (Bay Area, 1972)	4%
I will resort to violence and/or other illegal measures, if necessary (national sample age 18 to 24, 1973)	4%
Highly favorable to Black Panthers (national college sample, 1970)	8%
Highly favorable to SDS (national college sample, 1970)	6%
Political position: radical (University of California, Berkeley, senior males, 1973)	10%
Identify with the New Left (University of California, Berkeley, senior males, 1973)	10%

*Sources: Bay Area, 1973: Berkeley Religious Consciousness Project, 1,000 adults; Bay Area, 1972: Model Social Indicators Project, 1,000 adults; national sample age 18 to 24: *Gallup Opinion Index,* October 1973, Report No. 100; national college sample: George H. Gallup, *The Gallup Poll: Public Opinion, 1935-1971,* 3 vols. (New York: Random House, 1972), p. 2286; Berkeley senior males: Changing Life Styles and Values Among University Males, Institute for Research in Social Behavior.

students, and the other is a national sample of all youth age 18 to 21. All of the items shown suggest that no more than about 5 percent of the populations involved were committed to radical political experiments. And since none of these samples included groups such as older people from more conservative parts of the country, the overall proportion of radical political experimenters was probably even smaller than 5 percent. The upshot of this evidence seems to be that the political dimension of the counter-culture, even in terms of ideological devotion, consisted of an extremely small proportion of the population.

There is also some evidence that suggests that the numbers committed to extreme political experiments have declined in very recent years. For example, 55 percent of all senior men in the class of 1971 at the University of California, Berkeley, claimed they had taken part in a demonstration, but among their counterparts in the class of 1974 only 28 percent said the same. Likewise, 20 percent of the former but only 10 percent of the latter said they identified with the New Left.[5] This kind of evidence is, of course, risky to draw generalizations from. It is consistent, nevertheless, with more general observations that both the number of demonstrations and the number of people involved in radical political groups have dropped off drastically since the end of the Vietnam war.

That somewhere around 5 percent of the nation's youth or its college students were devoted to radical causes suggests that this aspect of the counter-culture was relatively insignificant in spite of all the publicity it received and even the consternation it caused the nation's political leaders. This figure is subject to different interpretations, though. One can say that *only* 5 percent were political experimenters. Or one can say that *fully* 5 percent were experimenters. Indeed, both interpretations have been made. The question, therefore, is what does it really tell us about the counter-culture, after all, to know that 5 percent were devoted to radical causes?

The answer to this question depends on several considerations, including one's notions about how political change comes about. But one of the most important things it depends on is what the other 95 percent, who were not committed to radical causes, were thinking. Experimentation with alternative social arrangements is clearly a matter of degree. Some become actively involved, others become ideologically committed although not behaviorally involved, still others become mildly interested in or supportive of the nonconventional, and others merely become disenchanted with the conventional without developing an actual interest in the nonconventional. The numbers who fall into each of these categories are what define the nature of social experimentation in its broader sense. Thus, a small cadre of political extremists is an entirely different phenomenon in a population highly tolerant of such activity and disenchanted with established political processes than it is in a population both satisfied with its government and more supportive of the police than of those working against the government. A more complete picture of political experimentation, therefore, depends on knowing what the broader climate of political opinion is.

5. Survey of "Changing Life Styles and Values Among University Males" by the Institute for Research in Social Behavior.

Looking first at mild support of nonconventional political means, there seems to be a sizable minority, if not a majority, who hold such views. For example, one question, a story-type question, in the Bay Area survey asked:

Betty Wilson thinks of herself as a "revolutionary." She is working to overthrow the U.S. government, but she has not broken any laws. Which of these answers best expresses your feelings about her?

The responses to this question were as follows:

Personally, I'm in favor of what she's trying to do, even if she does break a few laws.	4%
She should be treated like anyone else since she hasn't broken any laws.	47
The police should keep their eye on her.	30
The FBI should tap her telephone to get evidence against her.	4
She should be arrested immediately.	4
None of these.	11

Thus, 51 percent register some form of approval or tolerance while only 38 percent express some form of intolerance.

Other surveys have also found a fairly wide degree of tolerance toward, if not mild support of, nonconventional political experiments. As shown in Table 2, nearly half the Bay Area residents sampled in 1972, a year previous to the present study, were willing to consider illegal tactics to bring about political change. A similar proportion of college students in a nationwide study thought violence might be a necessary tool for political change. Another nationwide sample, this one of all young people, found over half of them interested in a range of nonviolent but still so-called activist methods of achieving change. Indeed, this proportion was greater than that for youth in any of the other ten countries who were asked the same question. And finally, a national sample of all Americans found that over half rejected a negative statement about student demonstrators.

This last finding is especially important because the same question that was asked in 1973 had been asked before, in 1969 and also in 1965, revealing the following trend. Between 1965 and 1969, as campus demonstrations grew to an all-time high, Americans became somewhat more intolerant of student demonstrations (7 percent more expressed a negative opinion). Then between 1969 and 1973, as campus confrontations virtually ceased, the public grew significantly less intolerant again (24 percent fewer expressed a negative opinion).

Table 2. **TOLERANCE OF POLITICAL EXPERIMENTATION***

Breaking the law is sometimes necessary to get action from the government (Bay Area, 1972)	40%
Violence is sometimes justified to bring about a change in society (national college sample, 1974)	40%
I will resort to a variety of measures, such as petitions, letters of complaint, demonstrations, sit-ins, etc., so long as the means are permitted by law (national sample age 18 to 24, 1973)	51%
Disagree that student demonstrators who engage in political activities do more harm than good for the country (national sample, 1973)	52%

*Sources: Bay Area, 1972: Model Social Indicators Project, 1,000 adults; national college sample: *San Francisco Chronicle,* May 13, 1974. Figures cited are from interviews with more than 1,000 full-time students at a sample of 60 campuses conducted by Gallup during January and March 1974; national sample age 18 to 24: *Gallup Opinion Index,* October 1973, Report No. 100; Harris poll reported in *Current Opinion* 1 (November 1973): 116.

The net effect, though, was that the public was significantly less intolerant of student demonstrators in 1973 than it had been in 1965. Perhaps this shift did not occur with regard to other forms of radical experimentation. The implication, however, is that the experience of the sixties probably left Americans more supportive of political experiments of various kinds than they had been before. In any case, the evidence from all these samples suggests that there is currently a large degree of sentiment among the American people which is open, if not conducive, to experimentation with nonconventional political activities. The people sharing these sentiments should perhaps not be considered as part of the counter-culture itself. And yet they clearly had an impact on it. Certainly the 5 percent who were devoted to radical political experiments were not faced with a solid wall of opposition to their efforts.

The other piece of information important for assessing the overall strength of the counter-culture is how satisfied or dissatisfied people were with established institutions. With regard to political attitudes, there is an ample amount of such evidence. In fact, trends in political disenchantment can be documented for nearly two decades.

Looking first at the Bay Area, dissatisfaction with established political arrangements is widely in evidence. Nearly half of the people interviewed said they feel our form of government needs a major overhaul. This is in comparison with only 14 percent who think our form of government is fine as is. The extent to which changes are valued is also evidenced by the proportion who personally think it important to work for major social changes. Nearly two out of three said this was of either great or fair importance to them. Questions asked in the 1972 Bay Area survey also tend to reveal the same degree of dissatisfaction. Over half said they felt they could trust the government to do what is right none of the time or at most only some of the time. And half also felt that the country is in poor shape or worse, with a third saying that something is very wrong.

Other polls and surveys have also shown that feelings of dissatisfaction with established political practices are widespread. In October 1973 a Gallup poll revealed that two out of every three Americans (66 percent) were dissatisfied with "the way this nation is being governed."[6] Only one in four (26 percent) was satisfied.[7] Somewhat surprisingly, a survey of youth (age 18 to 24) conducted about the same time revealed considerably less desire for change among this age group than in the nation at large, or so it seemed. Only 35 percent said they were more or less dissatisfied with "your society."[8] Still, this rate of dissatisfaction was higher in the United States than that for youth in every other country studied (Brazil, France, India, Japan, Philippines, Sweden, Switzerland, West Germany) except Japan and West Germany. Also in 1973, a national Harris poll which asked "Do you feel we always have one crisis or another in America, or do you feel there is something deeply wrong in America?" found that a majority of Americans (53 percent) believed there is something deeply wrong.[9] This finding reflected that of an earlier (1971) Roper study of the nation which asked "Do you feel that things in this country are generally going in the right direction today, or do you feel that things have pretty seriously gotten off on the wrong track?"

6. *San Francisco Chronicle*, October 15, 1973.
7. Only 53 percent similarly indicated they were satisfied with the future facing them and their families.
8. *Gallup Opinion Index*, October 1973, Report No. 100.
9. *Current Opinion* 2 (February 1974): 15.

Nearly two out of every three persons polled (64 percent) said the country had gotten seriously off track.[10]

From this evidence it seems clear that the radical political experiments that emerged during the last half of the sixties were but one manifestation of a much broader wave of discontent and desire for change. Although most of this sentiment never became mobilized into actual political activity, it certainly needs to be taken into account in any overall assessment of the counter-culture. It seems as important to seek explanations for why this degree of disenchantment with conventional political arrangements developed as it does to explain why more limited numbers of people actually experimented with nonconventional political activities.

It may be argued that political discontent has always been a characteristic of the American people. Indeed, one has only to look at the scores of reform movements that have been initiated over the course of the nation's history to place some credence in this argument. But at least since systematic poll data have become available, the political disillusionment evident in the most recent polls is unprecedented. Several periodic studies, in fact, reveal that a steady increase in dissatisfaction has been taking place for at least twenty years.

Table 3 summarizes the results of a dozen questions regarding political content or discontent, each of which was asked at least twice at different times during the past two decades. The first nine questions were asked of representative national samples, the last three of people in the Detroit metropolitan area. Reading across the table it can be seen that every question elicited more feelings of discontent in the second time period than in the first. For example, the first row shows that the proportion who feel the country is becoming more repressive rose from 35 percent in 1970 to 52 percent in 1973. Similarly, the last line shows that the proportion (in the Detroit area) who are dissatisfied with the federal courts rose from 37 percent in 1954 to 76 percent in 1971. The other questions reveal growing dissatisfaction with the executive branch of the government, with state governments, with community officials, and with the

10. *The Miami Herald,* July 14, 1971. An indirect indication of increasing dissatisfaction with American society is that the proportion saying yes when asked "If you were free to do so, would you like to go and settle in another country?" was 12 percent in 1971, three times as great as in 1946 and double what it was in 1959 (*Gallup Opinion Index,* May 1971, Report No. 71).

Table 3. TRENDS IN POLITICAL DISCONTENT*

	1954	1959	1964	1969	1973
(1) The country is becoming more repressive				35%	52%
(2) Do not feel a great deal of confidence in executive branch				59%	81%
(3) High on alienation index			29%		55%
(4) People running this country don't really care what happens to you			27%		56%
(5) The rich get richer and the poor get poorer			45%		77%
(6) Feel left out of things around you			8%		28%
(7) What you think doesn't count much anymore			38%		61%
(8) Can count on the government to do what is right only some of the time or never		22%	23%	36% 44%	
(9) Government is run for a few big interests			28%	39% 49%	

Table 3 Continued.

	1954	1959	1964	1969		1973
(10) State government not doing a good job (Detroit only)	37%				75%	
(11) No confidence in community officials (Detroit only)	46%				66%	
(12) Federal courts doing bad job (Detroit only)	37%				76%	

*Sources: (1) Current Opinion 1 (November 1973): 121; (2) The Harris Survey, September 13-22, 1973, survey conducted for the United States Senate Committee on Government Operations, copyright 1973, Chicago Tribune; (3-7) Current Opinion 2 (February 1974): 18, San Francisco Chronicle, December 3, 1973; (8-9) The Miami Herald, July 14, 1971; (10-12) Otis Dudley Duncan, Howard Schuman, and Beverly Duncan, Social Change in a Metropolitan Community (New York: Russell Sage Foundation, 1973), pp. 82-83.

responsiveness of government in general to the average person. Thus, by virtually every criterion, people have been becoming increasingly unhappy with the established political system.

In addition, Table 3 reveals that this rising sense of alienation has not been limited just to periods when events such as Watergate or the Vietnam war were causing people to be concerned. Disenchantment was already rising before Vietnam became a major issue, it continued rising during the Vietnam war, it has risen again since the end of the Vietnam war, it was already high before Watergate, and it has thus far shown no signs of reversing itself.

To summarize, the overall picture obtained from looking not simply at the more extreme political experiments of recent years but at the more general political climate as well is one of widespread and growing unrest. The movements that grew up during the late 1960s appear to be only the more visible top of a massive development. Established political institutions have clearly not toppled (although there may be some significance to the fact that each of the last three presidents to leave office did so under unusual circumstances). Nevertheless, there has clearly been a shift in the tenor of the American political climate. An atmosphere of strain has welled up which has led some to actually devote themselves to the cause of major political change and has left many others with desire for such change. Moreover, there are at this writing no signs that this development ended with the decline of the counter-culture in the early seventies. By every indication it is the result of deeper causes than simply such events as the Vietnam war or Watergate. Thus far it appears to show no major signs of diminishing, certainly not to the point of relative content evidenced by the polls of fifteen to twenty years ago. Before commenting further on the significance of this development, though, it will be helpful to examine what has taken place in other areas of the society.

ECONOMIC EXPERIMENTATION

The counter-culture is probably not as well remembered for its economic experiments as for its political experiments. Yet numerous such experiments were attempted. Among them were food conspiracies, agricultural communes, socialistically styled co-ops, free clinics, organic food stores, herbal medicine shops, as well as a new class, the self-employed "street artisans." Students of the counter-culture have identified several themes that seemed to be common to these experiments, among them the quest for community, the desire to facilitate ecological concerns, and feelings of alienation toward large bureaucracies.

Some of these experiments proved to be highly viable economic enterprises. Several communes, for example, became important in their particular geographic locales as suppliers of lumber and organic truck crops. Relative to the larger economy, though, most of these experiments never became strong enough to be considered serious threats to more established economic institutions. For whatever advantages they offered in terms of community or in terms of anti-bureaucratic values, they were easily smothered by the economies of large-scale production and distribution and the impact of large-scale advertising which only more established economic entities were able to afford.

There was another kind of economic experiment that took place during the sixties, however. It was importantly related to the counter-culture, but it was a movement that had a much broader social base as well. That was the movement for greater *economic equality* which took place primarily on three fronts: the movement for greater equality for *blacks,* the movement for greater equality for *women,* and the movement for greater equality for the *poor.* These movements involved significant numbers of people in such activities as sit-ins, marches, boycotts, racial and sexual encounter groups, volunteer welfare work, community organizing, and so forth. Indeed, much of the overall turmoil of the sixties has been attributed to the joint impact of these struggles.

The vast majority of people were not actually involved in these experiments, of course, just as they were not actually involved in the political experiments of the sixties. Just what the actual numbers were is impossible to say with any degree of certainty. Some marches involved hundreds of thousands of people. Some organizations, the National Organization of Women (NOW), for example, have been able to establish chapters in cities and towns all across the nation. Yet, as a proportion of the total American population, the number who have ever taken part in such events or organizations is undoubtedly minute.

But, in spite of the relatively small numbers of people who actually participated in them, the experiments that took place during the sixties in pursuit of greater economic equality must be considered one of the major social developments of our time. These experiments appear to have touched the lives of virtually all Americans, by affecting either their economic status in some way or their attitudes and values. Judging both from the changes in attitudes which have occurred over the past quarter century and from the actual successes that have been achieved toward greater economic equality for all, these experiments have had a tremendous impact on the society.

For instance, Table 4 reports the shifts in attitudes regarding racial inequality that have been documented since World War II. Every item shows a significant shift away from traditional racist perspectives to more equalitarian points of view, whether the issue is equality in employment, in education, in housing, or in public accommodations. Admittedly, these shifts are not all results of the more active racial experiments that took place between the middle 1950s and the late 1960s. Some of the early shifts in attitudes un- doubtedly helped pave the way for the more active attempts to achieve racial inequality. But whatever the relation, the past several decades have clearly been a major period of transition for many people's racial perspectives.

The same transition is also evident regarding sexual equality. As the items listed in Table 5 show, there has been a steady increase since at least the middle 1940s in the number of people who feel that women should have the same economic rights and opportunities as men.[11] And at present, there appears to be strong support for those who are working to further this cause. In the Bay Area, for example, the 1972 survey found that well over half (61 percent) of the respondents approved of the Women's Liberation Movement. And the 1973 Bay Area study found that nearly half (47 percent) considered it of at least fair importance to help women get equal rights. Obviously, there is still a large segment who do not share these sentiments. But their numbers have been steadily diminishing.

Along with these shifts in attitudes, there have also been im- portant shifts in the actual status of blacks, of women, and of other

11. Major shifts have also taken place in the extent to which women are actually included in the labor market, see Abbott L. Ferriss, *Indicators of Trends in the Status of American Women* (New York: Russell Sage Foundation, 1971), p. 89; U.S. Bureau of Labor Statistics, *Handbook of Labor Statistics, 1970* (Washington, D.C.: U.S. Department of Labor, 1970), p. 29. See also Stanley Lebergott, "Labor Force and Employment Trends," in Eleanor Bernert Sheldon and Wilbert E. Moore (eds.), *Indicators of Social Change: Concepts and Measurements* (New York: Russell Sage Foundation, 1968), pp. 97–143, esp. p. 104.

Table 4. TRENDS IN RACIAL ATTITUDES*

	1940	1950	1960	1970
(1) Negroes should have as good a chance at jobs as white people	42%		82%	
(2) Want equality for blacks			74%	89%
(3) Accept blacks working side by side with you (Texas)			56%	84%
(4) Ride in same buses (Texas)			49%	83%
(5) Eat in same restaurant (Texas)			40%	80%
(6) Send children to same schools (Texas)			41%	73%
(7) White students and Negro students should go to the same schools (Detroit)		62%		79%
(8) Not disturbed if a Negro moved into your block (Detroit)		46%		72%

Table 4. **TRENDS IN RACIAL ATTITUDES*** (Cont.)

1940	1950	1960	1970

(9) Disagree that blacks who demonstrate for civil rights do more harm than good

31%

60%

*Sources: (1) *Current Opinion* 1 (February 1973): 4; (2-6) Hazel Erskine, "The Polls: Interracial Socializing," *Public Opinion Quarterly* 37 (Summer 1973): 283-294; (7-9) Otis Dudley Duncan, Howard Schuman, and Beverly Duncan, *Social Change in a Metropolitan Community* (New York: Russell Sage Foundation, 1973), p. 99. National samples unless otherwise indicated.

Table 5. **TRENDS IN ATTITUDES TOWARD SEX ROLES***

	1940	1950	1960	1970
(1) Approve of women earning money in business	18%	18%		55%
(2) Would vote for a woman for president	31%			66%
(3) No kinds of work a woman shouldn't have (Detroit only)			20%	33%
(4) Both boys and girls should shovel walks (Detroit only)			34%	50%
(5) Both boys and girls should wash the car (Detroit only)			29%	69%

*Sources: (1) Hazel Erskine, "The Polls: Women's Role," *Public Opinion Quarterly* 35 (Summer 1971): 275-290; (2) *Gallup Opinion Index*, August 1971, Report No. 74; (3-5) Otis Dudley Duncan, Howard Schuman, and Beverly Duncan, *Social Change in a Metropolitan Community* (New York: Russell Sage Foundation, 1973), p. 25. National samples unless otherwise stated.

economically disadvantaged groups. Gains have been made in voter registration, housing rights, rights to public facilities, income and educational levels, and employment opportunities for blacks. Women have found it possible to move increasingly into higher education and into the labor market. More and more federal money has been spent on welfare, job training, and medical expenses for the poor, the handicapped, and the aged. And gross levels of poverty have apparently been reduced somewhat.

While recent decades have been a time of notable effort to relieve inequality and discrimination, it is clear that these efforts have often accomplished far less than was hoped for. But at least much of the attitudinal legitimacy that traditionally surrounded inequality and discrimination has been substantially reduced. Many legal changes have also been made which strip away legitimacy from these traditional practices. In this sense, it can be concluded that the past several decades have marked a major, perhaps decisive, turning away from certain traditional characteristics of the American economic system and toward a different set of standards that uphold the rights of all to full inclusion in the economic sphere.

The changes that have occurred appear to be only the beginning, rather than the end, of the experimentation that will take place in the economic sector. The more dramatic economic experiments of the sixties have largely died down, just as the more radical political experiments have. Sit-ins, marches, and bra-burnings have become mostly a thing of the past, although they have not ceased entirely. But there is still a great deal of dispute about how best to accomplish economic equality for all. The attitudinal shifts and the court decisions of recent years have created a climate of willingness to do something about inequality. But when it comes to the questions of who will pay the price and how much, there is evidence that a great deal of controversy and unrest still exist.

For instance, the vast majority favor educational equality; yet specific proposals such as busing are still hotly resisted. In the Bay Area, for example, only 17 percent oppose school integration, but nearly two-thirds oppose busing.[12] Greater equality in the job market is also widely favored currently, but proposals such as affirmative

12. Mailed questionnaire survey of approximately 700 randomly selected residents of the Bay Area, conducted by Richard Apostle with support from a grant from the National Science Foundation to the Survey Research Center for the study of "Model Social Indicators."

action, reverse discrimination, or quotas are experiments that only a few have as yet come to accept. And alleviation of poverty has also been widely favored, yet proposals for various guaranteed annual income plans or reverse income-tax programs are still in an extremely tentative phase. Thus, it seems likely that the unrest that was initiated in the economic sphere during the sixties is likely to continue for some time. The American dilemma Gunnar Myrdal saw between our equalitarian ideals and the presence of gross inequality in reality appears to be as much a problem today as when Myrdal first formulated the idea.[13] If anything, the equalitarian ideals have strengthened, and some gains in ending inequality have also been made; but the discrepancy between ideal and reality is as much present as ever.

In sum, the unrest in the economic sphere of American society appears to have been as significant, if not more significant, as that which took place in the political sphere. Neither was limited simply to the more dramatic outbursts which came to be identified as the counter-culture. Both involved major shifts in attitudes that eroded legitimacy from traditional institutional arrangements. Neither seems to be a process that has as yet ended.

RELIGIOUS EXPERIMENTATION

Perhaps even more dramatically than in the political and economic realms, radical social experiments have been much in evidence in the religious realm during the past decade or decade and a half. From the saffron-robed devotees of Hare Krishna to the Bible-toting Children of God, religious experimenters have been a trademark of the recent counter-culture. In the Bay Area over three hundred new religious movements have appeared since the middle sixties, ranging from the early Meher Baba cell groups, to the highly routinized Transcendental Meditation movement, to the dozens of small followings founded by various yogis and sikhs, to the more recent "premie houses" of the Divine Light mission. Some of the new groups espouse Christian doctrines not too dissimilar from those of the established churches. The majority, however, seem to take their cues either from Eastern traditions or from non-Christian philosophies of the West.

13. Gunnar Myrdal, *An American Dilemma* (New York: Harper & Row, 1944).

New religious experiments have clearly become highly visible. Just how significant a development they represent is still a matter of conjecture, however. Some students of the counter-culture have suggested that its most significant aspect may ultimately prove to be these new religious movements. Many of them subscribe to values and beliefs markedly different from those more common to American culture. If these groups were to become more widespread, the implication has been that they would alter the character of American values considerably, perhaps spearheading a new rapprochement between Eastern and Western thought. Some churchmen, in fact, have spoken out strongly for including these new groups in ecumenical discussions, which have traditionally been limited to Protestant, Catholic, and Jewish representatives. A few local churches have reportedly taken steps to incorporate ideas from yoga and from Eastern mysticism into their own services. The question that remains unclear, however, is whether these new groups are actually having an important impact in terms of actual numbers or whether they have simply made themselves seem much more prominent than they really are.

A few estimates have been made of the numbers involved in various new religious groups. For example, Transcendental Meditation has been estimated to have trained over 350,000 persons; 3HO (Happy-Healthy-Holy Organization), a group devoted to the principles of kundalini yoga, has been estimated to have processed over 200,000 participants; and Meher Baba has been estimated to have approximately 7,000 devotees.[14] These estimates should be regarded as highly unreliable, though. Some of them are based on the group's projections for the future rather than actual membership figures. Some have been calculated by casual observers visiting several local groups and then generalizing to the nation at large. In addition, it is often unclear whether the figures reported represent full-time devotees, members, occasional participants, or what. There appear to be no statistics from predefined populations stating how many people have taken part in such groups. Nor has there been any evidence on how these groups have been received by the public more generally. The average person can encounter Hare Krishnas,

14. *Oakland Tribune,* June 6, 1974; *San Francisco Chronicle,* March 17, 1974; Peter Rowley, *New Gods in America: An Informal Investigation into the New Religions of American Youth Today* (New York: David McKay, 1971).

for example, in virtually every large city. Yet, how many are enticed to take part, how many are attracted, how many are turned off, how many remain indifferent?

Since the larger Berkeley Religious Consciousness Project of which this study is a part included intensive studies of several new religious movements, specific questions were asked on the Bay Area survey about how the general public was responding to these movements. Thus, we are in a somewhat better position to say what the scope of this kind of experimentation is than any of the other kinds discussed in this chapter. It was not possible to ask specific questions about all the major religious movements in the Bay Area, let alone the minor ones. Yet the groups asked about give a rough sense of how prominent these groups have become on the average. Information was obtained about participation in and attitudes toward four Eastern groups and five Jesus People groups.

The Eastern groups asked about have been highly publicized in the Bay Area and elsewhere as well. *Transcendental Meditation* (TM) was founded by the Maharishi Mahesh Yogi and became familiar in the United States in the late sixties after the Maharishi made a series of public appearances in Western countries and after several well-known entertainers became attracted to it. *Zen Buddhism* has a somewhat longer history in the United States but also gained most of its diffusion during the sixties, especially through the writings of Alan Watts and D. T. Suzuki. *Hare Krishna* has become most familiar through the dancing and chanting of its saffron-robed, shaven-headed devotees on street corners, in campus plazas, and in other public places. The fourth offshoot of Eastern religions that was asked about—*yoga groups*—is not a single group but a variety of disciplines, among which Hatha is probably the most common, but which also includes Raja, Kundalini, Tantric, and other forms.[15]

It bears mentioning that these movements are not necessarily "religious" movements, depending on how the term is defined and who is defining it. The leaders of Transcendental Meditation, for example, have made an ardent effort to dissociate themselves from the label "religion." Many people who practice yoga, similarly, would probably regard it as more an exercise technique than a

15. For more detailed discussions of these groups and similar Eastern movements, see Rowley, *New Gods in America*; Jacob Needleman, *The New Religions* (Garden City, N.Y.: Doubleday & Company, 1970); Charles Y. Glock and Robert N. Bellah (eds.), *The New Religious Consciousness* (Berkeley and Los Angeles: University of California Press, forthcoming).

religion. The only reason for considering these movements in the context of religion is that each in one way or another has been derived from Eastern religious or spiritual disciplines.

The data show that relatively few people are seriously involved in these movements. On the average, only 4.3 percent have ever taken part in each one, only 3 percent claim to know a lot about each one, and only 2.6 percent are strongly attracted to each one. Considerably more people, however, are at least casually knowledgeable and attracted. On the average more than one out of every three persons (37.5 percent) claims to know a little about each of these movements and, of these, 34 percent are at least mildly attracted.

Yoga is clearly the best known and best liked of all the groups (see Table 6). Nearly half the sample claim to know at least a little about it; of these, almost half are either mildly or strongly attracted, and one in six has taken part in it. The relative popularity of yoga, of course, may be due either to the fact that a less specific term was used in the questionnaire to describe it or that it has actually been fairly widely popularized through the mass media, educational institutions, and even the churches. Hare Krishna ranks second highest in terms of the number of people who have heard of it, but it stands last in attraction and in participation. Zen and TM are about equally well known and attract about equal numbers of persons. TM, however, has recruited more participants than Zen.

Table 6. **KNOWLEDGE OF, ATTRACTION TO, AND PARTICIPATION IN EASTERN MOVEMENTS** (Total Weighted Sample)

	Yoga	Transcendental Meditation	Zen	Hare Krishna
Know at least a little about it	49%	32%	30%	39%
Number	(1,000)	(1,000)	(1,000)	(1,000)
Attracted (among those who have heard of it)	43%	39%	40%	13%
Number	(483)	(323)	(303)	(388)
Taken part	8%	5%	3%	2%
Number	(1,000)	(1,000)	(1,000)	(1,000)

Data were obtained for five Jesus People groups (or types of groups). *Groups that speak in tongues* have been much in evidence as part of the larger Jesus movement. They are, of course, not new to American culture. According to recent accounts, they have attracted new audiences, for example, among college students and members of both the Roman Catholic faith and main-line Protestant denominations where glossolalia has until now been viewed with skepticism. *Christian World Liberation Front* (CWLF) is a Berkeley-based group that has been an important part of the Jesus People movement since its inception in 1969. It tends to attract participants who are more highly educated and more theologically sophisticated than many Jesus People groups do, but much of its ministry has been to the Berkeley drug addicts, street people, and so-called burned-out radicals. *Children of God* is a now international Jesus People cult which commands extreme devotion from its young members, who live communally and who are governed in an ad-mittedly authoritarian style. Of the groups asked about, it has undoubtedly received the widest press coverage, partly because of its extremely ascetic life style and its harsh criticisms of the established churches. *Jews for Jesus* has consisted less of specific groups than of various clusters of converted Jews who have made themselves known through effective use of the mass media. In the Bay Area most of the Jews for Jesus campaign has been carried on by a specific (but appar-ently small) group which has loosely associated itself with other Jesus People movements such as CWLF. *Campus Crusade for Christ* was asked about for comparison rather than as a representative of the Jesus People movement. It was founded by William Bright, a successful businessman, in the 1950s to minister primarily to college students. Since then it has grown to be a large international organization, headquartered in Southern California, and has tried to keep itself distinct from the more recent Jesus People movement, directing its efforts more at so-called key students than at drop-outs, radicals, or alienated young people.[16]

16. For discussions of these groups and of the Jesus movement more generally, see Glock and Bellah, *The New Religious Consciousness*; Donald Heinz, *God's Forever Family* (forthcoming); Jack Balswick, "The Jesus People Movement: A Sociological Analysis," paper presented to the annual meeting of the American Sociological Association, New Orleans, 1972; Ronald Engels, Edward Erickson, and C. Breckinridge Peters, *The Jesus People* (Grand Rapids: Eerdmans Publishing Company, 1972); Mary Harder, James T. Richardson, and Robert Simmonds, "Jesus People," *Psychology Today* 6 (December 1972): 45–50, 110–113; Lowell D. Streiker, *The Jesus Trip* (Nashville: Abingdon Press, 1971); Bill Bright, *Come Help*

On the average, the data reveal much the same picture for these groups as for the Eastern groups. Serious involvement seems to characterize relatively few people. The average number of people who report knowing a lot about any one group is only 2.8 percent of the sample, the number who have ever taken part in each is only 2.3 percent, and the average number who claim strong attraction to any one group is only 1.8 percent. Again, a larger number are at least knowledgeable and supportive of these groups. Twenty percent on the average know at least a little about each group and of these 34 percent are either mildly or strongly attracted. In comparison with the Eastern groups, therefore, the Christian groups are less well known (20 percent versus 37.5 percent) and have attracted smaller numbers to take part (2.3 percent versus 4.3 percent). Among those with any knowledge of the groups, however, the same proportions for both kinds of groups have positive feelings (34 percent for each). There is one additional difference, though; namely, the Christian groups elicit negative feelings from a somewhat greater proportion than the Eastern groups do. Twenty-six percent compared with 20 percent claim to be turned off and, if the figure for Hare Krishna is left out, the proportion for the Eastern groups drops to 11 percent, less than half that for the Christian groups.

Groups that speak in tongues have made themselves known to the widest audience of all the Christian groups and have attracted the largest number of participants, perhaps not surprisingly, since they are a phenomenon that has been common elsewhere than just in the recent counter-culture (see Table 7). Positive rather than negative feelings toward tongues groups run relatively small, however, in comparison with the other Christian groups: nearly twice as many are turned off as are attracted. After tongues groups, Jews for Jesus is the most widely known, then Campus Crusade, Children of God, and CWLF. It is not surprising, of course, that a strictly local group like CWLF should be relatively unknown; that a group which has been publicized as much as Children of God is not better known, however, seems noteworthy.

With regard to positive and negative responses, Campus Crusade

Change the World (Old Tappan, N.J.: Fleming H. Revell Company, 1970); Thomas Robbins, Dick Anthony, and Thomas E. Curtis, "The Limits of Symbolic Realism: Problems of Empathic Field Observation in a Sectarian Context," *Journal for the Scientific Study of Religion* 12 (September 1973): 259–273.

Table 7. **KNOWLEDGE OF, ATTRACTION TO,
AND PARTICIPATION IN JESUS PEOPLE GROUPS**
(Total Weighted Sample)

	Groups that Speak in Tongues	Christian World Liberation Front	Children of God	Jews for Jesus	Campus Crusade
Know at least a little about it	27%	12%	15%	22%	20%
Number	(1,000)	(1,000)	(1,000)	(1,000)	(1,000)
Attracted (among those who have heard of it)	25%	35%	37%	29%	39%
Number	(262)	(113)	(149)	(215)	(195)
Taken part	6%	1%	1%	1%	3%
Number	(1,000)	(1,000)	(1,000)	(1,000)	(1,000)

has garnered the most favorable reaction. Children of God also stands relatively high on attraction, in spite of the generally negative press coverage it has received. CWLF ranks next, then Jews for Jesus, and finally tongues groups. Actual participation varies from 23 percent for tongues groups (among those who have heard of it) down to 4 percent for Jews for Jesus.

In addition to the Eastern and the Christian groups, one other group, which falls in neither tradition, was inquired about. *Satanism,* except to the sophisticated observer, covers a variety of phenomena, from witchcraft to actual devil worship. In the Bay Area its chief connotation is the much publicized Church of Satan in San Francisco, headed by Anton LeVay.[17] Thirty-seven percent altogether claim to know at least something about this form of religion, making Satanism better known than any of the groups listed except yoga and Hare Krishna. Not surprisingly, relatively few (3 percent) of these have ever taken part. And only 10 percent claim to be attracted, the smallest proportion for any of the groups, while 66 percent are turned off, the largest proportion for any of the groups.

17. See Randall H. Alfred, "Who is Rosemary's Baby's Father?" chapter 9 in Glock and Bellah, *The New Religious Consciousness.*

All in all, the data indicate that in terms of sheer numbers these movements have in no way taken the Bay Area by storm. If the same questions had been asked of the nation at large, the numbers would have probably been even smaller. Even though the numbers of relatively serious experimenters are small, though, they are undoubtedly sufficient for many of these groups to maintain themselves and perhaps even to grow. Some of the oldest religious groups in America have never attracted more than a small proportion of the total population. The 4 percent who say they know a lot about TM and a lot about Campus Crusade, for example, would probably compare favorably in size if similar questions were asked, for example, about Episcopalians or United Presbyterians (judging from the fact that only 2.5 percent of the sample identifies with the former and 2.9 percent with the latter).

The larger body of persons who are at least somewhat supportive of these movements is also something to reckon with. Altogether, one out of every four persons is attracted to at least one of the Eastern movements. These are the people who may never become serious devotees, but who are nevertheless likely to have their lives influenced in some way by the presence of these groups and who, in turn, are indirectly likely to help these groups perpetuate themselves. Students of social movements have come increasingly to recognize the role of this larger constituency in the course of every movement.[18] That some of the groups have elicited favorable responses in ratios of 4 to 1 over negative responses, therefore, seems to be of significance.

Whether attraction to new religious experiments is currently growing or declining is something about which the Bay Area data afford no indication. That they have grown in comparison with a decade or two ago goes without saying. In 1960 questions such as those just examined could not even have been asked, for many of the groups did not exist or had not yet arrived in the West. Whether they are currently growing or declining is, of course, more difficult to judge. There is some evidence, however, that sheds a little light on this problem. The studies of Berkeley senior males already referred to included several questions about familiarity with some of these groups. Only two, however, were asked on both the 1971 and the

18. See, for example, Ralph H. Turner, "Determinants of Social Movement Strategies," in Tomotsu Shibutani (ed.), *Human Nature and Collective Behavior: Papers in Honor of Herbert Blumer* (Englewood Cliffs, N.J.: Prentice-Hall, 1970), pp. 145–164.

1973 studies, one about Transcendental Meditation, the other about Zen meditation. What these questions reveal is a clear increase in the numbers who are familiar with these two disciplines. For Transcendental Meditation the proportion who knew nothing about it dropped from 33 percent to only 3 percent during this two-and-one-half year period and the comparable proportion for Zen dropped from 33 percent to 9 percent.

Experimentation with new religious groups may continue to flourish and even to attract wider and wider audiences as these groups become more generally well known. This experimentation, however, is but a fraction of the larger amount of unrest which has been taking place in the religious realm. There is a much broader climate of ferment evident than that which has surfaced in the form of new religious movements. Just as traditional political arrangements appear to have been losing legitimacy in recent decades, so traditional religious institutions appear to be undergoing a gradual, yet serious, process of erosion. While relatively few people are joining new religious groups, large numbers are abandoning the established churches and becoming essentially nonreligious. Indeed, the major form of religious experimentation that warrants attention is probably not experimentation with new groups at all, but experimentation simply with *nonreligion*. The two kinds of experimentation are undoubtedly related. Both reflect increasing dissatisfaction with the traditional church. But the major thrust of this dissatisfaction appears to be simply a climate of religious apathy rather than one of religious renewal.

Students of American religion have speculated for some time that the churches are gradually ceasing to be effective at recruiting committed members. In the past, much of this speculation has been conducted without any solid information either to prove or disprove it. Within the past several years much evidence has become available, however, most of it showing clearly that the churches have, indeed, been losing influence, especially during the past two decades, and that more and more people are content to live their lives nonreligiously.

In the Bay Area the extent to which nonreligion is emerging as a way of life for many is brought into sharp relief by comparing the religious preferences respondents give for themselves and for their parents. Nearly a fourth of the sample choose to dissociate themselves from any religion (11 percent, no religious beliefs; 7 percent, agnostic, 4 percent, humanist, and 2 percent, atheist). Only half this many say their fathers were nonreligious. And only one fourth this many say their mothers were nonreligious.

The extent of religious defection in the Bay Area can also be seen in what respondents report about their churchgoing habits. At present 62 percent never attend religious services. But while they were growing up, only 12 percent never attended. In other words, fully half the sample has adopted a nonreligious life style since growing up.

More people are probably nonreligious in the Bay Area than in most other parts of the country. Yet the trend away from the churches is clearly evident in national statistics as well. Although overall church membership has remained fairly stable in recent years, church attendance rates have dropped steadily.[19] Annual polls have registered declines in weekly church attendance almost every year for the past two decades. The high in weekly attendance was 49 percent in 1955 and the low was 40 percent in 1974.[20] This trend, moreover, has been most pronounced among the young and the relatively more educated, that is, precisely among those who will in the future have the most influential roles in American life. Since 1957, when church attendance was at a high point for all age levels reported, until 1971 (the last year in which comparable age categories were reported) church attendance declined by 23 percentage points for persons age 21 to 29, but only 11 points for persons age 30 to 49, and only 4 points for persons age 50 and over. The trends for different educational levels are somewhat more complex, but they also suggest that religious commitment is dropping off most rapidly among those who are gradually coming to occupy more prominent places in the society, i.e. the better educated. Among persons with only grade school educations there has been a somewhat erratic pattern since 1957, with an overall decline of only 5 percentage points by 1973. Among persons with only high school educations there has been

19. Between 1960 and 1970 church membership declined by only 2 percent, from 64 percent to 62 percent. This was still higher than the 1950 figure of 57 percent (U.S. Bureau of the Census, *Statistical Abstract of the United States: 1973,* Washington, D.C.: Government Printing Office, 1973, p. 46).

20. *Current Opinion* 2 (February 1974): 14; *San Francisco Chronicle,* January 15, 1972; George H. Gallup, *The Gallup Poll: Public Opinion, 1935–1971,* 3 vols. (New York: Random House, 1972), pp. 902, 1222, 1252–1253, 1389, 1479, 1530, 1584, 1649, 1663, 1697, 1746, 1796, 1856, 1863, 1912–1913, 1978–1979, 2040–2041, 2095, 2173–2174, 2229, 2276.

a steady decline since 1957, totaling 14 percentage points. And among college-educated persons, church attendance stayed remarkably the same from 1955 to 1963, but since then it has dropped dramatically, a total of 13 points in the past decade. It is also noteworthy that what has appeared to be a leveling off of the decline in church attendance since 1971 (at 40 percent) actually seems to be attributable to a slight rise in church attendance among the less well educated while those with higher education have continued to decline in their church attendance.

Another indication that people are becoming less and less committed to traditional religious institutions is that the value of new construction of religious buildings, often considered a gauge of the strength of organized religion, has undergone a marked decline in recent years.[21] Between 1955 and 1965 expenditures for new buildings rose steadily, nearly doubling from $736 million to $1.2 billion. Since 1965, however, this trend has reversed. In 1971 expenditures were back down to $813 million. If adjustments are made to take inflation into account, 1971 expenditures amount to only 57 percent of those just four years previously. The major reason for this decline appears to be declining contributions from members. Adjusting for inflation, the members of nine major Protestant denominations, for example, gave $47 million less in 1971 than they had in 1970.[22]

Finally, the Detroit Area studies cited earlier also afford evidence suggesting a shift toward more nonreligious life styles.[23] Between 1958 and 1971, the proportion who said they attended religious services less often than they did ten or fifteen years earlier rose from 37 percent to 52 percent. During this same time period those who indicated they were less interested in religion than ten or fifteen years earlier also rose, from 6 percent to 27 percent. And a similar question which asked whether persons' interest in religion had decreased over the ten or fifteen years past also showed an increase, from 7 percent to 30 percent.

Admittedly, this evidence may not convince some readers that religious institutions are coming to be less and less influential in

21. Constant H. Jacquet, Jr. (ed.), *Yearbook of American and Canadian Churches, 1973* (New York: Abingdon Press, 1973), p. 266.
22. Ibid., p. 241.
23. Otis Dudley Duncan, Howard Schuman, and Beverly Duncan, *Social Change in a Metropolitan Community* (New York: Russell Sage Foundation, 1973), pp. 56–57.

American society.[24] It is perhaps important to note, however, that the vast majority of the American people have come to share this belief in the past few years.[25] As recently as 1957 Gallup polls showed that only 14 percent of the American public thought religion was losing its influence on American life. But in 1965 this figure had already climbed to 45 percent and by 1970 an overwhelming 75 percent believed the influence of religion to be declining. To the extent that such beliefs often come to be self-fulfilling prophecies, this may be one of the most important signs of all that American religion is in a significant period of unrest.

To summarize, the new religious movements that grew during the late sixties and early seventies, mostly as part of the counter-culture among youth, appear to be only one unusually visible part of the unrest and experimentation that have taken place in the religious realm of American society. In themselves, they represent what seems to be a viable, though still relatively minor, new force in American religion. But besides the relatively few who have taken part in these

24. Most of the statistics generally cited date back only to the middle fifties, a time widely recognized as an unusual period of religious revival accompanying the Cold War. If available church attendance figures from a few years earlier are taken into account, this revival period can easily be seen. In 1950, for example, weekly church attendance was only 39 percent, rising to 46 or 47 percent in 1954, and then to 49 percent in 1955. Church attendance in 1973, therefore, was no lower than it was in 1950. The decline evidenced during the sixties, consequently, may turn out to be part of a cyclical fluctuation rather than part of a linear trend that will continue into the future. Indeed, there is already some evidence that religion may again be regaining loyalty. Whereas a 1972 Harris poll showed that the proportion expressing "a great deal of confidence" in religion had declined 11 points from a 1966 figure of 41 percent, a 1973 poll showed that this proportion had risen 6 points within a single year, back to 36 percent. See Charles Y. Glock, "The Religious Revival in America?" in Jane C. Zahn (ed.), *Religion and the Face of America* (Berkeley: University Extension, University of California, 1959), pp. 25–42; Seymour Martin Lipset, *The First New Nation* (New York: Basic Books, 1963), pp. 159–162; Gallup, *The Gallup Poll*, pp. 902, 1222, 1252–1253; *The Harris Survey*, September 13–22, 1973, survey conducted for the United States Senate Committee on Government Operations, copyright 1973, *Chicago Tribune*. See also *Current Opinion* 2 (February 1974): 24.

25. *Gallup Opinion Index*, February 1969, Report No. 44; Gallup, *The Gallup Poll*. Similarly, in 1963, when a national sample was asked to compare people then with people a generation before, 42 percent said people were less religious at present and only 21 percent thought their contemporaries were more religious. See Hazel Gaudet Erskine, "The Polls: Personal Religion," *Public Opinion Quarterly* 29 (Spring 1965): 145–157.

movements, many more have come to be somewhat attracted to them, creating a significant reservoir of potential members and supporters. And beyond this latter group, many others have simply become dissatisfied with the churches and have abandoned all commitments to organized religion. Thus, the religious realm shares some of the same characteristics that have been seen in the political and economic sectors in recent years. Although religion is still a strong social institution, its legitimacy has been eroded, like that of the political order, to the extent that many people currently express dissatisfaction with it. The American religious institution has also come to a point, like the economic system, where new groups are vying for inclusion. Americans have gradually redefined the character of the economic system so that blacks, women, and other minorities might come to be more fully included in its rewards. Similarly, Americans appear to be on the verge of expanding their definition of what constitutes an acceptable religious commitment so that Eastern religions and, indeed, nonreligious orientations, may take their place alongside Christianity as legitimate faiths.

FAMILY ARRANGEMENTS AND SEXUAL STYLES

A fourth area in which highly visible counter-cultural experiments occurred during the sixties is in family patterns and sexual conduct. For a time, the Sexual Freedom League made the headlines as frequently as the antiwar movement. Free speech and free universities seemed to imply free love as well. The "hippie commune" became a symbol of novel sexual experiments. Group marriages and trial marriages caught the imagination of the press. Agitation for homosexual freedom, gay liberation, came to be nearly as familiar as liberation movements for women and racial minorities.

These experiments provoked, and have continued to provoke, considerable debate about what broader trends might be taking place with regard to family and sexual values. Most young people were obviously not living in communes or cohabiting with the opposite sex. Yet there was speculation that subtle shifts in sexual mores might be occurring on a wide scale.

Available data on family and sexual patterns is too sparse to draw firm conclusions about the extent of change. Clearly the dominant pattern of living arrangements still remains the nuclear, conjugal family. The proportion of people who marry and who have children has remained virtually the same for over a century.[26] But there is also evidence that the family, like other institutions, may be in the midst of profound unrest and transition. This evidence suggests that there have been important shifts both in the numbers who are experimenting with alternative family and sexual styles and in the attitudes of those who are not experimenting.

The trial marriage is one such alternative to more conventional marital arrangements that seems to be gaining in acceptance, if not in actual practice. According to census figures, cohabitation between unmarried members of the opposite sex has increased dramatically in the last decade.[27] In the 1960 census only 17,000 persons reported they were living with a partner of the opposite sex to whom they were not married. By 1970, however, this figure had increased to 143,000 persons, an increase of over 700 percent in a single decade. Millions more, the Census Bureau estimated, were also practicing cohabitation. Either the number choosing this arrangement has substantially risen, therefore, or the arrangement has become more socially acceptable so that larger and larger numbers are acknowledging it.

There are no figures from national polls to show whether approval of cohabitation has actually increased. One recent poll, however, shows that about one fourth of the population currently approves of "living together out of wedlock" and 15 percent say they would be likely to do it themselves.[28] That approval in some parts of the country is even more widespread is shown by the Bay Area data. When asked their opinion of "an unmarried couple living together," 55 percent said they were mostly in favor, compared with 35 percent who said they were mostly opposed (the remainder were undecided).

Another alternative living arrangement that has also received much publicity is the commune. To date, no one has attempted to estimate how many communes there are altogether in the United States. Such an estimate, indeed, would be virtually impossible to make since many communes are small and often without a name, consisting perhaps of only several couples living together. Even census figures on group living arrangements are too crude to sift out those who are actually living in a communal relationship. One rough

26. U.S. Bureau of the Census, *Statistical Abstract of the United States: 1973* (Washington D.C.: Government Printing Office, 1973).

27. William Safire, "Couples Who Don't Get Married," *New York Times,* October 18, 1973.

28. Institute of Life Insurance, national adult sample, June 1973.

estimate provided by the National Institute of Health in 1970, nevertheless, suggested that there were approximately 3,000 communes in urban areas alone and probably a substantially larger number in rural areas.[29] If this were the case, the number was undoubtedly larger than it would have been a decade before and, according to all indications, even larger than what it would have been in the middle of the nineteenth century, the other time in American history when communes, such as the Fourierist and Owenite sects, came into the public eye.[30]

In the Bay Area the number reporting at present living in communes is extremely small—only nine in a thousand. There is a substantial amount of acceptance of communes, however. Seventy-six percent altogether express some form of approval, 1 percent saying they are now living in a commune, 12 percent saying they "would like to try living in a commune for a while," and 63 percent saying communes are "OK for others, but they're not for me." Only 22 percent say they "dislike the whole idea." Although there is no evidence over any time span on these attitudes, one finding from a national study of college students helps at least to put the present figures in perspective. When asked how they regarded communes, 38 percent said they'd be interested in living in one for at least a few years.[31]

Besides alternative living arrangements, experimentation with new standards of sexual conduct has also emerged as an apparently growing phenomenon. In some ways this experimentation does not represent as great a departure from traditional family patterns as new kinds of living arrangements do, but it has undoubtedly involved more people directly. This shift in attitudes and behavior is documented in a number of recent polls and surveys.

One attitude that has clearly changed is that concerning premarital sex. Between 1969 and 1973, for example, the proportion of persons on national Gallup polls saying premarital sex is wrong dropped from

29. Herbert A. Otto, "Communes: The Alternative Life-Style," *Saturday Review* (April 24, 1971): 16–21.
30. See for example, Rosabeth Moss Kanter, *Commitment and Community: Communes and Utopias in Sociological Perspective* (Cambridge, Mass.: Harvard University Press, 1972).
31. Daniel Yankelovich, *The Changing Values on Campus: Political and Personal Attitudes of Today's College Students* (New York: Washington Square Press, 1972).

68 percent to 48 percent.[32] This drop is especially significant in light of the fact that somewhat similar questions in 1937 and in 1959 had shown no change during that period. Twenty-two percent on each poll said premarital sex is all right.[33] Much of the shift in this attitude, in other words, has apparently taken place only since the beginning of the 1960s.

Changes in attitudes regarding premarital sex have also been documented by polls taken among young people. National surveys of noncollege young people between the ages of 16 and 25, conducted in 1969 and 1973 by Daniel Yankelovich, for example, show a drop from 57 percent to 34 percent in the number who think "casual premarital sexual relations are morally wrong.,"[34] This shift in attitude is also evident in practice. For instance, the proportion of college students nationally who said they had had premarital sex rose from 51 percent to 63 percent between 1969 and 1971 alone.[35]

Another form of sexual experimentation that has aroused a considerable degree of public attention is homosexuality. Regardless of whether the extent of homosexual relations has actually increased, public acceptance of these relations has clearly risen. The number of respondents on national Harris polls who think homosexuals "do more harm than good for the country," for example, decreased from 70 percent in 1965, to 63 percent in 1969, and then to 50 percent in 1973.[36] The Yankelovich surveys of noncollege young people show a similar shift, from 72 percent in 1969 to 47 percent in 1973 who think "relations between consenting homosexuals are wrong."[37] And the 1971 and 1973 surveys of senior men at the University of California, Berkeley, show an increase in the number who strongly approve of "legalization of homosexual relations between consenting adults," from 49 percent in 1971 to 62 percent

32. *Current Opinion* 1 (September 1973): 93. While attitudes toward premarital sex are becoming more liberal, it is interesting to note that an eleven-nation survey of young people still found U.S. youth relatively conservative, ranking seventh in the proportion approving of premarital sex (*Gallup Opinion Index*, October 1973, Report No. 100).

33. Hazel Gaudet Erskine, "The Polls: Morality," *Public Opinion Quarterly* 30 (Winter 1966–1967): 669–680.

34. *San Francisco Chronicle*, May 20, 1974.

35. *Gallup Opinion Index*, July 1972, Report No. 85.

36. *Current Opinion* 1 (November 1973): 116.

37. *San Francisco Chronicle*, May 20, 1974.

in 1973. In the Bay Area a somewhat similar question found 45 percent in favor of "more freedom for homosexuals" and 42 percent opposed.

Other scattered questions on sexual relations, it might be added, also show similar trends. For example, the Yankelovich surveys of noncollege youth show that the proportion who "would welcome more acceptance of sexual freedom" rose from 22 percent in 1969 to 47 percent in 1973.[38] Similarly, a nationwide Harris survey found a large decline in the proportion who think prostitutes "do more harm than good," from 70 percent in 1965 to 46 percent in 1973.[39]

Regardless of how much change in sexual conduct there has actually been, it is perhaps also significant that the vast majority of Americans *believe* a change is taking place. In 1965, a national sample was asked: "In general, would you say people are more liberal in their attitudes toward sex now than fifty years ago, or more strict?" An overwhelming, though not surprising, 84 percent said "more liberal." Only 2 percent said "more strict."[40] The same sample was also asked whether or not "teenagers today have different attitudes toward sex than when you were a teenager." Nearly two out of three (62 percent) said yes. And when asked: "Many people say there has been a great change in attitudes toward sex in the last fifteen or twenty years, say, since the end of World War II. How much change do you think there has been in people's attitudes toward sex?" more than half (57 percent) said "great change" and almost eight out of ten (79 percent) said at least "some" change.

If a change is, indeed, taking place toward a greater acceptance of a wider variety of sexual activities, it obviously has not reached all parts of the society. Substantial segments of the population still hold to more traditional values. Yet there is to date no indication of a reversal in the trends away from these values.

Another trend which should be mentioned in the context of alternatives to traditional family and sexual patterns is the increasing amount of experimentation with divorce, remarriage, and what has been termed "serial monogamy" as alternatives to the lifelong marital bond. Increasing acceptance of these alternatives is well evidenced both in values and in practice. Statistics on attitudes

38. Ibid.
39. *Current Opinion* 1 (November 1973): 116.
40. Hazel Gaudet Erskine, "The Polls: More on Morality and Sex," *Public Opinion Quarterly* 31 (Spring 1967): 116–128.

toward divorce in the Detroit area, for example, have shown a decline in the proportion who believe divorce is wrong from 43 percent in 1958 to 18 percent in 1971.[41] A similar decline is evidenced from two national studies of Roman Catholics, one in 1952 which found 51 percent disapproving of divorce and another in 1965 which found 36 percent expressing disapproval.[42] The divorce rate itself has also increased, as is well known, especially in recent years. In 1960 it was 2.2 per 1,000 persons; in 1965, 2.5; in 1970, 3.5; and in 1972, 4.0, nearly double the 1960 figure.[43]

Finally, another kind of alternative to the conventional nuclear family that is increasingly being experimented with is the childless marriage. The advent of more effective birth control methods, a growing number of women in the work force or in school, and other factors have combined to make this a viable alternative. One indirect indication that it is being chosen increasingly is simply the declining birth rate, which has dropped since 1960 from 23.7 per 1,000 persons to 19.4 in 1965, to 18.2 in 1970, and to 15.6 in 1972.[44] Perhaps a better indicator of this trend is the number of young women who remain childless. This number has varied over the years because of economic conditions, wars, and other factors. In the last decade (1960 to 1971), however, there has been a steady increase in the proportions, from 12.6 percent to 15.0 percent for women age 25 to 29, from 24.2 percent to 35.6 percent for women age 20 to 24, and from 43.6 percent to 52.0 percent for women age 15 to 19.[45]

The overall picture drawn from these various pieces of evidence is one of an increasing degree of interest in alternative family arrangements, whether they be trial marriages, communes, premarital sexual relations, homosexual relations, divorce or separation, or marriage without children. Indeed, one corollary to this development has been an increase in the number of people who think conventional family arrangements are actually passing out of existence. For example, a 1971 poll of college students across the nation found 34 percent who

41. Duncan et al., *Social Change in a Metropolitan Community*, p. 72.
42. Andrew M. Greeley, *The Denominational Society: A Sociological Approach to Religion in America* (Glenview, Ill.: Scott, Foresman & Company, 1972), p. 140.
43. U.S. Bureau of the Census, *Statistical Abstract of the United States: 1973* (Washington D.C.: Government Printing Office, 1973), p. xiii.
44. Ibid.
45. U.S. Public Health Service, *Vital Statistics of the United States* (Washington, D.C.: Government Printing Office, 1972).

thought marriage is obsolete, an increase of 10 percent from only two years previously.[46] And a follow-up study in late 1973 found that even among young noncollege women, generally more conservative than college women, 34 percent also thought marriage is obsolete.[47] Even so, for a majority, the traditional conjugal family will undoubtedly continue to take precedence over these alternatives. Still, it seems likely that these other arrangements will continue to be available for those who want them and that increasingly they will be regarded as acceptable styles of life. As one text on family relations summarizes:

Barring some sort of massive state interference, there is unlikely to be one family pattern which everyone will automatically follow on pain of being labeled deviant, in the manner of the nuclear family. There will probably be families, there will be couples, there will be communes, homosexuals, some homosexual marriages, there will be many free individuals, men and women, who choose to spend their lives, or part of them, outside of families.[48]

ALTERNATIVE LEISURE STYLES

Thus far it has been seen that every area of society examined shows signs of relatively widespread ferment, partly manifesting itself in experiments with nonconventional arrangements and partly evident simply in an erosion of confidence in traditional social arrangements. The final area to be examined—leisure—is one in which there simply is not enough evidence to say what kind of trends may or may not be taking place. Nevertheless, it bears consideration, since this was also an area of life in which much counter-cultural experimentation emerged during the last decade. Drug use, meditation, encounter groups, ecology programs, all appeared as new ways in which at least a few people were spending their free time.

The term "leisure" is perhaps somewhat misleading. Once a variety of living arrangements and sexual styles become socially acceptable, many of them involving no kinship relations at all, the term "family" is not entirely suitable to describe them. By the same token, the term "leisure" is clearly inadequate to encompass what

46. Yankelovich, *The Changing Values on Campus*, p. 43.
47. *San Francisco Chronicle*, May 20, 1974.
48. Arlene S. Skolnick and Jerome H. Skolnick, "Rethinking the Family," pp. 1–32 in *Family in Transition: Rethinking Marriage, Sexuality, Child Rearing, and Family Organization* (Boston: Little, Brown & Company, 1971), see esp. p. 30.

some people consider merely recreational activities but others consider serious spiritual quests or personal efforts to grow or express oneself. Thus, leisure, as used here, includes a variety of activities, such as drug use, or encounter groups, or nature hikes, which from the standpoint of the broader culture might be considered activities pursued solely for the sake of relaxation, but which to those involved in them might have entirely different meanings.

Leisure has not been studied as systematically over the years as political discontent or sexual standards have been and, therefore, it is difficult to discern precisely how much turmoil and change may have been taking place in this area. The few studies that have been done have focused on more conventional forms of leisure and suggest that these are still the choices of a vast majority of persons. A national study of American young people, age 18 to 24, for example, showed that 60 percent say they usually include movies, the theater, or sporting events in their weekend activities, 71 percent get together with friends or neighbors, 44 percent go shopping, and 37 percent take part personally in sports.[49] TV, hobbies, music, and books are also often mentioned. For instance, TV viewing is the favorite way to spend an evening for 46 percent of the American population.[50] Evidence from the Bay Area also reveals a relatively strong commitment to such conventional activities. Thirty percent, for example, say they like to watch sports events a lot, and over half (59 percent) say they like to do this at least some part of the time. Nearly half (44 percent) say they watch television more than ten hours a week.

Many observers of the contemporary culture, while not denying the continued salience of conventional leisure activities, have nevertheless been impressed by a new set of leisure activities that seems to have become appealing to many people, especially the young.[51] Among the more familiar of these activities are drug use, sensitivity sessions, encounter groups, body-awareness groups, "back-to-nature" movements, organic gardening, and similar pursuits.

49. *Gallup Opinion Index*, October 1973, Report No. 100.
50. *The Gallup Poll*, February 1974.
51. See for example, Charles A. Reich, *The Greening of America* (New York: Bantam Books, 1970); Theodore Roszak, *The Making of a Counter Culture* (New York: Doubleday & Company, 1969); Philip Slater, *The Pursuit of Loneliness* (Boston: Beacon Press, 1970); Gibson Winter, *Being Free* (New York: The Macmillan Company, 1970); Henry Malcolm, *Generation of Narcissus* (Boston: Little, Brown & Company, 1971); William Braden, *The Age of Aquarius* (New York: Pocket Books, 1971).

Unfortunately, it isn't known precisely how widespread these activities are, nor whether they are gaining popularity or remaining about the same. Many such activities have obviously had precedents. Still, it is clear that new organizations have been formed in recent years, such as the many growth-group centers, to encourage people in these activities. Some trends, such as trends in drug use, have actually been documented. And others of these activities, like the "back-to-nature" movement, have had new meanings ascribed, even if the form they take is not entirely different from leisure activities of the past.

In the absence of other data on these phenomena, we decided to obtain at least some information about their current popularity in the Bay Area. It was not possible to obtain data on a whole variety of leisure experiments, since the Bay Area survey was concerned with obtaining information about other kinds of experiments. Three kinds of leisure experiments were singled out for inclusion as possible representatives of other kinds as well. These are drug use, growth groups and introspective values, and the "back-to-nature" movement.

Taking drugs has been one of the most widely discussed of the current leisure experiments. It is also the one activity for which figures covering a period of time are available. Nationally, the number who have ever tried marijuana, for instance, remains relatively small (12 percent in 1973), but this number is three times what it was just four years previously.[52] Among college students, the late sixties and early seventies also showed a remarkable increase in marijuana experimentation, from only 5 percent in the spring of 1967 to a majority (55 percent) in the spring of 1974.[53] And between 1967 and 1971 the proportion of students who had tried LSD grew from 1 percent to 18 percent.[54] Substantially larger numbers of persons, as might be expected, approve of drug use, even though they have never tried drugs themselves, and think such drugs as marijuana should be legalized. These numbers have also been increasing. Nationally, support for the legalization of marijuana has edged up from 12 percent in 1969 to 27 percent in 1974, and national studies of high school students have shown approval of the "sale

52. *Gallup Opinion Index,* March 1973, Report No. 93.
53. *Gallup Opinion Index,* February 1972, Report No. 80; *San Francisco Chronicle,* May 13, 1974.
54. *Gallup Opinion Index,* February 1972, Report No. 80.

and possession of marijuana" more than doubling, from 11 percent in 1969 to 28 percent in 1972.[55]

In comparison with these figures the Bay Area shows a remarkable amount of interest in and experimentation with drugs. Forty-four percent altogether claim they have "smoked dope," nearly four times the national figure, and among respondents under 30 this proportion is an amazing 70 percent. Much of this proportion, however, seems to be relatively casual experimentation, for only 27 percent even among the young people say they like to smoke dope either a lot or some. Still, 53 percent of the young people say they have experienced a "high" on drugs at one time or another, and about one third of these say it has had a lasting effect on their lives. Among those youths who have had a lasting experience from drugs, a high degree of involvement with drugs is also indicated by the fact that eight out of ten have had a "high" within the past year and about three out of four say they have taken drugs many times. There is also a relatively high degree of more general tolerance in the Bay Area toward legalizing marijuana. Forty percent say they are mostly in favor of it.

The second kind of spare time activity about which data was obtained is the growth group or encounter group. T-groups, sensory awareness groups, bioenergetics, sensitivity training, and similar group activities are all phenomena that have emerged largely since World War II and have come to function as alternatives to more conventional uses of free time, at least for some people.[56] The numbers involved in such activities appear to be relatively small as a percentage of the total population, yet they are fairly substantial in absolute terms. Seventeen percent of the Bay Area sample (28 percent of the youth subsample) say they have taken part in some kind of encounter group, sensory awareness group, sensitivity training, T-group, or growth group. About 6 percent say they have taken

55. *Gallup Opinion Index,* March 1973, Report No. 93. The Purdue Opinion Panel, December 1972, Purdue Research Foundation, West Lafayette, Indiana (mimeo). Similar trends have also been shown by The California Poll: between 1969 and late 1973, the proportion favoring the legalization of marijuana grew from 13 percent to 29 percent, the proportion agreeing that marijuana is no more dangerous than alcohol rose from 16 percent to 32 percent, and the proportion agreeing that marijuana should not be considered in the same class as LSD mounted from 29 percent to 47 percent.

56. See for example, Kurt W. Back, *Beyond Words: The Story of Sensitivity Training and the Encounter Movement* (Baltimore: Penguin Books, 1973).

part many times. And virtually all who have taken part believe that their experience has been helpful rather than harmful.

A somewhat more detailed assessment of interest in growth groups was also obtained from the Bay Area respondents by asking them about the extent of their familiarity with, attraction to, and participation in three specific growth groups that have been much publicized in the Bay Area as well as elsewhere: Synanon, Scientology, and EST. Synanon consists of a string of communities, located primarily in California, in which an estimated 15,000 persons have resided at one time or another. Originally a therapeutic community for the rehabilitation of drug and alcohol addicts, it has evolved into a social movement intended to provide an alternative way of life for anyone who wants such a collective style of living. Besides "life-stylers," it also attracts more casual experimenters who attend encounter sessions offered by the organization.[57] Scientology, founded by L. Ron Hubbard in the fifties, claims to be a religious organization promising "total freedom of the soul through wisdom." It is reputed to have over 250,000 disciples in California alone.[58] EST, a group that originated in San Francisco in the early seventies, stands for Erhard Seminars Training, named after its founder and central figure, Werner Erhard. It falls generally within the bounds of the so-called human potential movement, ostensibly providing people with new insights about themselves through a series of weekend and/or evening training sessions. In the first three years of its existence approximately 20,000 people participated in its weekend training sessions.[59] These groups are, of course, only a sampling of the growth centers in the Bay Area. Sources close to these phenomena estimate there are about twenty major growth centers in the Bay Area, plus scores of less formal groups.

Judging from the responses to these three movements, there is a fairly substantial amount of interest in growth groups, although only a few people actually participate in them. Synanon, for example, is something about which over half the people in the Bay Area (52 percent) claim to know at least a little, and of these nearly half

57. Richard Ofshe, "Synanon: The People Business," in Glock and Bellah, *The New Religious Consciousness.*
58. George Malko, *Scientology: The Now Religion* (New York: Dell Publishing Company, 1970).
59. Donald Stone, forthcoming dissertation on EST and the Human Potential Movement, Department of Sociology, University of California, Berkeley.

(47 percent) are strongly or mildly attracted while only 13 percent are "turned off." Still, only 3.1 percent of the sample claim to have ever taken part in Synanon. EST is considerably less well known than Synanon, probably because of its preference for communication through personal contacts rather than the mass media. Only 6 percent of the sample have heard of it. Among these, however, there is a fairly favorable response, 54 percent being mildly or strongly attracted and only 16 percent being repulsed. There is also a relatively high rate of participation (24 percent) among those familiar with EST, although only 1.5 percent of the total sample have ever taken part in it. Scientology is less well known than Synanon but better known than EST. Twenty-four percent claim to know at least a little about it. In comparison with the other groups, it elicits a fairly negative response, however, with only 25 percent being attracted but 37 percent being repulsed. It also has tempted the fewest number to take part (1.1 percent) even though it has been in existence the longest.

This evidence in combination with that about encounter groups suggests that perhaps no more than about 5 percent of the Bay Area residents are, or have been, at all seriously involved with new kinds of growth or sensitivity groups. Somewhere around a fourth of the population, however, seems to be attracted to these groups and has perhaps experimented with them casually. Twenty-four percent, for example, are attracted to at least one of the three growth groups.

If relatively few persons say they actually participate in growth groups or sensitivity training, other evidence from the Bay Area, however, suggests that getting to know the inner self or the body is an activity that substantial numbers of Bay Area residents deem important. For example, 33 percent say that "spending time getting to know your inner self" is of great importance to them, and 28 percent say that "learning to be aware of your body" is of great importance. Although these are not large proportions, they are larger than the proportions who attach great importance, for example, to more conventional activities such as "having a beautiful home, a new car, and other nice things," "having a high paying job," or "taking part in church or synagogue."

The other kind of free-time activity the Bay Area survey asked about is nature-oriented pursuits. Such pursuits are by no means new to American culture, but social observers have noted what seems to be a renaissance of such interests, as evidenced by the founding of rural communes, the "natural" foods and other natural products craze, and even an apparent rebirth of interest in Wordsworth, Blake, and the pastoral poets.[60]

Some of the extent to which "back-to-nature" has become an appealing pursuit can be seen in several recent polls of college students. For example, a national survey of college students in 1971 found 43 percent "interested in living off the land," 9 percent as a permanent arrangement.[61] Similarly, the 1971 survey of senior men at the University of California, Berkeley, found that, while only 11 percent had been raised in a rural area, 39 percent chose this as the location in which they would most like to live.

The Bay Area survey asked two questions about nature-oriented activities. One was how important "living close to nature" is. Thirty-eight percent said it was of great importance to them, and another 32 percent said it was of fair importance. Twenty-two percent listed it as one of their three most important values. In comparison with other activities asked about, living close to nature is actually one of the more widely held values in the Bay Area. The proportion attributing great importance to it is larger than that for 12 of the 17 activities listed. The other question, posed in the form of a story, asked respondents to choose between the appeal of the wilderness and a chance to make a contribution to society:

Jim Smith was a talented young scientist doing research on cancer; then he moved away to the Alaskan wilderness with some of his friends and made plans to spend his life there living off the land. Without knowing anything else about him, do you think that Jim is someone you would probably admire or probably not admire?

On this question the Bay Area is about evenly split, with 54 percent saying they would admire Jim and 44 percent saying they would not admire him.

These questions evidence a fairly widespread interest in nature-oriented activities. Whether there was more or less interest in such activities in the past is a question that must be left open. Whether or not there has been a change in these interests, however, the present data does hint that interests in nature may be taking on a

60. See for example, Reich, *The Greening of America*; Theodore Roszak, *Where the Wasteland Ends* (New York: Doubleday & Company, 1973); John J. McDermott, "Nature Nostalgia and the City: An American Dilemma," *Soundings* 55 (Spring 1972): 1–20; Maynard Kaufman, "The New Homesteading Movement: From Utopia to Eutopia," *Soundings* 55 (Spring 1972): 63–82.
61. Yankelovich, *The Changing Values on Campus*.

different meaning than they have had in the past. This hint comes from comparing the data on young people with those of older people, so it is not a firm indicator of change. But change is always one possibility that must be entertained when generational differences are discovered.

Slightly more younger people than older people hold nature as a value, but the main difference between the young and the old is in the kinds of things that go along with holding this value. One difference is that, for young people, exploring nature seems to be part of a more general interest in self-expressive and introspective activities, while for older people it isn't. In the youth subsample, for example, there is a moderate relation between valuing a life spent close to nature and a life spent getting to know the inner self, but in the older subsample there is virtually no relation between these two values.[62] Similarly, there is a moderate relation with valuing body awareness among youth but hardly any among older persons.[63] Another difference between the generations is that for younger people exploring nature seems to be a value that has implications for social policy, but for older people it hasn't. For instance, youths who admire Jim Smith for going to live in the Alaskan wilderness are significantly more likely than youths who do not to choose a conservationist solution to energy problems when the question is posed:

In another political race, Adams is running against Brown. Their state has been growing rapidly and experts say there will soon be a shortage of electrical power.

ADAMS is in favor of building a new atomic plant and argues that it won't hurt the environment any.

BROWN argues that we could do without a new power plant and that we should start conserving our natural resources.

Which candidate would you vote for?

Older persons, in contrast, show virtually no relation between this policy question and their attitudes toward Jim Smith.[64] The implication is that a generational change may be occurring in the *meaning* of nature-oriented activities, regardless of whether there are any trends in the extent of interest in such activities.

62. Goodman's statistic gamma, which varies between ± 1.000, but which in social science research seldom exceeds ± .500 is a moderate .209 for young people but only .075 for older people.
63. The gamma for young people is .203, for old people .033.
64. The gamma for young people is .211, for old people .026.

All in all, the evidence on alternative leisure styles suggests that a relatively small number of people have actually become involved with such activities as drug use or encounter groups. But perhaps as many as one in every four persons expresses some degree of interest in these activities. With respect to drug use, there is evidence of growing approval, although the proportions are still relatively small. No evidence exists on other nonconventional leisure activities to indicate whether they have increased or not. Still, it is clear that the founding of centers such as Esalen and Synanon or even the publication of guides such as the *Whole Earth Catalog* have made some of these activities more available to the casual experimenter than they were fifteen or twenty years ago. In contrast to the other aspects of society examined, there is no evidence that suggests that large numbers of people are somewhat dissatisfied with traditional leisure styles. Perhaps other kinds of questions would disclose such feelings. But the data that now exist suggest that most people are still relatively committed to traditional leisure activities. To the extent that something new of significance is happening in this area, therefore, it appears to be more an expansion of the kinds of leisure activities that are available than an erosion of traditional leisure forms.

CONCLUSIONS

This chapter has attempted to outline some of the kinds of "radical" or "counter-cultural" social experimentation that have taken place in recent years. This has been in preparation for the task of discovering why this experimentation has occurred.

The data examined indicate that experiments with nonconventional social forms have taken place in virtually every area of American society. These experiments appear to reflect at least partly a broader erosion of confidence in traditional social arrangements. This erosion has by no means led to massive withdrawals of commitment from conventional social arrangements. It has, however, become manifest in relatively widespread feelings of dissatisfaction with the performance of traditional social institutions and in relatively pronounced expressions of interest in bringing about some form of change.

Thus far, one of the chief outcomes of the recent unrest has been a noticeable expansion of the range of life styles and commitments that are considered legitimate forms of behavior. Although traditional patterns of life still command the loyalties of the vast majority, other patterns have also become acceptable alternatives. At the same time, there are signs that the social fabric is also being expanded in another direction, namely, to include minority groups and minority interests on a more equitable basis than in the past.

As for the actual magnitude of social experimentation, the data tend to confirm one widely held suspicion about the recent counter-culture: even though it was highly visible and of considerable fascination to social observers, it actually involved only a tiny fraction of the American people. Most of the experiments for which data exist involved no more than about 5 percent of the public. Beyond this group, though, there is a larger minority who express interest in or approval of these experiments. This minority appears to average about 25 percent of the American people, whether the issue involved is major political change, women's liberation, communes, or some other issue. Then there is the larger segment who in some way express a lack of commitment to traditional social arrangements. The scope of these feelings varies considerably depending on the issue involved, but often the proportion of the population holding them seems to run as high as 50 percent.

The available data permitting comparison over time indicate consistently that unrest and experimentation have also increased gradually over the past fifteen or twenty years, indeed, probably ever since the close of World War II. This is not to say that unrest hasn't been at even higher levels at previous times in American history. But the present data raise forcefully the question of why unrest and experimentation of so many kinds have been increasing in almost linear fashion in recent years.

Even though their numbers are few, the small minority who have actually become committed to alternative life styles is extremely significant. Without them, much of the recent disenchantment and unrest might well have been passed off as having little effect on actual behavior. Yet, in seeking an explanation for the emergence of social experimentation, we shall not be concerned exclusively with this small minority. Rather, our interest will also focus on the more general shifts in attitudes and values that have clearly been taking place in recent years. In the chapters that follow we shall attempt to discover if there may be some shifts taking place in our basic under-standings of ourselves that may be nourishing these more specific forms of unrest and experimentation.

CHAPTER 2

Consciousness and Meaning Systems

The question that lies central to this study is whether there is a relation between two phenomena: the counter-cultural experimentation that has appeared in recent years and the general understandings with which Americans make sense of their lives. We have been concerned thus far with describing what the first of these two phenomena was and is. Our attention turns now to the second.

Terms such as "consciousness," "meaning systems," "understandings of life," express abstract concepts that are subject to much misinterpretation and confusion. Unlike more familiar concepts (social class, for example) they have not been used systematically enough to have acquired meanings to which most people would readily agree. But since these are the terms that most accurately describe the phenomena we will be considering in all the remaining chapters, it is of central importance that their meaning be clearly understood.

This chapter introduces and defines the concept "meaning system" as a more precise term for what has thus far been loosely referred to as understandings, world views, creeds, and so forth. To delineate accurately what is meant by this concept, it will be necessary to describe it in relation to the more general human process of reality construction that will be referred to here as "consciousness." This chapter, of necessity, digresses from the more immediate problem of accounting for contemporary social experimentation. But it will facilitate clarity, as a matter of procedure, to establish the *general* philosophical parameters of meaning systems before turning to the specific meaning systems whose relations to social experimentation we shall be examining empirically.

The delimiting characteristics of meaning systems are developed in extensive detail in the pages which follow. This degree of detail is dealt with for two reasons. First, meaning systems are not phenomena that can be defined in terms of such commonly used concepts as attitude, belief, or value. The use of the term itself derives from a distinct philosophical tradition which emphasizes the role of symbolism and the meanings that inhere in particular symbolic configurations. This philosophical tradition has been advanced in several areas, perhaps most clearly in the work of Susanne Langer, Ernst Cassirer, and Alfred Schutz. While it will not be necessary to expand at length upon this tradition, the concept of meaning systems can best be described in relation to it. Second, the dominant thrust of work to date on matters related to what will be considered here as meaning systems has been concerned with the meanings that derive from everyday life or what Schutz termed everyday reality. The emphasis in the present study runs directly counter to the emphasis of this previous work. We shall here be concerned with those meaning systems that *transcend* everyday reality. There is need, therefore, at a conceptual level to establish that these transcendent meaning systems have significance over and against the more specific meanings of everyday reality and to indicate generally what this significance is. This is even more so the case since the role of transcendence has tended to be minimized in modern culture. In developing the concept of meaning systems we shall be especially concerned, therefore, with contrasting these meaning systems with that level of consciousness concerned exclusively with everyday reality.

This chapter considers, first, the character of consciousness as a general reality construction process; second, the specific characteristics of everyday reality; and third, the distinguishing characteristics of transcendent meaning systems. The purpose of the first section is to indicate simply that reality is indeed a product of consciousness rather than simply a "given." The second section seeks to demonstrate the incompleteness of everyday reality taken by itself. The third section describes the nature and functions of transcendent meaning systems as compared with everyday reality. Having established what meaning systems are and in general terms what their functions are, we shall be in a position in Chapter 3 to examine the four meaning systems that appear to be especially germane to the problem of accounting for the recent social unrest and experimentation.

CONSCIOUSNESS AS THE CONSTRUCTION OF REALITY

In the normal round of daily affairs reality does not appear as a product of consciousness, but as an independent entity. Like Sancho Panza, we are persuaded that our eyes do not make the world; they only see it. Reality presents itself as "the way things are," as actuality, fact, truth. It tends to become cloaked in a vesture of authority that evokes a willing suspension of doubt that things may not actually be what they seem. Reality seems sufficiently obvious that others besides ourselves would vouch for its existence.[1] It is something more than the private ruminations of our minds, for these may be illusions. Reality exists in space and time and consists primarily of objects and events which have specified forms and durations. It forms the permanent, familiar world in which we live.

But reality is like this because we construct it to be so. Reality is an entity that depends for its very existence upon human consciousness. Through the selective organization of objects and events into patterns, and through the location of objects and events in symbolic frames of reference, reality is molded and given its basic identity. So fundamental is this process to human consciousness that consciousness itself may be defined, among other ways of defining it, as *the ongoing process of constructing reality out of symbols and experience*. The manner in which this process operates can be seen in a simple example.

In front of me is a desk, an object so familiar that for the most part it can merely be taken for granted. Yet it is not something that I perceive in all of its pure complexity and ambiguity. It exists as a meaningful reality only through human construction. I discount the fact that it is actually more like a table, having but one small drawer and four long legs, than a desk. It could be used for eating and the drawer for silverware, but I interpret its significance for me as something upon which to write. It obviously has a blotter instead of a tablecloth and is located in an office rather than in a dining room. By emphasizing some of its features and disregarding others and by perceiving it in one context rather than another, I am able to categorize it with other objects which I know to be used for writing. Consequently, it becomes a reality for me as a "desk."

1. In Alfred Schutz' terms, reality is "intersubjective" (*Collected Papers,* Vol. I, The Hague: Nijhoff, 1962).

To say that consciousness is the process of constructing reality and, thereby, that reality is a product of consciousness, is not to deny the objective existence of phenomena or actualities. But "actuality" is not synonymous with what is perceived and interpreted as "reality."

The processes by which reality is humanly constructed consist principally of *selection* and *organization*. Merely because of the physiological limitations of the human senses, objects and events are never preceived as the complete sum of their diverse characteristics. Not all frequencies of sound can be heard. Not all hues of color can be seen. But selectivity is also involved in the construction of reality beyond that which is imposed by the limitations of the senses. Reality is selectively constructed according to one's purposes, predispositions, past experiences, and the symbols and imagery one brings to bear upon it.

The degree to which selective processes of human consciousness operate to mold reality is clearly illustrated by the extent to which recurrent rather than erratic events, and stable rather than unstable objects, become the primary ingredients of one's definition of reality. Psychological research has shown that from early childhood stable events and objects elicit signs of pleasure rather than fear, even when they may have no practical use, simply because they become familiar.[2] They give an aura of permanence and security to the infant's world. Then, as the child develops, they function as landmarks in relation to which new realities are defined. In adulthood reality also tends to be constructed to provide a fairly high degree of permanence and familiarity. Unusual events are often more likely to be disbelieved than the familiar objects surrounding us in home and office day after day. These soon become realities that are simply taken for granted.

Selectivity plays an important role in human consciousness, because the only way in which some constructions of reality can be maintained is by excluding or denying other aspects or interpretations of reality. One can look at a figure-ground drawing, for example, and see a picture of an old woman only by excluding from perception the lines that turn the drawing into a picture of a young woman. The selective aspect of human consciousness means that reality, as it is perceived, is always something less than what might

2. Jean Piaget, *The Construction of Reality in the Child* (New York: Ballantine Books, 1954).

have been perceived. It also means that different realities can be constructed from the same objects and events, depending on the characteristics upon which attention is centered.

The process by which reality is constructed consists not only of selectively emphasizing objects and events, but also of organizing them into patterns. Five identical words create quite different realities when organized in different ways: the dog bit the postman; the postman bit the dog. Like words in sentences, experiences are always related to form patterns rather than standing as isolated events. They are assigned labels which become the basis for categorizing them with like experiences and distinguishing them from dissimilar experiences. Connections are posited which relate categories in broader constellations. For example, events may be interpreted as the causes or consequences of one another, as mere coincidences, or as indications of some broader experience. Without organization, objects and events stand as isolated, meaningless phenomena. The organization of experience is therefore not simply something that occurs only upon reflection, not simply a matter of recalling events and trying to cast an interpretation upon them, but it is constitutive of meaningful experience itself. Even the pure "unorganized" experience of the mystic who claims, for example, to transcend "time" or to go beyond both "time" and "timelessness" does not exist apart from the distinctions that such organizing concepts as "time" make possible. The experience of reality consists of an endless stream of nearly automatic interpretations which organize and thereby make meaningful otherwise incomprehensible objects and events.

The process of selecting and organizing things to form reality is accomplished at least in part simply through *repetitive behavior*. The infant develops his first sense of reality through recurrent overt interaction with it.[3] He discovers that some realities are nourishing through the repeated trial-and-error process of sucking. He develops a tacit understanding of the principle of gravity by experimenting repeatedly with different ways of dropping things. In later stages of development the infant constructs more complex patterns of reality, again through repetitive behavior. His play takes the form of acting out social roles and relationships over and over again until their structure becomes an integral part of his consciousness. Through

3. Ibid.

imitation he brings together different experiences so that he can construct more complicated realities.[4] This behavior precedes the capacity to use symbols. In fact, it is out of such repetitive behavior that mental representations of reality that form the basis for using symbols first seem to develop. Recurrent interaction with objects gradually produces mental images that allow these objects to be understood with a greater degree of self-awareness and, from this self-awareness, images or "representations" develop which then form the basis for the use of verbal symbols.[5]

In adulthood reality is also constructed at least partly through repetitive behavior alone. New aspects of reality are not always learned through language, but often impress themselves upon consciousness simply through recurrent events. Many of the most familiar aspects of daily reality have been learned in this fashion. The faces of our associates, for example, tend to become recognizable realities more through recurrent interaction than through verbal descriptions. Once constructed, reality is also maintained by repetitious behavior. We maintain the reality of our home by living in it as much as by talking about it, the reality of our job by performing the many small tasks it requires each day as much as by consciously thinking about it.

Beyond patterned behavior, the processes of selection and organization by which reality is constructed also involve, of course, the use of *verbal symbols*. More complex patterns of reality can be constructed with symbols than with overt action alone. Things which are experienced at one time and place can be brought together with experiences from different times and places, allowing new concepts of reality to be defined.[6] Symbols also permit concepts of reality to be communicated. Definitions of reality do not have to be invented afresh by each person but can be learned from others. Thus reality

4. Jean Piaget, *Play, Dreams, and Imitation in Childhood* (New York: W.W. Norton & Company, 1962).

5. See inferences drawn from maze experiments by G. Mandler, "From Association to Structure," *Psychological Review* 69 (1962): 415–426; and the more general discussion found in Jerome S. Bruner, Rose R. Oliver, and Patricia M. Greenfield, *Studies in Cognitive Growth* (New York: John Wiley & Sons, 1966), pp. 1–66. See also Jean Piaget and Bärbel Inhelder, *The Psychology of the Child* (New York: Basic Books, 1969), p. 4.

6. Experimental evidence on these characteristics of symbols is reviewed in O.J. Harvey, David E. Hunt, and Harold M. Schroder, *Conceptual Systems and Personality Organization* (New York: John Wiley & Sons, 1965), pp. 24–49.

comes to be a product of the culture in which one lives and its definition varies according to the symbols that prevail in different cultures.

Besides the influence of different cultures, the character of reality is also shaped merely by the act of using symbols. The act of naming things tends to create a response set, as the Sapir-Whorf research has shown, that predisposes persons to experience reality in one way rather than another.[7] Once past experiences have been labeled, moreover, they tend to be recalled from memory in the form in which they are named, rather than in their initial state of raw complexity.

That symbols are characteristically embedded in language also means that the construction of reality is influenced by grammatical and syntactical structure. The discursive character of language alone, which strings words end to end in sequence, tends to reinforce a concept of reality that consists of events happening sequentially in linear time rather than a concept of reality based upon some other notion of time.[8] The organization of language into "hierarchically nested" categories and subcategories also molds reality. Things tend to be perceived, not as isolated fragments, but in relation to other things: as a manifestation of a larger category, as similar to this thing but different from that category of things.[9] Cognitive psychologists have, in fact, observed that children apparently learn the hierarchical structure of language and then only slowly learn to adapt their experience to this structure so that they can use language effectively.[10] Both the structural arrangement of symbols and their cultural content, then, as well as behavior alone, selectively mold reality into what it is.

7. Edward Sapir, "The Status of Linguistics as a Science," in David G. Mandelbaum (ed.), *Selected Writings of Edward Sapir* (Berkeley and Los Angeles: University of California Press, 1958); Benjamin Lee Whorf, *Language, Thought, and Reality* (New York: John Wiley & Sons, 1956).

8. Susanne K. Langer, *Philosophy in a New Key: A Study in the Symbolism of Reason, Rite, and Art* (New York: New American Library, 1942), ch. 4; H. Werner and Edith Kaplan, "The Acquisition of Word Meanings: A Developmental Study," *Monographs of Social Research on Child Development* 15 (1950): no. 51.

9. "Any sign is made up of constituent signs and/or occurs only in combination with other signs. This means that any linguistic unit at one and the same time serves as a context for simpler units and/or finds its own context in a more complex linguistic unit" (Ramon Jakobson, "Two Aspects of Language and Two Types of Aphasic Disturbances, Part II," in R. Jakobson and M. Halle, *Fundamentals of Language*, The Hague: Mouton, 1956).

10. Bruner et al., *Studies in Cognitive Growth*.

If reality is constructed rather than simply given, it follows that it can be constructed in a variety of different ways. And to some extent it is. Each of us lives in a world that is somewhat different from the worlds of those around us. Yet it is evident that there is also a high degree of agreement regarding the nature of reality. Each person may have his private worlds of fantasy and dream, but in daily life we define and experience reality sufficiently alike for communication and social interaction to take place. We make appointments and keep them. We earn our livings and buy products. We drive our cars, vote, raise our children and send them to school, all of which presuppose some common definition of reality. The process of constructing reality is not merely an idiosyncratic process, in other words, but tends to take on shared characteristics. It is for this reason that human consciousness, as the process by which reality is constructed, needs to be recognized as not simply a psychological phenomenon, but as a process linked in important ways to the functioning of society.

In the normal world of workaday life reality tends to be constructed in a relatively distinct way which is conducive to the conduct of ordinary social affairs. The manner in which reality is constructed in everyday life reveals, however, that there are also other levels of consciousness, constituted by more transcendent forms of symbolism, which must also be taken into account if the relation between consciousness and society is to be understood.

The nature of everyday reality has been discussed extensively by Alfred Schutz and more recently by Peter Berger, Thomas Luckmann, Burkhart Holzner, and others.[11] By drawing on this work it is possible to see the extent to which everyday reality is tailored to meet the exigencies of ordinary events, but also the extent to which it is of necessity rooted in more general understandings of life.

THE CONSCIOUSNESS OF EVERYDAY LIFE

In everyday life reality tends to be constructed in such a way, first of all, that primacy is given to the here and now. The immediate

11. Schutz, *Collected Papers,* Vol. I; Peter L. Berger and Thomas Luckmann, *The Social Construction of Reality: A Treatise in the Sociology of Knowledge* (Garden City, N.Y.: Doubleday & Company, 1966); Burkart Holzner, *Reality Construction in Society* (Cambridge, Mass.: Schenkman Publishing Company, 1972). See especially Alfred Schutz and Thomas Luckmann, *The Structures of the Life-World* (Evanston: Northwestern University Press, 1973).

concerns, events, and objects occupying our mental landscape from day to day are in a sense most real to us. To be sure, we live intentionally, we perceive and evaluate the here and now according to its future utility. But our long-range goals, our dreams, our ultimate purposes, tend to be much less a part of our everyday consciousness than our more immediate tasks. We become absorbed in the daily details of work and play and only peripherally concern ourselves directly with the distant future. We look around and consider our surroundings to be reality beyond question. Objects and events removed in space and time are more likely to take on an aura of unreality. Events experienced while vacationing, for example, often seem to have occurred in a dream world once they have become removed from us in space and time. We do not trust our memories to reconstruct the past nor our imaginations to envision the future as much as we tend to trust our perceptions of the present. By the same token, we tend to trust actual personal experience more than we trust hearsay reports about events happening in distant places. This is not to say that everyday reality is constituted exclusively by the here and now. I know my family to be real even when I am at work and my work to be real when I am at home. Yet that which is removed tends to fade into the horizon and becomes overshadowed by that which is immediately present.

The here and now of everyday reality is based upon conventionally accepted conceptions of time and space. Events happen in minutes, hours, and days that can be measured by clocks and calendars. This sort of time is subject to common definition and interpretation, which facilitates collective action. Time in everyday life is not the telescoped time of dreams or fiction, nor the timeless time of eternity, nor the cyclical time of the aboriginal world. Neither are there leaps forward or backward as in stories. It is linear, sequential time that can be broken into measurable, additive units. Space is also defined in standard units of measurement. Objects occupy space that can be measured and located in relation to one another in terms of distance. Space is limited to three dimensions. Additional planes are inconceivable in everyday reality.

Part of the reason for everyday reality being organized around standard definitions of time and space with emphasis upon the here and now is that it is dominated by pragmatic concerns. Everyday reality is the realm in which the physical provisions of life must be secured; consequently, it is oriented to the efficient attainment of these necessities. Egocentric concerns tend to reign. Things tend to be defined in terms of their utility for gratifying immediate needs. Persons tend to be defined in terms of the roles they perform. One's concept of self, too, is ordinarily defined chiefly in terms of the functions one fulfills. The objects and events that make up everyday reality tend not to be defined merely as things in themselves but as a product of this or an influence upon that. Perceiving reality through such an organizational filter provides immediate cues about what to manipulate to produce desired results.

The necessity of fulfilling practical needs in everyday life makes it difficult to detach oneself from this reality. The "real world" is where things count; either you win or you lose. You become immersed within it. The reality of fantasy or games may be absorbing for a time, but there is a way to escape it, an ending when one can, and should, come back to the real world. One can be a detached observer there in a way that is not normally available in everyday life. It is more difficult to gain distance from the problems of real life.

Pragmatic motives produce an everyday reality that is relatively regimented, fixed, or established. Generally it is more efficient to perpetuate existing definitions of reality than to create new ones. There is an economy in marriage, for example, that is not known to courtship. Routine streamlines the pursuit of practical objectives by reducing the number of considerations that must be taken into account in making decisions. Alternative definitions of reality which might arouse questions about the "proper" way of doing things are avoided by confining action to the realm of the familiar and the habitual. While the assembly line of life cranks out the necessities, thought is freed to focus on other things.

The pragmatic, here-and-now design of everyday reality generates, not a unitary reality, but one which is compartmentalized into discrete *spheres of relevance*. Factors which have to be taken into account for the achievement of particular goals tend to be organized into a pattern that specifies the necessary relations among them. Aspects of reality relevant to other goals are not systematically incorporated into this sphere of relevance. To cook dinner requires the construction of a culinary reality patterned out of recipes, food-stuffs, and perhaps even a quick trip to the supermarket. But this reality is compartmentalized separately from the volume of standard math tables used to solve a problem at work, from the political leaflet one finds placed on the car's windshield, and from the sexual practices one follows. These are relegated to other spheres of relevance. Their exclusion facilitates the efficiency with which dinner is prepared. Intrusion of another reality into the reality of cooking, such as a call from a colleague concerning a business deal, is both unwelcome and disorienting.

To prevent one sphere of reality from intruding upon another, boundaries, both physical and mental, are established. As Erving Goffman's work has shown, a considerable amount of physical stage-managing is used in everyday life to maintain the integrity of different parts of reality.[12] Home and office tend to be kept separate. Within each there are also demarcations between public places where social interaction may take place and backstage areas where it may not. Walls, geographic distance, secretaries and security guards, desks interposed between professionals and their clients, different modes of attire—all serve as physical barriers between different segments of everyday reality. Mental fences are also erected to keep different segments of reality corraled; for example, those which isolate one's self-identity as a mother from that as a career woman, or eating habits from health concerns, or business decisions from personal scruples.

In combination the characteristics of everyday reality make it a highly stable, highly efficient world in which to live. Ambiguities that may hamstring practical behavior are excluded. Irrelevant portions of reality are carefully bracketed. Standard definitions of time and space make collective, as well as personal, functioning possible. Reality is constructed in such a way that it can be shared and can largely be taken for granted. Everyday reality tends to be a secure and sheltering house in which to live.

But the reality of everyday life is also a taskmaster demanding an awesome price for its favor. The world is infinitely richer than the manner of construction of everyday reality allows us to experience. From birth, the multifaceted complexity of objects and events is selectively reduced through collectively imposed definitions of reality. Those things that are most practical, most stable, and most readily organized are filtered into perception with the greatest facility. Others tend to be filtered out. Selective perception reduces the

12. See especially Erving Goffman, *The Presentation of Self in Everyday Life* (Garden City, N.Y.: Doubleday & Company, 1959), ch. 3.

potential spectrum of consciousness to a narrow band of awareness which is identified as the real world.

Experiences alien to the *modus vivendi* of everyday reality, which cannot be filtered out through selective perception, tend to be defined as irrelevant or unreal. Fantasy, fiction, dreams, ecstasy, religious experiences—all tend to be boxed and labeled as a subordinate kind of experience, relevant, if at all, chiefly as means of refreshing oneself for the work of everyday life.[13] Persons are enjoined not to tarry too long in their midst. The mystery of life which such experiences attempt to convey tends not to be taken as the way things are. Or, if taken seriously, it is a mystery which is not really a mystery at all, but rather a "structured mystery," one that knows its place and that stays there until called upon. The rest of the time everyday reality tends to be where we would prefer to make our home. In the words of Wallace Stevens:

> We keep coming back and coming back
> To the real: to the hotel instead of the hymns
> That fall upon it out of the wind.[14]

Hymns falling out of the wind are too unpredictable, too ambiguous, too inefficient, too uncategorized to be of relevance to the pragmatic structure of everyday reality.

Ultimate experiences—suffering, pain, the grief of loss, the threat of death—also fail to find a way of receiving full expression and resolution within the confines of everyday reality. The here and now provides a compulsive way to avoid them, but not a way to find meaning in them. To the pragmatic, they are threats to be circumvented by whatever means possible.

Everyday reality inevitably succumbs to these experiences, however. Although it is a secure world, it is not one that can be lived in exclusively. Death and suffering creep into it with utter disregard for its fortifications. Without dreams and fantasy it becomes unbearable. Religious or ecstatic experiences periodically break through and expose its surface existence. The aesthetic survives in spite of being inefficient. Routine symbols and habitual behavior that hold ambiguity at bay eventually fail to hold back the tides of new

13. This is, of course, more the case in American culture than in many societies.
14. Wallace Stevens, "An Ordinary Evening in New Haven," in Holly Stevens (ed.), *The Palm at the End of the Mind: Selected Poems and a Play by Wallace Stevens* (New York: Vintage Books, 1972), p. 336.

symbols and experiences. The unexplained and the mysterious perpetually knock at its doors demanding entry. In sum, the world of everyday reality crumbles precariously around the edges.

Everyday reality is also cracked and fragmented within. The compartmentalized, here-and-now spheres of relevance in everyday life do not provide any overall sense of wholeness or integration in and of themselves. Each supplies only limited amounts of meaning. James Sellers has described this condition well:

> Most men find life neither meaningless nor productive of final ends—but rather reasonably well furnished with small meanings and incidental ends. Life is neither barren of goals nor decisively organized about a final goal. It is, instead, a mosaic of tidbits, small morsels of meaning and value. Life is a process of browsing or moving around in a very small orbit.[15]

The small orbit of sexuality may have meaning with respect to a limited sphere of reproductive or leisure concerns. But its meaning is disconnected from the realm of work; and even more so, until Freud at least, from the reality of dreams. By itself, the world of practical, immediate reality provides no schema for integrating these diverse spheres so that each becomes part of some larger constellation of meaning.

The need that the individual experiences for meaning and wholeness is experienced variously as the sense that one is more than the sum of his parts, a personality rather than a mere functionary, a being having continuity from the past and into the future rather than a mere object moving sporadically in time and space. The desire for wholeness is the desire to be a person amidst the many diverse and often conflicting roles one is called upon to play in everyday life. As one of the respondents in the survey expressed it, "All your life is a process of affirming a basic unity that gets by-passed along the way of everyday life."[16] The quest for wholeness is manifested in the feeling that one's experiences should somehow make sense in relation to one another. Negatively, it is the desire to resolve inconsistencies among the spheres of life, to escape the anxiety and emptiness of purposelessness. Wholeness tends to be manifested subjectively as a realization of well-being, inner harmony, fulfillment. It is this desire for wholeness that gives birth to experiences

15. James Sellers, *Theological Ethics* (New York: The Macmillan Company, 1966), pp. 62–63.
16. This and subsequent quotes from respondents in this chapter are by no means meant to be representative of the comments from the larger Bay Area sample.

and symbols which constitute a level of consciousness transcending everyday life, placing it in broader perspective and giving it larger meaning.

SYMBOLIC EXPRESSIONS OF WHOLENESS

Beyond the consciousness of everyday reality, or perhaps more accurately, beneath it, submerged below the stream of thoughts and perceptions that occupy normal waking attention, lies a system of symbols and images that evokes a larger coherence and meaning than that found in everyday reality. This level of consciousness derives from the impulse for "something more" in which to embed the reality of day-to-day existence. The assumptions and beliefs that occupy it may be called "holistic" or "transcendent" in that they express a reaching out for wholeness and fulfillment that exceed everyday life and affirm it. They constitute overarching frames of reference for the integration and interpretation of life.

In order that a sense of wholeness be grasped amidst the fragmented spheres of everyday life, commonalities that crosscut diverse experiences must be recognized—commonalities of purpose, similarities of structure, of content, of causation. Symbolism concerning Being, Life, Karma, Nature, Will, has functioned over the centuries as an archetypal expression of what have been perceived as the most basic dimensions shared by all spheres of reality. The symbol "Will" expresses the supposition that freedom of choice is a principle that operates throughout the pragmatic realms of day-to-day existence and in other realities besides, for instance, as a determinant of eternal destiny. "Being" symbolizes the common feature of reality simply as its existence, which may be understood as rooted further, as in Tillich's formulation, in a deeper "Ground of Being." Symbols and myths that center around totem animals or around ancestral deities tie things together as blood relatives having a common origin. Notions of fate or luck imply a universal condition to which persons and things are subject. Concepts of harmony or interconnectedness articulate an assumed unity and mutual dependence among things as parts of a larger totality or universe.

That dimension of consciousness which consists of understandings about life in a holistic or transcendent sense is the immediate focus of the present study. Philosophically, these understandings are conceived to be rooted in the need the individual experiences for meaning and wholeness not found within everyday reality alone. Their significance for social affairs is understood as deriving to a certain extent from the role they play within the individual personality.

Symbolism and imagery which express fundamental commonalities in life theoretically provide a means whereby communication between isolated spheres of reality can take place, a point of tangency that eases the passage from one to another as persons move through life. They can provide a common basis for resolving tensions and inconsistencies between spheres of reality and for organizing them into more meaningful complexes. The consequences of behavior in one realm upon that in another can be given expression in terms of their common denominator. Thereby discrete spheres of behavior can be coordinated toward greater personal fulfillment. Will power, for example, practiced in one sphere may be seen as producing success in another, which in turn becomes a sign of one's good fortune in ultimate matters. Mystical knowledge gained from one realm of experience may be understood as the key to illuminating all realms of experience. Holistic symbols tend to provide a way in which the diverse areas of reality can be expressed as functions of one another. Each can be made part of an equation that stands for the whole. Symbolization allows the whole to be brought into consciousness. Once the common edges of the puzzle pieces of life have been symbolized, the whole picture can be envisioned. As one person interviewed commented, "Whenever things meet, there is some aspect that is common to them. This lets people know that everything alive is one being." Or, in the words of another respondent, "Once you become more aware of the oneness of things, of the fact that we—plants, animals, man—are all enjoying life together, you become more sensitive to the universe itself and to the life-giving force within all things."

The broad perspective this level of consciousness tends to evoke is capable of providing a sense of detachment from the immediate events of daily life. Specific spheres of relevance can be viewed, not as paramount realities in themselves, but as single among multiple realities within a larger constellation. Personal freedom to move from one sphere of reality to another and from everyday reality to other realities, and to see each from new perspectives, can be gained.

The perspective of the whole tends to put specific experiences in proportion. One respondent remarked, "Trying to see myself in relation to mankind, society, and the universe makes me feel generally good about life. So when I have bad times I see them as little bad spots in a predominantly good life. It helps make the problems smaller." The urgency and immediacy of everyday events tend to be devalued in light of a more general outlook.

Symbolic expressions of wholeness and transcendence, it seems, should not be understood as denying or as standing simply outside of the realm of everyday life. Rather, they seem to represent, if a phrase may be borrowed from Dietrich Bonhoeffer, "the beyond in the midst of life." Conceptually speaking, they both encompass and exceed everyday reality. They tend to point to something beyond everyday reality and, indeed, beyond themselves. For symbolizing the whole takes attention away from exclusive fascination with the parts of life. But ironically, a perception of the whole also tends to create an awareness that there must be some larger, undefined context in which the whole is situated. On the one hand, symbolic expressions of wholeness are, as Schutz argued, rooted in the experience of everyday life and grow out of its need for meaning and unity.[17] They give acknowledgment to the empirical, the here and now, the pragmatic, the knowable. But on the other hand, they also tend to leave open a place for the supra-empirical, the eternal, the hidden dimensions of life. As Wilfred Smith has put it in discussing the nature of sacred symbols, "The sacred must always be not only ambiguous but unlimited: it is a mystery, so that no specific significance can exhaust it—there is always more wanting to be explored."[18]

It is this openness, relating the here and now to the beyond, that makes understandable the "staying power" and appeal of transdendent forms of symbolism. For instance, "luck" almost, but never quite, reveals the principles by which it operates. The Judeo-Christian God is personally knowable, but also awesomely unfathomable. Scientific law is "there" in the minutest particle of life, yet it is also a mystery which is only minusculely understood. Metaphorically speaking, the sheltering canopy that is constructed by symbolic expressions of wholeness and transcendence is not closed

17. Schutz, *Collected Papers*, Vol. I.
18. Wilfred Cantwell Smith, *Problems of Religious Truth* (New York: Charles Scribner's Sons, 1967), pp. 16–17.

but has an opening that leads into the open air above.[19] One respondent in discussing his general understanding of his life put it in these words: "Existence is an endless god-flow. Matter expands out of nothing and goes back into it. The two are one. Life is real not only now, but with a whisper of infinity in it. Simply being here, therefore, with infinity in me makes me full." Another respondent, in discussing the symbols and imagery that give meaning to her life, also captured with unusual poetic eloquence the sense in which these images point to an openness beyond themselves: "The rhythm of the seasons, the way day and night are, how people grow and change, the clouds in the sky, the light that lights up little children— there's so much that can't be explained when you start thinking about the nature of life. There's a lot of mystery around us."

TRANSCENDENT MEANING SYSTEMS

The sense of wholeness that these transcendent forms of symbolism express bestows added meaning upon the discrete realms of everyday reality. Meaning,.in the classic words of Wilhelm Dilthey, is "the relation of the parts of life to the whole, which is grounded in the nature of life."[20] The common "nature of life" which holistic symbolism attempts to articulate provides an overarching pattern in which discrete experiences can be located so that each becomes meaningful in relation to all the others. Within such overarching "systems of meaning" each realm of life is no longer discrete, but perceived as connected with and as having significance for other realms. Mutual effect and countereffect among realms of experience are expressed by the larger pattern that is perceived. Meanings are, as Susanne Langer has shown, not inherent in objects or events themselves, but functions of the patterns formulated among objects and events.[21] The meaning of any object or event is defined in terms

19. The metaphor of "sacred canopy" is from Peter L. Berger, *The Sacred Canopy: Elements of a Sociological Theory of Religion* (Garden City, N.Y.: Doubleday & Company, 1969); see Mircea Eliade, *The Sacred and the Profane: The Nature of Religion* (New York: Harcourt, Brace & World, 1959), pp. 172–179, for a discussion of the significance of the house with a hole in the roof in primitive mythology.
20. Wilhelm Dilthey, *Gesammelte Schriften,* VII, p. 233, quoted in H.A. Hodges, *The Philosophy of Wilhelm Dilthey* (London: Routledge & Kegan Paul, 1952), p. 143.
21. Langer, *Philosophy in a New Key,* esp. p. 56.

of its identity in relation to other objects and events and in terms of its significance for them. Thus, the total stock of meaning with which an object or event is invested is dependent upon the scope of the pattern or system in which it is located. Herbert Fingarette's discussion of meaning in psychotherapy has clearly illustrated this principle.[22] The therapist, by providing a larger frame of reference in which experiences can be reinterpreted, helps to make things "hang together" in a new way. Experiences that previously had no meaning in relation to other experiences are brought together so that latent ambiguities or anxieties can be seen. Previously unintelligible experiences make sense when viewed subsequently from the enlarged perspective that the new frame of reference provides. And a renewed and enlarged sense of subjective well-being and significance presumably results. A sense of coherence among the pieces of life can be grasped, facilitating a more unified rather than a divided concept of self-identity. One respondent, for instance, described this larger coherence in these terms: "To me it's been important to see how everything in life ties together, to recognize the inner ties between man and the universe. Consequently, I feel I know who I am and what I can do. This makes me more relaxed with myself. I don't get hung up about a lot of things."

Symbols and images concerning life in a holistic sense tend to generate an overall sense of meaning in life by enabling the person to locate himself in a context larger than himself and larger than his immediate experience of here and now reality. They locate one's experience, in Susanne Langer's words, "not only in a place, but in Space, not only at a time, but in History."[23] Discrete experiences remain no longer isolated events but become part of an encompassing "cosmic drama." Everyday realities tend to be transformed from ends in themselves to experiences interconnected with objects and with other persons both in space and throughout time.

Locating oneself in a system of meaning that surpasses immediate events and experiences seems to provide a sense of attachment, a sense that one is an integral part of something larger than himself rather than an isolated entity. In response to the question "What gives meaning to your life?" one respondent commented, "The feeling of unity I have with those around me—being part of others.

22. Herbert Fingarette, *The Self in Transformation: Psychoanalysis, Philosophy and the Life of the Spirit* (New York: Harper & Row, 1963).
23. Langer, *Philosophy in a New Key*, p. 241.

It's a feeling of interdependence—like in a building where each part depends on another.'' Perceiving oneself in a broader frame of reference, whether the frame be defined in terms of ''nature'' symbols, supernatural concepts, or social imagery, also seems to provide a mirror in which personal identity can be groomed. As this respondent went on to say, ''I can see myself in other people and other people in myself. We are like mirrors of one another.'' Another respondent summarized well the relationship between holistic imagery and personal identity and significance in commenting: ''Everything in the universe is connected. If someone wants to take a journey, then my life should be like a little footprint along the way. Everybody lives in relation with other people and things. It's possible to recognize yourself in everything that exists.''

The psychological connection between personal meaning and a larger frame of reference is also expressed frequently in terms of purpose. Imagery involving holistic purposes specifies some ultimate goal toward which day-to-day action is or should be moving. In the service of such a goal discrete acts assume a larger significance. For example, one respondent who perceived the meaning of her life in terms of service to God commented, ''We are created by God and sent by God to make the world a better place to live in. We are like co-workers with God to help his will be done in this world. So when we help people to know God, it gives our lives meaning and purpose.'' Commitment to a holistic purpose tends to transcend the limited spheres of relevance of everyday reality and pervades all the various aspects of personal identity. Day-to-day goals are made means to a larger goal rather than ends in themselves. As a result, theoretically, a sense of overarching personal meaning is provided which is impervious to the fate of more limited goals. As one respondent summarized, ''People need to remember that there are goals which give meaning to everything else you do, long-range goals I would say. Because of these goals, the other things you do will be important.'' The meaning of specific behavior henceforth is no longer defined only within a limited sphere of relevance but in conjunction with other spheres of action. Consequently, activities in different parts of life can be coordinated and unified.

In sum, transcendent systems of meaning, viewed from the standpoint of the individual, are the components of consciousness which both overarch the compartmentalized spheres of everyday reality and include other realities that lie beyond its boundaries as well. Theoretically, their function is to integrate the discrete realms of personal life and to provide a larger frame of reference in relation to which personal meaning can be perceived.

MEANING SYSTEMS IN SOCIETY

The symbolism that provides an overarching system of meaning for individuals appears to perform a similar function for societies. Every society tends to be divided into relatively distinct institutional sectors—family, polity, medical care, education, law, recreation. Each sector is governed by a number of specific assumptions regarding those aspects of reality unique to it, assumptions about the disciplining of children, for example, or about the techniques of plea bargaining. These assumptions constitute much of what is taken for granted as everyday reality within each institutional sphere. They provide clues about what kinds of behavior are likely to be most productive or most reasonable and, thereby, make it possible for social interaction to take place within each sphere with a minimum degree of confusion. But these specific assumptions are of necessity rooted in more general understandings of reality, for the institutional sectors of society must have some basis for interaction to take place among them. They require standards of conduct to govern their interrelations for the pursuit of larger social purposes. The assumptions about reality within each sphere do not necessarily provide the cues for this larger form of interaction.

Understandings of reality which are based on symbolism such as Fate, Luck, Will Power, God, Evolution, Karma, and so forth are capable of transcending the various sectors of society. God is the God of the marketplace and the palace as well as the home. Fate applies both to the just and the unjust, to the stock market and the foxhole. The sanctity of the Will requires safeguarding in the pulpit and the poverty program alike. Such symbolism tends to integrate collective behavior by pointing to some broader, or more basic, order of reality which crosscuts as well as permeates the institutional sectors of society. The common understandings and feelings it evokes make it possible for collective goals, the allocation of collective resources to those goals, and the distribution of collective rewards to be decided upon with reference to broader assumptions and principles than those governing single institutions. It provides a potential basis for coordinating institutional behavior for the achievement of more general societal goals as well as a higher court of appeal for the resolution of conflicts between institutional sectors.

Symbolism which defines overarching frames of reference not only facilitates the integration of sectors of society but also helps to maintain the integrity of society against the limiting conditions that threaten its collective functioning. Societies inevitably fail to operate in an entirely just and equitable manner or to fulfill all the expectations of their members. Transcendent frames of reference facilitate accommodation to these conditions. Often they provide transvaluing reasons explaining why disappointment and misfortune have come: there is suffering in the world because men do not obey the gods or because they don't take responsibility for themselves; there is injustice because society operates by natural laws which perpetuate it; there is evil because men and women don't try to find inner peace and fulfillment. By providing explanations for suffering, misfortune, untimely death, and so on, these frames of reference increase the chances that collective tasks will be performed. They explain why men should work even if in the end they are only to die or why personal sacrifices should be made for the collective good even though it seems that "the wicked prosper while the good die young." They suggest answers which explain, for example, that there can be no happiness apart from service to others, or that things *can* be changed through hard work or greater knowledge, or that the world is actually *maya* and such problems illusions.

From the standpoint of the individual member of society, overarching assumptions about life facilitate the accomplishment of social objectives by integrating different role demands and by softening the shocks involved in functioning among different realities. During the normal trajectory of daily life such symbols facilitate the transition of the individual through the various social roles he performs and into other realities. The passage from dream life to family life, to work life, and to the world of games or fantasy during a typical day contains generically a considerable degree of shock and disorientation as one moves from one reality to the next. These shocks are softened by the assumptions which crosscut different realities. The principle of luck, for example, can be counted upon to operate in each reality, or each can be assumed to function according to common social psychological laws, or each can be understood as adding a unique dimension to the holistic experience of fulfillment in life.

Because of these integrating and facilitating functions, meaning systems that concern reality in a holistic sense tend to be accorded special status in societies. A considerable amount of authority tends to be vested in them and energy is expended to preserve them and to apply them to the changing contingencies of behavior in different societal realms. In the broad usage of the term, such symbols and images acquire "sacred" status in societies. Symbols such as God, Fate, Natural Law, reside on a plane that is clearly distinct from mundane symbols. The sacred character of such symbols may or may not involve being regarded explicitly with reverence. They may be accorded conscious devotion, as in the case of many religious symbols. But, perhaps more likely, their sacred character may consist more of simply being taken for granted, of being assumed so readily that they are seldom questioned. In other words, their sacred quality may involve a de facto taboo status. Since they are taken for granted, they become inviolate and self-confirming. Specific events tend to be taken for granted as examples of more general assumptions: "He was just lucky"; "Praise God"; "It's just human nature." Such succinct epithets and proverbs provide the links between concrete events and the complex, tacit assumptions by which reality is patterned.

Transcendent meaning systems appear to derive their sacred quality partly from their extraordinary efficacy in giving social reality its basic definition and meaning. They specify the superordinate frame of reference which, in Mircea Eliade's words, "founds the world in the sense that it fixes the limits and establishes the order of the world."[24] Transcendent symbols provide keystones around which more specific experiences can be organized and interpreted. As highly generalized assumptions about the nature of life, they provide ready clues about how specific events should be interpreted. For example, the meaning of a ghetto riot, given one set of transcendent symbols, may be that evil spirits have been unleashed by the devil; given another, that the inherent contradictions of the economic infrastructure have finally earned their due; given another, that the participants have been raised without proper regard for moral principles. Out of the same event, quite different realities are molded. Put differently, the understandings of life that constitute this general level of consciousness significantly influence the manner in which everyday reality is constructed. Whereas everyday reality

24. Eliade, *The Sacred and the Profane*, p. 30.

emphasizes immediately observable characteristics of the here and now, the manner in which these characteristics are interpreted—their meaning—is to a degree dependent on "higher order" assumptions about life which locate them in a broader context. The fact that these same assumptions can then provide the keys for interpreting behavior in other realms of society, ranging from sex-role relations to the latest craze in the world of sports, gives them an extraordinary role in the molding of social realities.

Not only the definition of situations tends to be influenced, but the actual behavior that follows as well. Depending upon the broad frames of reference within which specific events are located, different responses are likely to follow. Whether ghetto riots result in collective rituals to exorcise the demons provoking them, in class-based conflict, or in redoubled efforts to teach moral virtues depends upon the way in which reality is initially defined.

Transcendent forms of symbolism also stand out from ordinary symbols and acquire a "sacred" character in society because of their *enduring* quality. Collective energies tend to be expended to maintain their stability since they impinge upon the basic definition and integration of social reality. Pressures to keep out alternative interpretations of ultimate reality that may shatter prevailing assumptions are likely to be in evidence in any given society. Since specific events can be defined in different ways depending upon the frame of reference in which they are located, the legitimacy of any one definition is enhanced by simply excluding access to other frames of reference or by discrediting them. In extreme situations force may be used to drive out alternative interpretations of ultimate reality, as in religious pogroms. More commonly, alternative frames of reference are merely discredited by being labeled heresy, deviance, false consciousness, delusion, illusion, and so forth.

The stability of transcendent meaning systems is also maintained by being "acted out," so to speak, in the organization of social relations. An appropriateness of "fit" seems to develop between symbols and social organization so that each is mirrored in the other. Societies organized around paternalistic authority relations within the family, for example, are more likely than societies devoid of such structures to find "god-the-father" symbols meaningful. Paternalistic authority, in turn, tends to be articulated and legitimated by such concepts of deity. The existential situation of social life makes the overarching symbols intuitively meaningful and the nature of the symbols, in turn, articulates and legitimates the experience of social life.

Against the tendencies that stabilize transcendent symbols, though, there are also inevitable pressures that promote change. The development of new ideas within the culture of a society can reveal inconsistencies in prevailing formulations of ultimate reality or at least pose new problems that must be taken into account by systems of meaning which attempt to encompass the entirety of life. Pressures for change can also be initiated by the transmission of existing scientific, philosophical, or aesthetic ideas to new and broader constituencies within society. Changes in the existential social conditions in which transcendent symbols are grounded can also set up strains that motivate change. To understand the relationship between the level of consciousness that consists of transcendent or holistic symbols and social transformation, then, attention must be paid to both the conserving and the transforming strains which operate upon these symbols.

Apart from determining what causes change in transcendent symbols themselves, it is also an empirical question to discover what changes in specific values and social policies can be inspired by different transcendent symbols. On the one hand, transcendent meaning systems, because of their integrating and legitimating potential, would appear to perform a conservative function in society. On the other hand, transcendent meaning systems can point to realities not normally attended to in everyday life, thereby creating visions of ways in which the limitations of current social conditions can be overcome. Which of these two outcomes is most likely seems to depend upon the specific historical and cultural contexts in which different meaning systems are found, implying that their role in social change must be determined through empirical rather than impressionistic investigation.

CHAPTER 3

Meaning Systems and Experimentation: Some Propositions

Having obtained a sense of how much support for nonconventional social alternatives there is and the extent to which this support has increased over the past several years, and having indicated what is meant by the terms "consciousness" and "meaning systems," our attention can now be directed to the central question of this study: Why has support for social experimentation increased in recent years? More specifically, has it been nurtured by some deeper shift in the basic understandings of life that give us our sense of meaning and purpose?

In this chapter, four propositions will be introduced: that the appearance of widespread social experimentation has been nurtured by a decline in *theistic* meaning systems, that it has been nurtured by an erosion of *individualistic* meaning systems, that it has been nurtured by the rise of *social science* as a meaning system, and that it has been nurtured by an increase in *mystical* meaning systems. These propositions will be treated for the time being as entirely tentative. In the subsequent chapters the Bay Area data will be used to test them insofar as this is possible. But for the present our attention will be devoted to merely considering reasons why each proposition is a tenable assertion. Reasons will be stated for suggesting that there has been a decline in the prominence of the first two meaning systems and an increased prosperity among the latter two, and each meaning system will be examined for ideas that seem either conducive or resistant to social experimentation.

Proposition 1: A decline in theism has contributed to the rise of social experimentation.

Theism is an understanding of the meaning and purpose of life that places God at the center. It assumes that reality was created and given meaning by God and that the individual, by following God's will, finds meaning and purpose. Although there are many variations to this form of consciousness, it lies at the core of every major American religious faith. It implies a distinct understanding of life, one that sees God as the agent chiefly responsible for governing reality, and that finds in this understanding of God answers to life's ultimate problems.

Students of American religion have often noted the near universality with which Americans affirm their belief in God.[1] And yet there is currently a widely held view among students of religion that theism is gradually becoming less and less a vital part of the American culture. There are divergent perspectives on the exact nature of this erosion and about the reasons why it is·taking place, and not all students of American religion share the view that theism is declining. But the dominant thrust of opinion seems to be that some form of erosion has been occurring and that it has become even more prominent in the last three or four decades than in previous years.[2]

Among the conclusions to which scholars have come regarding theism, one is that it is simply withering away entirely. This conclusion is based on several observations. One is that people who came to maturity after World War II seem to be noticeably less likely to believe in God and to hold related beliefs than people who reached maturity before World War II.[3] Another is that patterns of interdenominational switching among Protestants show that most of this movement is, first, from conservatively theological denominations to liberal denominations and, second, from liberal de-

1. Gallup polls typically find over 90 percent affirmative responses to simple yes or no questions regarding belief in the existence of God.
2. This view is also widely shared by historians of religion, for example, Sydney E. Ahlstrom, *A Religious History of the American People* (New Haven: Yale University Press, 1972); Martin E. Marty, *Righteous Empire: The Protestant Experience in America* (New York: Dial Press, 1970); Langdon Gilkey, *Naming the Whirlwind: The Renewal of God-Language* (New York: Bobbs-Merrill Company, 1969).
3. Rodney Stark and Charles Y. Glock, *The Poor in Spirit: Sources of Religious Commitment* (forthcoming).

nominations to no religious affiliation at all.[4] A third observation that has led to the conclusion that theism is simply on the way out is that church attendance has been, as we have seen in Chapter 1, declining over at least the past fifteen years. Finally, there are some direct data which show declines over time in the proportion who believe in God and who hold similar beliefs. For instance, periodic surveys of the Detroit area show that between 1958 and 1971 the proportion saying they are very sure of God's existence dropped from 68 percent to 48 percent.[5] On a related subject—life after death—Gallup polls of the nation have shown a similar decline: in 1944, 76 percent believed in the existence of life after death; in 1971, 53 percent subscribed to this belief.[6] Surveys of college students over the years also show this pattern. Dean Hoge's research, for example, suggests that theism was at a high point in the 1920s when college students were first studied, that it declined during the thirties, rose again in the early fifties, and has declined steadily ever since.[7]

Scholars who feel that theism has definitely been declining have also offered compelling reasons why this decline may be expected to continue. It has been argued that supernatural revelation will increasingly be recognized to be at odds with the rational-empirical emphasis of science. The claim has also been made that modern man will increasingly find it impossible to reconcile the concept of God with an image of the universe that is no longer three-storied. Another argument is that the dogmatism and particularism presumably

4. Rodney Stark and Charles Y. Glock, *American Piety: The Nature of Religious Commitment* (Berkeley and Los Angeles: University of California Press, 1968), chs. 10 and 11. This pattern does not contradict but is consistent with the thesis put forth in Dean M. Kelley, *Why the Conservative Churches Are Growing* (New York: Harper & Row, 1972).

5. Otis Dudley Duncan, Howard Schuman, and Beverly Duncan, *Social Change in a Metropolitan Community* (New York: Russell Sage Foundation, 1973), p. 70.

6. George H. Gallup, *The Gallup Poll: Public Opinion, 1935–1971,* 3 vols. (New York: Random House, 1972), p. 2174. This shift may simply be a result of some polling differences; until 1968 responses to belief in life after death were remarkably stable. Cross-cultural studies, however, show similar declines in Norway, Finland, the Netherlands, France, Sweden, and Great Britain (Hazel Gaudet Erskine, "The Polls: Personal Religion," *Public Opinion Quarterly* 29 (Spring 1965): 145–157.

7. Dean Richard Hoge, *College Students' Religion: A Study of Trends in Attitudes and Behavior* (unpublished doctoral dissertation, Harvard University, 1969).

inherent in theism are increasingly out of tune with the dominant pluralism of American culture.[8]

That theism is gradually withering away and being replaced by some form of atheism or humanism is clearly an argument to be taken seriously, because of both the empirical and the theoretical bases upon which it rests. But throughout history theistic beliefs have shown an amazing capacity to adapt and to survive. The argument may be stated, therefore, and indeed has been, that in the present case theism will not actually fade from existence but that it will instead simply change in character. The notion of a transcendent God "out there" may be replaced, as Bishop Robinson has suggested it should, by a concept of an immanent God "in here." The distinction between a natural realm and a supernatural realm may fade to make way for a more multiplex concept of reality which can contain many kinds of reality. The traditional emphasis upon dogma and Biblical revelation may be replaced by an emphasis upon personal religious experience.[9]

It is not yet clear whether the dominant trend in theism is currently toward its complete extinction, whether a change in character is in store, or, more likely, whether some combination of these trends will continue to take place. But it is clear that in certain segments of the population large numbers have already come to understand the ultimate conditions of their lives in ways which do not include reference to God. In the Bay Area one in three no longer believes

8. See N.J. Demerath III and Phillip E. Hammond, *Religion in Social Context: Tradition and Transition* (New York: Random House, 1969), pp. 169–173; Louis Schneider, *Sociological Approach to Religion* (New York: John Wiley & Sons, 1970), ch. 9; Will Herberg, "Religion in a Secularized Society: Some Aspects of America's Three Religion Pluralism," pp. 591–599 in Louis Schneider (ed.), *Religion, Culture and Society: A Reader in the Sociology of Religion* (New York: John Wiley & Sons, 1964); compare Guy E. Swanson, "Modern Secularity," pp. 801–804 in Donald R. Cutler (ed.), *The Religious Situation* (Boston: Beacon Press, 1968) for a dissenting perspective.

9. John A.T. Robinson, *Honest to God* (Philadelphia: Westminster Press, 1963); Robert N. Bellah, *Beyond Belief: Essays on Religion in a Post-Traditional World* (New York: Harper & Row, 1970), esp. pp. 39–44; Thomas Luckmann, *The Invisible Religion: The Problem of Religion in Modern Society* (New York: The Macmillan Company, 1967); Charles Y. Glock, "The Study of Non-Belief: Perspectives on Research," in Rocco Caporale and Antonio Grumelli (eds.), *The Culture of Unbelief* (Berkeley and Los Angeles: University of California Press, 1971).

definitely in God and another 11 percent believe in "something more or beyond" but feel uncomfortable about using the word "God" to describe it. Almost one fourth (24 percent) say it is of no importance to them to follow God's will. And almost half feel that God has only a small influence on their lives.[10] Whether these proportions have increased, the Bay Area data do not say. Given the more general evidence and theoretical arguments just considered, however, it seems more than likely that they probably have.

It seems beyond question that the erosion of theism, if it is happening at all, has been taking place for at least several centuries.[11] But putting aside longer trends, the last quarter century, during which systematic data have been collected, tends to indicate that theism has been declining as a vital element in American culture, or at least has been undergoing a process of reinterpretation, during precisely the same period in which social unrest and experimentation with alternative social arrangements has been increasing.[12] If we are interested in accounting for the recent growth of unrest and experimentation, it seems obvious that one explanation that warrants serious consideration is the possibility that this unrest and experimentation has been nourished by the subsidence of theistic beliefs from their traditional place of importance in American culture. As with any simultaneous historical events, these two developments may have coincided by chance and otherwise be in no way connected. But if there is reason to believe that theism has been a restraint against social unrest and experimentation, then it becomes plausible to suspect that its fading may have permitted unrest and experimentation to grow. The critical question, therefore, is whether or not there is reason to think that theism fosters resistance to social experimentation.

On the surface it is quite apparent that theism does not *necessarily* militate against nonconventional social experiments. Christianity itself was such an experiment, as was the Protestant Reformation, the Puritan errand in the American wilderness, and countless similar undertakings. In more recent times there are certainly notable

10. Figures cited are based on the total *weighted* sample.
11. Longer-range shifts will be considered subsequently.
12. For a discussion of some of the theological events constituting this development, see Sydney E. Ahlstrom, "The Moral and Theological Revolution of the 1960's and Its Implications for American Religious History," pp. 99–118 in Herbert J. Bass (ed.), *The State of American History* (Chicago: Quadrangle Books, 1970).

examples of major social experiments being conducted in the name of theistic principles, the civil rights movement in its early period being one such instance. But such cases appear to be more the exception than the rule. What little systematic evidence has been collected suggests that the dominant tendency is for theism to be not a source of social experiments, but primarily a factor in creating opposition to them.[13] Strong theistic beliefs have typically been found to be related to low interest, low involvement, and low approval of everything from civil rights activity to radical politics to sexual experiments.[14] For the most part church leaders have simply remained silent on such issues, even though they may have favored them, fearing criticism from their parishioners. The few who have been outspoken in their support have tended to be least committed to the traditional tenets of their faith.[15] But resistance to nonconventional social experiments is by no means a recent development in American theism. Indeed its roots lie within the teachings of the early Puritan fathers themselves.[16]

From colonial times to the present an important element of

13. Many studies have simply found no correlations of general expressions of political and social conservatism with theism; those that have found correlations are overwhelmingly positive rather than negative, however. See Robert Wuthnow, "Religious Commitment and Conservatism: In Quest of an Elusive Relationship," pp. 117–132 in Charles Y. Glock (ed.), *Religion in Sociological Perspective: Essays in the Empirical Study of Religion* (Belmont, Calif.: Wadsworth Publishing Company, 1973).

14. For some recent corroborating evidence see Robert Wuthnow and Charles Y. Glock, "Religious Loyalty, Defection, and Experimentation Among College Youth," *Journal for the Scientific Study of Religion* 12 (June 1973): 157–180; "The Shifting Focus of Faith: A Survey Report," *Psychology Today* 8 (November 1974): 131–136.

15. See Rodney Stark, Bruce D. Foster, Charles Y. Glock, and Harold E. Quinley, *Wayward Shepherds: Prejudice and the Protestant Clergy* (New York: Harper & Row, 1971), esp. ch. 5; and Harold E. Quinley, *The Prophetic Clergy: Social Activism Among Protestant Ministers* (New York: John Wiley & Sons, 1974).

16. To suggest this is not necessarily to contradict Michael Walzer's well-known thesis, since we are concerned with a somewhat different time period and a somewhat different kind of social experimentation. Walzer himself provides part of the reason for suggesting that Puritan theology may lead to at least an aloofness if not a disdain for experiments designed to change society: "With the intense moral discomfort of the righteous and the high minded, Puritans sought desperately to separate themselves from the chaotic sinfulness that they imagined to surround them." Michael Walzer, *The Revolution of the Saints* (Cambridge, Mass.: Harvard University Press, 1965), p. 209.

American theism that has tended to reduce the legitimacy of social experiments is the assumption that man is inherently sinful. While the secular philosophers of the Enlightenment had high hopes for man's ability to perfect himself and the society in which he lived, the Puritan fathers took a much more skeptical view of man's inherent capacities.[17] This view of human nature played a vital part in the formation of American society. Among other places, its impact is clearly evident in the Constitution itself.

There is [wrote James Bryce] a hearty Puritanism in the view of human nature which pervades the instrument of 1787. It is the work of men who believed in original sin, and were resolved to leave open for transgressors no door which they could possibly shut. Compare this spirit with the enthusiastic optimism of the Frenchmen of 1789. It is not merely a difference of race and temperaments; it is a difference of fundamental ideas.[18]

The strong emphasis upon an omniscient creator God which became so vital a part of American culture led naturally to the assumption that man apart from God could do little that was right and good. Left to his own volition man would, it tended to be assumed, become the victim of his own base desires. "When the restraints of religion are dissolved," wrote the Reverend Uzal Ogden in a counterargument to Thomas Paine's optimistic *Age of Reason,* "what can be expected, but that men should abandon themselves to the impulse of their passions? Human laws and penalties will be insufficient to restrain men from licentiousness, where there is no just sense of the Deity; no regard to a future state, or to the due punishment of vice, and the rewards of virtue hereafter."[19] To prevent man from becoming the unhappy product of his own

17. With regard to the extent to which Puritan thought and, more generally, Calvinism were dominant influences in colonial America, Sydney Ahlstrom's recent compendium on American religious history estimates that by the time America had established itself as an independent nation approximately 85 to 90 percent of its people bore the "stamp of Geneva" (Ahlstrom, *A Religious History of the American People,* p. 124). Perry's estimate is smaller although he too concludes that a majority of Americans at the time of the Revolution were in the Puritan heritage (Ralph Barton Perry, *Puritanism and Democracy,* New York: Vanguard Press, 1944, p. 80).

18. James Bryce, *The American Commonwealth* (New York: Macmillan & Company, 1910), I, p. 306.

19. Uzal Ogden, "Antidote to Deism," quoted in Yehoshua Arieli, *Individualism and Nationalism in American Ideology* (Cambridge, Mass.: Harvard University Press, 1964), p. 248.

dissipation, God had established rules of conduct for men to follow.[20] These rules were assumed to be found clearly in the Scriptures and could be discerned without difficulty by all who walked within the will of God. Dissension or controversy over what was established as the proper interpretation of Scripture tended to be regarded with suspicion as a possible sign of unregeneracy.[21] To experiment with nonconventional life styles or social forms was to violate the moral law. At minimum such experimentation was nonsense, since God had already revealed how men ought to live. His ordinances had been tested throughout time. Attempts to improve upon them had been futile. At maximum such experimentation was likely to prove truly harmful, since God knew much better than men did what was right and good.

The Puritan view of human nature was also conducive to the establishment of strong social control mechanisms to prevent men from violating what were agreed to be God's laws. God had instituted systems of authority whereby societies should be governed. Those in positions of power operated under divine sanction, legislating regulations that had been prescribed for the common good of mankind. Rulers were always subject to the authority of Scripture, but as long as they did not blatantly violate God's law they were able to exercise a great deal of social control. Without them it was assumed that all semblance of social order would cease as each man pursued his own selfish interests.

Puritan theism also tended to legitimate a strict hierarchical order for the economic structure of society, thereby rendering meaningless experiments to bring about economic reform. God had recognized, it was assumed, that a great variety of tasks needed to be fulfilled to accomplish the goals of his kingdom. To ensure that these tasks be fulfilled, he had called men to occupy different estates in life and had given them different talents appropriate to their callings. William Hubbard in 1676 argued in his *Happiness of the People* that God had divided his overall plan for mankind into different tasks "which necessarily supposes that there must be differing places, for those differing things to be disposed into, which is Order."[22]

20. Ahlstrom, *A Religious History of the American People*, p. 129.
21. Alan Simpson, *Puritanism in Old and New England* (Chicago: University of Chicago Press, 1955), p. 24.
22. Quoted in Perry Miller, *Nature's Nation* Cambridge, Mass.: Harvard University Press, 1967), p. 44.

Some had been called to exercise leadership, others to serve; some to become wealthy, others to remain poor. To fail in one's calling was recognized as a possible sign that one had not been foreordained to God's eternal favor. But merely the fact of occupying a higher or lower station in life tended to be considered a natural part of God's order. Moreover, it was understood in Calvinistic thought that a by-product of such inequality was to ensure that each member of the corporate body of believers would be dependent upon, and therefore more considerate of, his fellow members. The fact of wealth and poverty meant, as John Winthrop explained to his following in the Bay Colony, "That every man might have need of other, and from hence they might be knitt more nearly together in the Bond of brotherly affeccion: from hence it appeares plainely that noe man is made more honourable than another or more wealthy etc. out of any particuler and singuler respect to himselfe but for the glory of his Creator and the Common good of the Creature, Man; . . ."[23] If economic inequality was both divinely instituted and humanly beneficial, there was clearly no reason to support experiments with alternative economic arrangements.

Perhaps even more importantly than the idea of the calling, the idea of the covenant also provided a powerful deterrent to social experimentation. In virtually every colony it was assumed that God had entered into a covenant that sanctioned the founding of the colony. Before the *Arbella* landed in Massachusetts harbor, John Winthrop admonished those aboard that "We shall be as a Citty upon a Hill, the eies of all people upon us."[24] Writing in his diary, he commented further that the sole purpose of the migration was "to serve the Lord and worke out our Salvacion under the power and purity of his holy Ordinances."[25] To William Penn, the founding of Pennsylvania was a "holy experiment." And to the founders of Virginia, theirs was a mission designed by God to further extend the Christian message to the world. The idea of the covenant was not simply that God made general covenants or that he made specific covenants with individuals, but that he had singled out each

23. Quoted in Loren Baritz, *City on a Hill: A History of Ideas and Myths in America* (New York: John Wiley & Sons, 1964), p. 14.
24. Quoted in Winthrop S. Hudson, *Religion in America* (New York: Charles Scribner's Sons, 1965), p. 48.
25. Quoted in Baritz, *City on a Hill*, p. 16; see also Hudson, *Religion in America*, pp. 19–21.

colony in particular to play a special role in his plan. In these colonies God's precepts were to be instituted and lived as an example to the rest of the world.

All persons who were part of the colony were understood to have entered voluntarily into a covenant with God and with each other.[26] This was the bond which, above all else, held society together for, in Thomas Hooker's words, "there is no man constrained to enter into such a condition, unlesse he will: and he that will enter, must also willingly binde and ingage himselfe to each member of that society to promote the good of the whole, or else a member actually he is not."[27] Each person was to be subject to the jurisdiction that God had established and was under the admonition that whatever he did would accrue to either the benefit or the harm of the whole community. In living morally and in obedience to established laws and customs, he helped to assure the continuance of God's blessings; in living contrary to the moral law, he was endangering the community of God's judgment and punishment. Nonconventional behavior on the part of any person, in other words, became a threat not only to the individual himself, but to the divine mission of the entire colony. Just as God had smitten Israel of old for the sins of one man when he had allowed them to be defeated at Ai for the impiety of Achan, so he might rain punishment upon the New Israel for the misdeeds of any of its members.

The power of this assumption to restrain nonconventionality is well evidenced by the plea of a young girl of Middlesex County who, in 1656, having been found guilty of the sin of fornication, confessed to the Court that "by this my sinn I have not only donn what I can to Poull doune Jugmente from the lord on my selve but allso apon the place where I live." About this incident Edmund S. Morgan comments, "In view of such a belief the reason for restraining and punishing sin is obvious. Since the whole group had promised obedience to God, the whole group would suffer for the sins of any delinquent member, unless that member were punished."[28]

Even with the strong sense of collective purpose and mutual

26. Perry Miller, *Errand into the Wilderness* (New York: Harper & Row, 1956), p. 91.
27. Thomas Hooker, *A Survey of the Summe of Church Discipline* (London, 1648), I, p. 50.
28. Edmund S. Morgan, *The Puritan Family: Religion and Domestic Relations in Seventeenth Century New England* (New York: Harper & Row, 1944), p. 10.

responsibility plus the sense of respect for authority which were implied by the theistic understanding of life, its ability to deter social experimentation could probably not have operated, however, without the additional idea that God had revealed clearly the specific commandments he wished his people to obey.[29] To the regenerate, it was assumed that the Holy Spirit would illuminate the message of the Scriptures in such a way that there could be no error and no controversy.[30] The theistic orientation, in other words, did not merely concern ultimate questions of meaning and purpose but was also a scenario for the government of everyday affairs. And to the extent that these affairs bore on the collective destiny of the community, God would ensure that his will was made clear, whether the issue concerned matters of church membership, personal morality, or economic policy. Moreover, God's will was thought to be both wise and just and, therefore, understandable and acceptable. Although his will was in the end inscrutable, beyond human comprehension, and sometimes difficult to follow, as when suffering and hardship struck, God was also assumed to be rational and committed to the system of law and order which he had placed in the natural universe.[31] Thus, it was not for man to experiment with ways to improve upon or change this order, but to uphold it in whatever way possible. In 1636 when the Antinomian controversy broke out in Massachusetts, the clergy argued against leniency for Anne Hutchinson and her comrades on the grounds that God's law is immutable and must not be bent to fit particular circumstances. "Crook not God's rules to the experience of men," one Puritan divine had written, "but bring them unto the rule, and try men's estates herein by that."[32] Deviations from the established beliefs and conduct of the community, such as the Antinomians represented, were not to be regarded with interest or curiosity, or even with sympathy, but were viewed as a kind of sore on the community which had to be excised before it festered and spread. Especially since

29. The idea of the covenant was, of course, most pronounced in Calvinistic traditions.

30. Simpson, *Puritanism in Old and New England*, p. 24.

31. In the words of one early American spokesman: "All the Commandments of God, are grounded upon cleare reason, if we were able to find it out." And another wrote: "It is his will and good pleasure to make all laws that are moral to be first good in themselves for all men, before he will impose them upon all men" (quoted in Miller, *Errand into the Wilderness*, pp. 65–66).

32. Quoted in Kai T. Erikson, *Wayward Puritans: A Study in the Sociology of Deviance* (New York: John Wiley & Sons, 1966), p. 187.

it was assumed that God's law was clear and could be interpreted in the same manner by all, deviance of this sort constituted a dangerous challenge to the very legitimacy of the accepted system of authority.[33]

The combined impact of the particular way in which God's relation to man tended to be understood by the Puritan founders produced, in sum, an image of society that gave a high degree of legitimacy to law, to order, and to authority. It implied that conformity to established patterns of conduct was clearly to be valued over attempts to deviate, to strike out on one's own, to challenge or to revolutionize the existing social order. Because of the idea that all members of the community were under a common covenant with God to fulfill the special mission he had given them, this sense of conformity and obedience to authority was not to be simply a matter of fear or of unthinking loyalty, but of mutual concern and responsibility for one's brothers and sisters under the covenant.

That this image of society should have become as pronounced as it did is ironic in light of the fact that many of the early American settlements had been founded by dissenters from established authority and seekers of religious, personal, and economic freedom.[34] Moreover, it was out of these early settlements that a national government of democracy and a creed of toleration came to be molded and institutionalized. In part the colonists' resistance to social experimentation can be understood in terms of their need, as a group facing increasing opposition from without, to maintain solidarity within their own ranks. Lewis Coser's remarks about the characteristics of "struggle groups" are helpful in this regard:

A group that, from its inception, is conceived as a struggle group is especially prone to engage in violent heresy-hunting; and its members are obliged to participate continuously in the selection and reselection of those who are "worthy," that is, those who do not question or dissent, precisely because its very existence is based on the "purity" of its membership.[35]

And yet, the resistance to social experimentation that developed in the nation's early formative stages must also be attributed to the very meaning system that had inspired the American experiment in the first place. Wherever strong theistic views were present, as they were most clearly in those colonies in which Calvinism was the dominant

33. Ibid., p. 194.
34. For this side of the story see Walzer, *The Revolution of the Saints.*
35. Lewis Coser, *The Functions of Social Colnflict* (New York: The Free Press, 1956), pp. 100–101.

theological influence, nonconventional behavior tended to be staunchly opposed. New Amsterdam, for example, under the tutelage of a strict Dutch Reformed interpretation of Calvinism, came to be known for its intolerance of alternative faiths such as Lutheranism and Judaism, while in Pennsylvania, in contrast, Quakerism afforded a sanctuary for such diversity of belief and became an early experiment in democracy, although even in Penn's political thought there tended to be a strong emphasis on authority and obedience.[36] Similarly, Massachusetts struggled against granting tolerance for religions other than Puritanism (especially Anglicanism) and occasionally was able to resolve internal disputes over proper belief and conduct only by the banishment of heretics, while Rhode Island with a less articulate formulation of God's sovereignty and calling became a gathering place for such outcasts.

As the colonies moved toward becoming a nation, the problem of coping with the diversity of belief among them did much to hamstring the rigid image of society implied by Puritan theism and to create a more democratic and libertarian spirit. Even before the end of the eighteenth century, theism and the social ethics implicit in it had begun to undergo an important transformation. Speaking of the eighteenth century, Edmund S. Morgan has ventured that "The most pervasive intellectual change was the withdrawal of God from His place in the forefront of all thinking."[37]

The gradual erosion of strict Puritan theism consisted primarily of two partially independent developments. On the one hand, a gradual erosion of the legitimacy and credibility of the theistic world view occurred as the result of the rise of alternative understandings of reality which grew especially out of the rationalistic spirit of the Enlightenment and which became an important intellectual force especially during the Revolutionary period. This development did not constitute the most serious challenge to the theistic mode, however. Even the leading defenders of such beliefs had early established at least a tentative peace with rationalism, since it could be readily argued that God himself had instituted rational laws in creating an orderly universe and that he himself abided by these laws.[38]

36. Hudson, *Religion in America*, p. 50.
37. Edmund S. Morgan, *Puritan Political Ideas, 1558-1794* (New York: Bobbs-Merrill Company, 1965), p. xxxv.
38. Miller, *Errand into the Wilderness*, p. 65.

On the other hand, and more profound than the impact of rationalism, deism, and other contemporary philosophical challenges, was the gradual shift that occurred *within* religious thought itself toward a greater emphasis upon the role of the individual relative to God in the shaping of human affairs. One of the early steps in this direction was the doctrine set forth by Thomas Hooker, Cotton Mather, and others that the individual is not totally at the mercy of God's grace for his salvation but can prepare himself, live righteously, and make overtures to God to see whether or not the covenant applies to him.[39] Another early step toward establishing the individual as master of his own destiny was what became known as the Halfway Covenant, which acknowledged the importance of human *desire* relative to divine foreordination in the redemption process.[40] It permitted the unregenerate to make known their desire to become regenerate, enter into a halfway covenant, and as a result obtain the right to have their children baptized. While this procedure usefully served the church by allowing it to incorporate a greater proportion of the populace, an unintended consequence was the eventual weakening both of the authority of the church in governing community affairs and of the legitimacy of a strong predestinarian image of God.

Throughout the eighteenth century more and more emphasis gradually came to be placed upon the role human choice and especially human preparation played in the salvation process, so that by midcentury, for example, considerable emphasis was beginning to be placed on the value of evangelists to prepare the hearts of men and women and arouse them to heed God's calling.[41] It was not until after the beginning of the nineteenth century, however, that a distinct and pervasive shift began to be evident in the nature of the theistic meaning system. Essentially this was a shift away from the strong theocentrism of Calvinism to a more "Arminian" world view which gave the individual a more independent role in his relation to God.

An important stage in this shift was the Second Great Awakening, which spread through western New York, Pennsylvania, eastern Ohio, and parts of Kentucky during the first half of the nineteenth

39. Miller, *Nature's Nation*, pp. 50–77.
40. The Halfway Covenant was officially approved in Connecticut and Massachusetts in 1657.
41. Ibid., p. 82.

century. Its most important result was to bring about a major shift in the balance of religious power in America. Whereas religious bodies espousing Calvinistic doctrines had been in the vast majority at the time of independence, the balance of power shifted radically during the next three quarters of a century. By 1844, for example, Methodism, which (though retaining some of the principles of Calvinism) was recognized as primarily Arminian in belief, had become the largest single religious body, with over a million members, and other so-called "popular" denominations, such as the Disciples of Christ and the Baptists, who were also leaning more towards Arminianism than Calvinism, were also appearing as significant new religious bodies.[42] More generally, the schisms in established denominations and the new sects that emerged during the Second Great Awakening instituted a new freedom on the part of the believer which shifted a major part of the responsibility for his eternal destiny, in effect, from the will of the supernatural to the will of the individual. For a period of at least thirty years, this new emphasis upon man's freedom was associated with widespread social experimentation in virtually every area of social life, an indication that the ability of theism to deter such behavior as it had in the past had weakened, although a good many other factors were involved as well.[43]

Historians of the period tend to agree that throughout the remainder of the nineteenth century the erosion of strict theism continued, to the extent that by the end of the century many theologians could echo Washington Gladden's remark that what some people still called Calvinism was "no more the Calvinism of Calvin than the astronomy which is taught in our colleges today is the astronomy of Ptolemy."[44] The increasing emphasis that came to be placed on the role of man relative to the role of God during this period did much to modify American theism. Yet there are still themes implicit in it reminiscent of its Puritan origins which still appear to militate against social experimentation. Three of these themes might be mentioned.

42. Ahlstrom, *A Religious History of the American People*, p. 437.
43. Linda Pritchard, forthcoming dissertation on the Second Great Awakening (Department of History, University of Pittsburgh).
44. Washington Gladden, *How Much is Left of the Old Doctrines? A Book for the People* (Boston: Houghton Mifflin Company, 1899), p. 211: quoted in Paul A. Carter, *The Spiritual Crisis of the Gilded Age* (Dekalb, Ill.: Northern Illinois University Press, 1971), p. 46.

First, the negative image of man evident in Puritan theism continues to be much a part of the theistic meaning system. If man could perfect himself and his society through his own efforts, there would be little need for preachments about salvation and redemption through Christ.[45] Second, there is still a strong degree of other-worldlyism in many contemporary theologies. Social experimentation tends to be regarded with disinterest because it is assumed that either God is going to bring about the end of the world soon, that only God's miraculous intervention can solve the problems of today, or that God must have a reason for the problems we experience.[46] Finally, there still tends to be a considerable degree of belief in the literal truth of the Bible, which serves as a source of opposition to many specific social experiments, such as premarital sex, homosexuality, Eastern religions, "atheistic Communism," radical violence, and drug use.[47]

Summarizing briefly, the theistic meaning system seems capable of legitimating either social experimentation or opposition toward such experiments. But as it has developed in American culture it seems most likely to do the latter. The few studies that have attempted to relate religious beliefs to contemporary social and political issues clearly suggest this. The reasons for this being so are not entirely clear, but they seem to lie at least partly in the beliefs themselves rather than simply in extraneous factors. Some social experiments may be opposed simply on the grounds of specific

45. See for example Rodney Stark and Charles Y. Glock, *By Their Fruits: Consequences of Religious Commitment* (Berkeley and Los Angeles: University of California Press, forthcoming).

46. See for example Stark et al., *Wayward Shepherds*. The otherworldly motif may not be as important a successor of Puritan theism as what Max Weber termed "inner worldly asceticism." But other-worldlyism is clearly in evidence in the teachings of many of the more fundamentalistic and evangelical denominations at present. Among the sample of California ministers in *Wayward Shepherds*, otherworldly orientations appear to be the chief link between theism and apathy regarding social problems.

47. For some discussion of the social consequences of Biblical literalism, see Jeffrey K. Hadden, *The Gathering Storm in the Churches* (Garden City, N.Y.: Doubleday & Company, 1969). It has, of course, been evident that Biblical literalism has also led to support of social experimentation in history, as in the antinomian movements in pre-Reformation Europe and the Oneida community in America. Biblical literalism allows traditional injunctions to be taken out of their cultural context as one source of support for conservative views. It also permits the Scriptures to be cited out of their larger theological context, leading to biased interpretations.

scriptural passages which appear to impute moral wrong to them, although other scriptural passages might be found to support these same experiments. But there is a more general level of opposition to experimentation within American theism. Especially its emphasis upon *God's governing power and man's weakness* seems capable of deterring interest in all kinds of social experiments, whether they are concerned with religion or politics or economics or leisure styles or the family. If theism has been declining or undergoing some major reformulation, this could be an important factor contributing to the recent social unrest and experimentation.

Proposition 2: A decline in individualism has contributed to the rise of social experimentation.

Individualism is a form of consciousness in which the person occupies the position of authority. The individual himself is the agent responsible for governing his own destiny. Not God or some other force, but the individual's own choices determine the meaning and purpose he finds in life. His will power and effort determine whether he will succeed or fail. Harold Laski once aptly described this form of consciousness as "the secularized form of American puritanism [which] leaves the individual face to face with his fate, as the chief forms of puritanism left the individual face to face with his God."[48]

The philosophical underpinnings of American individualism are to be found in European thought well before the nineteenth century, especially in Locke, Hobbes, Rousseau, Adam Smith, and in the Protestant reformers.[49] In political philosophy the idea had been put forth clearly that the ultimate legitimacy of the state derives solely from the consent of equal and independent individuals. In religious doctrine the Reformation had established the idea that the individual is related to God directly rather than through any institutional intermediaries and is held personally accountable for each of his thoughts and deeds. As a clearly distinguishable philosophy, however, individualism did not come to be recognized until early in the nineteenth century.[50]

The term itself came into being as a negative concept to describe

48. Harold J. Laski, *The American Democracy: A Commentary and an Interpretation* (New York: The Viking Press, 1948), p. 43.
49. Steven Lukes, *Individualism* (New York: Harper & Row, 1973).
50. Arieli, *Individualism and Nationalism in American Ideology.*

what was perceived as a lamentable fragmentation of the "natural" order of society, a form of disintegration that would inevitably accompany attempts to institute popular liberty and equality. The first known use of the term was by the French Catholic restorationist, Joseph de Maistre, who wrote in 1820 of "this deep and frightening division of minds, this infinite fragmentation of all doctrines, political protestantism carried to the most absolute individualism."[51] Among de Maistre's contemporaries, especially the followers of Saint-Simon, the term became associated with, if not a substitute for, disorder, atheism, and egoism. Tocqueville, who is credited with first applying the term to American society, used it in a similar sense, perceiving it both as an inherent product of democracy and as a condition of weakened social ties, political apathy and irresponsibility, and the triumph of self interest over public welfare.[52]

In American intellectual thought the notion of individualism took a decidedly different and distinctly positive cast, however. Scholars, perhaps the most notable of whom was Emerson, defended it against its European critics, claiming that it represented a value system capable of fulfilling the best interests not only of the individual but of society as well. If each person merely developed his innate talent to the best of his ability and used it to pursue his own self-interest (by which "material" self-interest was typically implied) benefits, it was assumed, would accrue to all.

The pervasiveness of these understandings is clearly in evidence in the literature of the nineteenth century. They are well evidenced in travelers' reports, in fiction, in sermons, and in school books. Ruth Miller Elson, who has analyzed the content of over a thousand school books of the nineteenth century, concludes that individuals tend to be portrayed in these books in terms of easily discernible, inherent characteristics of their race and nationality and in terms of their own character. "Virtue is always rewarded, vice punished. And one can achieve virtue and avoid vice by following a few simple rules."[53]

51. Ibid., p. 4.
52. Alexis de Tocqueville, *Democracy in America* (New York: Vintage Books, 1945), II, p., 105.
53. Ruth Miller Elson, *Guardians of Tradition: American Schoolbooks of the Nineteenth Century* (Lincoln: University of Nebraska Press, 1964), pp. 189–195; see also Cornelia Meigs, Anna Thaxter Eaton, Elizabeth Nesbitt, and Ruth Hill Viguers, *A Critical History of Children's Literature,* rev. ed. (New York: The Macmillan Company, 1969).

Nowhere was the prevailing individualism more evident than in the famed McGuffey readers. And perhaps no other medium had more impact on the mind of the nineteenth century American. Certainly, few books had ever before gone through four hundred separate editions or been read and studied by over 122 million school children.[54] "The road to wealth, to honor, to usefulness, and happiness," admonished the newly revised *Fourth Reader* which appeared in 1853, "is open to all, and all who will may enter upon it with the almost certain prospect of success. In this free community, there are no privileged orders. Every man finds his level. If he has talents, he will be known and esteemed, and rise in the respect and confidence of society."[55] Elsewhere the school child of the nineteenth century was taught to follow the rugged examples of men like Benjamin Franklin, William Tell, Daniel Boone, and Abraham Lincoln. He learned, above all, the importance of strong self-determination, willpower, and individual effort.[56]

As a value system, American individualism espoused achievement, ambition, diligence, and moral discipline.[57] It was not simply a system of values, though, but a broader understanding of the way in which reality was thought to be constructed. In it the individual tended to be regarded as the active agent who decides his own destiny. He does so amidst a constellation of essentially benign and predictable laws of nature. By drawing upon the store of resources that exists within himself, the individual activates the forces of nature on his own behalf. These forces operate according to laws assuring the individual of being rewarded for his efforts. Another important assumption, therefore, was that if God exists he would not, except perhaps in extraordinary circumstances, intervene in human affairs to upset this system of rewards. By the same token, other factors that might interfere with the calculated relation of the individual to his world, such as luck or social conditions, also tended to be discounted. Either by design or through fiat the world that

54. Ray Ginger, *Age of Excess: The United States from 1877 to 1914* (New York: The Macmillan Company, 1965), p. 284.
55. William Holmes McGuffey, *McGuffey's Newly Revised Eclectic Fourth Reader* (Cincinnati: Sargent, Wilson, and Hinkle, 1853), p. 205.
56. See Henry Steele Commager, *The American Mind: An Interpretation of American Thought and Character Since the 1880's* (New Haven: Yale University Press, 1950), ch. 1.
57. Irvin G. Wyllie, *The Self-Made Man in America* (New York: The Free Press, 1954).

"really matters" tended to be reduced to talents presumed to lie within the individual himself, plus the tacit laws that guaranteed the fruits of these talents. In Emerson's words, "A man contains all that is needful to his government within himself. He is made a law unto himself . . . Good or evil that can [befall] him must be from himself . . . Nothing can be given to him or taken from him but always there is a compensation."[58]

The image of society in nineteenth century individualism was one almost totally devoid of content. In one sense society tended to be regarded chiefly as a tabula rasa on which each individual etched his own fate. For the laws of nature always to reward virtue and punish vice it was important that no social forces interfere. What a person accomplished in life was assumed to be the product solely of his choice, effort, and talent. Society was merely the land of opportunity in which the individual functioned. Above all, it posed no barriers to the individual who wished to succeed. Travelers visiting America from Europe during the nineteenth century were quick to note this prevailing assumption. Frances Trollope, whose *Domestic Manners of the Americans,* written in 1832, became one of the most widely read accounts of nineteenth century American society by any European traveler, concluded that "Any man's son may become the equal of any other man's son, and the consciousness of this is certainly a spur to exertion."[59] In a similar vein Frederick Marryat, who visited America late in the 1830s and who, as a former British naval officer and a Tory, was particularly sensitive to the notions of social ranking held by the people he visited, wrote:

The Americans used to tell me with exultation that they never could have an aristocracy in their country from the law of entail having been abolished. They often asserted, and with some truth, that in that country property never accumulated beyond two generations and that the grandson of a millionaire was invariably a pauper.[60]

Society was not so naively understood as to deny that there were such things as government, laws, commercial transactions, families, all of which influenced the individual. But there was little sense of

58. Ralph W. Emerson, *Journals* (Boston: Houghton Mifflin Company, 1912), III, pp. 200–201.
59. Frances Trollope, *Domestic Manners of the Americans* (New York: Alfred A. Knopf, 1949), p. 121.
60. Frederick Marryat, *A Diary in America with Remarks on Its Institutions* (New York: Alfred A. Knopf, 1962), p. 467.

society being composed of social *structures,* that is, of patterns of behavior which become entities in themselves beyond the individuals who created them. Writing in the 1880s, James Bryce described the prevailing view that "the nation is nothing but so many individuals. The government is nothing but certain representatives and officials, agents who are here to-day and gone to-morrow."[61]

If society tended to be devoid of complex social structures, there was a sense in which even the more immediate, face-to-face social relations tended to be minimized. Another European observer, Henry Unwin Addington, visiting the United States in the early 1820s commented:

The social ties sit looser upon them than upon any other people, and like well-boiled rice they remain united, but each grain separate. Yet an American is an excellent father, husband, neighbor, and performs all his family and social duties to admiration. But [in] spite of this his nature is essentially solitary, and he casts off his social ties with greater facility than another man, and leans less on others for his comforts or necessities.[62]

A popular adage of the day had it that if you could see your neighbor's smokestack he was too close. This was not to imply, as Addington warns, that the nineteenth century American was a poor family man or irresponsible to his community. But there was clearly, at least in popular mythology, a tendency to extol the independent entrepreneur, the rugged frontiersman, and the hearty pioneer, more than the loyal family member, the communard, or the socialite.

The individualistic understanding of society represented a radical departure from the earlier image of society implied by the Puritan understanding of the world. Perry Miller has expressed this distinction so clearly in his discussion of the Puritans of Massachusetts that it is appropriate to quote his statement in full:

The lone horseman, the single trapper, the solitary hunter was not a figure of the Puritan frontier; Puritans moved in groups and towns, settled in whole communities, and maintained firm government over all units. Neither were the individualistic business man, the shopkeeper who seized

61. James Bryce, *The American Commonwealth* (New York: Macmillan & Company, 1910), III, pp. 267–269.
62. Bradford Perkins (ed.), Henry Unwin Addington, *Youthful America: Selections from Henry Unwin Addington's Residence in the United States of America, 1822, 23, 24, 25* (Berkeley and Los Angeles: University of California Press, 1960), p. 40.

every opportunity to enlarge his profits, the speculator who contrived to gain wealth at the expense of his fellows, neither were these typical figures of the original Puritan society. Puritan opinion was at the opposite pole from Jefferson's feeling that the best government governs as little as possible. The theorists of New England thought of society as a unit, bound together by inviolable ties; they thought of it not as an aggregation of individuals but as an organism, functioning for a definite purpose, with all parts subordinate to the whole, all members contributing a definite share, every person occupying a particular status.[63]

In many other respects individualism was akin to Puritanism and more generally to Calvinism and was a natural outgrowth from it. Both belief systems tended to place high value on hard work, sobriety, diligence. Both upheld strict moral codes. Both recognized that the individual was ultimately responsible for his own condition, even if in the one instance this responsibility was tempered by the idea of predestination. Both tended to deny that social structures took on independent lives of their own apart from God and the individual, and therefore needed to be confronted and changed directly rather than indirectly. But in the matter of a sense of solidarity with one's comrades, the two understandings were mirror opposites, the one espousing solidarity, the other solitude; the one cooperation, the other competition. To whatever extent the one provided the foundation for the other, and to whatever extent the two had similar implications for other matters, on the issue of community and the mutual responsibility that derives from having a common purpose, theism and individualism were clearly different.[64]

Because of this difference it might be expected that individualism and theism would have had different implications regarding social experimentation. Whereas the Puritan doctrines of God's calling and God's covenant tended to imply the necessity of obedience to the authorities of society and conformity to its standards of conduct, the individualistic understanding of reality, it would seem, should imply a spirit of nonconformity, of tolerance for a wide range of social experimentation and diversity. But, although American society did come to be more diverse (especially religiously and ethnically)

63. Miller, *Errand into the Wilderness*, p. 143.
64. Another important difference between theism and individualism is the idea of *covetousness*, emphasized greatly in the former but almost totally absent in the latter (see Richard L. Bushman, *From Puritan to Yankee: Character and the Social Order in Connecticut, 1690–1765*, New York: W. W. Norton & Company, 1967, esp. ch. 2).

during the nineteenth century, it was not its diversity or nonconformity that impressed its visitors, but just the opposite. The Polish
scholar, Adam G. de Gurowski, for example, writing in 1857 of his
visit to America, emphasized that "Even now, although new and
more diversified elements are mingled in American life, a certain
sameness still pervades it. The circle extends, the horizon enlarges,
and nevertheless monotony dominates the whole."[65] Other visitors,
including Marryat, Tocqueville, and, later, Richard Müller-Freienfels,
made similar observations.[66] What these commentators observed
was that even though there was a tendency for Americans to
romanticize the rugged nonconformity of heroes such as Davy
Crockett, William Tell, and Ben Franklin, there was also a certain set
of standards that placed strict limitations on the kind of nonconformity or diversity that could be tolerated.[67] Obtaining social approval
for what one did was not explicitly enjoined, for one was to be
independent of others; yet, there was a limit beyond which one's
independence could not go.

There are undoubtedly a number of reasons other than individualism why deference to a limited range of life styles could be observed
in the nineteenth century even in the midst of the great geographical
and ethnic diversity that was also evident: ethnic groups attempting
to develop new identities and become part of what was later to be
called the melting pot, democratic notions about equality and the
common man, then later the effects of technology and mass
production. The degree of conformity or, perhaps more accurately,
uniformity that was observed could also be regarded as a product of
the theistic understandings which were still widely in evidence,
especially with regard to intolerance of experimentation in religious
belief and in morality.[68] But the sanctions against social experimenta-

---

65. Adam G. de Gurowski, "The Practical Genius of the American," pp. 157–170
in Henry Steele Commager (ed.), *America in Perspective: The United States
Through Foreign Eyes* (New York: Random House, 1947), p. 164.

66. Marryat, *A Diary in America*; Tocqueville, *Democracy in America*; Richard
Müller-Freienfels, "The Mechanization and Standardization of American Life,"
pp. 310–319 in Commager, *America in Perspective,* p. 316.

67. Elson's content analysis of school books also emphasizes the strict codes of
conduct to which individuals were expected to adhere (Elson, *Guardians of
Tradition,* pp. 45, 47, 82, 83, 98).

68. See, for example, Commager, *The American Mind,* and T. Hamilton, *Men and
Manners in America* (London: T. Cadell, 1833), II, pp. 394–395.

tion did not derive solely from theistic understandings. The individualistic mode of consciousness also appears to have reinforced the degree of uniformity that was observed in values and in standards of conduct.

Perhaps much of the impetus toward social uniformity that derived from individualism was simply a by-product of the stress it placed upon the pursuit of material success. People were admonished to seek their fortunes, not engage in social reform movements or become devotees of new religious movements or spend time exploring their inner selves. Becoming successful was more than simply one path a person could choose. It was in a very real sense a badge of one's intrinsic worth. Since there were no social or natural forces to interfere, one was bound to succeed if he was of good character. To fail or to pursue some other goal than the goal of material success was an indication that one was not of good character. Elson concludes that this line of reasoning probably did more to make Americans concerned with material success than even the concept of aristocracy had done in European societies.[69]

Conformity to the predominant success ethic was also required for the health of the society. Adam Smith had performed the ultimate alchemy when he proved that selfishness was really altruism, that the pursuit of individual success benefited not only the individual but the entire society as well.[70] This was an especially strategic assumption, by no means limited to the readers of *The Wealth of Nations*. For material wealth and power to be regarded as marks of great personal accomplishment, the competitive game to attain them had to be played by everyone. What reward would there have been in scrambling to the top if one then discovered that his peers had all the time been playing a different game? By making success a social virtue as well as a personal virtue everyone was given not only the opportunity, but had placed upon them the responsibility as well, to bend their efforts in the direction of material success.

Individualism legitimated not only the pursuit of success but also the inequities that resulted from it. There was no reason to engage in political or economic experiments to rectify inequality, for inequality was deserved. Those who succeeded did so by their own talents,

69. Elson, *Guardians of Tradition*, p. 337.
70. See also in this regard, John Locke, *Two Treatises of Government* (New York: New American Library, 1960), Treatise II.

those who failed had done so by their own design. School books of the day bear evidence of this understanding:[71]

Misfortune is mostly the result of misconduct.

Remember that all the ignorance, degradation and misery in the world is the result of indolence and vice.

Declining prosperity is the usual attendant of degenerate morals in individuals, in families, and in larger communities.

Poverty is the fruit of idleness.

From this point of view it was but natural for the unfortunate to be regarded less than sympathetically. "When persons are reduced to want by their own laziness and vices, by drunkenness, gambling and the like," queried Daniel Webster, "is it a duty to relieve them?" "In general," he concluded, "it is not."[72] By the theistic mind misfortune had been viewed with ambivalence, for, even though misfortune was a possible sign of unregeneracy, the community of believers was enjoined to look after and to help each other. This rationale for charity tended to be absent in the individualistic mind.

This view of misfortune left society free of blame for its ills. Efforts to change the society made no sense from this perspective. "He who has so little knowledge of human nature, as to seek happiness by changing anything but his own disposition," wrote Webster, "will waste his life in fruitless efforts, and multiply the griefs which he proposes to remove."[73] Indeed, to suggest that social reforms should be experimented with was to challenge the whole notion that individuals were in complete control of their own destinies. To experiment with alternative social arrangements was likely to upset the delicate harmony that prevailed in the free market economy. Consequently, social experiments were not simply regarded as nonsense but were actively opposed. Those who participated in Shays' Rebellion, for example, were regarded in the history books of the nineteenth century not simply as misguided visionaries but as criminals. This is not to say that reform movements were absent in the nineteenth century. Obviously, comments like those of Webster were occasioned by the existence of such movements, which were especially notable in the first half of the century. But even though there were reform movements, they tended to be

71. Elson, *Guardians of Tradition*, pp. 253–254.
72. Quoted ibid., p. 273.
73. Quoted ibid., pp. 300–301.

directed much more at reforming the poor and the misfortunate themselves than at reforming the larger society.

Individualism also appears to have discouraged social experimentation by placing a premium on strong law and order. In one sense individualism tended to be associated with weak government. As in the popular adage, "the best government is that which governs least," it was assumed that the welfare of the society depended upon freedom of interference from the state. But this theory applied much more to the economic activities of those who were pursuing material success than it did to those who might be engaging in nonconventional activities. Minimal governmental interference might be valued with regard to business codes, but the story was different when it came to movements aimed at organizing labor unions. In asserting that every individual was free to choose his own course in life, it was recognized that some would choose badly. Some would become criminals or drunkards or social reformers. Rather than pursuing self-interest through conventional means they would simply prey upon the property of others. They would disrupt the natural laws that guaranteed freedom of choice to individuals and social welfare to the society at large. Consequently, it was necessary to have strict laws against socially deviant behavior and even against some personal vices that were thought to lead to more public forms of deviance. It was also necessary to have strong law enforcement agencies to support these laws.

By the end of the nineteenth century individualism was in certain respects at a high point. Ideologically it was enjoying widespread acclaim. In academia what was to become known as Social Darwinism had become a popular apologetic for an essentially individualistic interpretation of history. In the popular press the individualistic creed of writers like Horatio Alger and Russell Conwell was widely read and discussed well into the twentieth century.[74] Nevertheless, by the end of the nineteenth century individualism was already beginning to be undermined. The simplistic assumptions of individualism were beginning to fall visibly out of step with the social

74. Richard Hofstadter, *Social Darwinism in American Thought* (Boston: Beacon Press, 1944); Wyllie, *The Self-Made Man in America*; Richard Weiss, *The American Myth of Success: From Horatio Alger to Norman Vincent Peale* (New York: Basic Books, 1969), p. 53; Frank Luther Mott, *Golden Multitudes: The Story of Best Sellers in the United States* (New York: The Macmillan Company, 1947), pp. 158–159.

complexity of a rapidly developing industrial economy. The health and welfare of the society at large were clearly more problematic than the invisible hand of self-interest had promised. By the time Herbert Hoover delivered his famous "rugged individualism" speech, ironically just before the great financial crisis of 1929, it could no longer be assumed that society automatically functioned for the best of all when each looked only to his own self-interest; nor could it be assumed that the American Way automatically guaranteed all individuals equal opportunities to make of themselves whatever they wished.[75]

At about the same time, a nascent social science was in the process of developing that would present an understanding of life distinctly different from the individualistic mode of consciousness. Early American sociologists were beginning to reject the assumptions that natural laws and innate talents were the primary ingredients of human behavior and in their place to substitute theories that emphasized the culturally and socially conditioned nature of men. Charles Horton Cooley, for example, was advancing notions about the primacy of social forces in determining human conduct which were almost mirror opposites of many of the individualistic theories with which intellectuals had become familiar during the nineteenth century. John Stuart Mill, whose ideas became popular in America during the latter half of the nineteenth century, had argued forcefully that

Men . . . in a state of society, are still men; their actions and passions are obedient to the laws of individual human nature. Men are not, when brought together, converted into another kind of substance with different properties as hydrogen and oxygen are different from water. . . . Human beings in society have no properties but those which are derived from, and may be resolved into, the laws of individual men.[76]

But Cooley countered with the notion that, contrary to popular impressions, society is an entity distinct from individuals, is logically antecedent to them, and significantly shapes their very identities. "Most people," wrote Cooley at the turn of the century, "not only think of individuals and society as more or less separate and anti-

75. Herbert Hoover, *American Individualism* (Garden City, N.Y.: Doubleday & Company, 1928).

76. John Stuart Mill, *A System of Logic,* Book VI, chapter vii, quoted in Harry K. Girvetz, *The Evolution of Liberalism* (New York: Collier Books, 1950), p. 43.

thetical, but they look upon the former as antecedent to the latter. That persons make society would be generally admitted as a matter of course; but that society makes persons would strike many as a startling notion. . . .''[77]

At about the time Cooley was developing ideas about the social shaping of personal identity, a whole array of pioneering works in the social and behavioral sciences was taking shape. Franz Boas in anthropology and Lester F. Ward in sociology were explicitly challenging the notions that differences in inborn talents are responsible for the inequities one could observe throughout society. William James and Stanley Hall were pushing the study of psychology in new empirical directions. Historians such as Frederick Jackson Turner were putting forth new ideas about the social, cultural, and geographical forces that had helped to shape American society. In addition, Thorstein Veblen's *Theory of the Leisure Class* appeared as a new interpretation of economic behavior. And John Dewey was becoming interested in the relations between education and the societal pressures influencing it. For all the impact these studies were to have, most of them would be read and discussed by only a relatively small number of people, mainly by academicians and by some college students. To the extent that they were being read, it was also the case that they were sometimes being interpreted as defenses of individualism, as for example in the case of Dewey's pragmatism. And yet, it is possible to see that these and other ideas were gradually becoming diffused to wider and wider audiences and that in the process individualism was seriously being challenged.

By the 1950s there was still agreement that individualism was an important element of American culture. The most prominent social observers (Ralph Barton Perry, Harold Laski, Robin Williams, Talcott Parsons, Clyde Kluckhohn, Clifford Case, Arthur Schlesinger, among others) all placed individualistic values and assumptions at the cornerstone of American culture.[78] But to a man they also suggested that individualism was on the decline or at least under-

---

77. Charles H. Cooley, *Human Nature and the Social Order* (New York: Charles Scribner's Sons, 1902), p. 7.
78. For a review, see Clyde Kluckhohn, ''Have There Been Discernible Shifts in American Values During the Past Generation?'' pp. 145–217 in Elting E. Morison (ed.), *The American Style: Essays in Value and Performance* (New York: Harper & Row, 1958).

going important modifications. The most widely read sociological treatises of this period, which included Riesman's *Lonely Crowd,* Mills' *White Collar,* and Whyte's *Organization Man,* concurred that a new understanding of the forces governing reality was coming into prominence.[79] The fiction of the period also reflected this view. "Man was no longer free, as he had been in the mind of Emerson, to vault into his throne and lord it over the creepers and crawlers of the conventional world," concludes Howard Leon. "The weight of a complex social organization was depressing the confidence of even those who were most determined to declare their independence. . . ."[80] The traditional emphasis that Americans had placed upon success and self-interest appeared to remain strong. But the forces that had to be taken into account to achieve these goals were changing. No longer could one look only to the talents that lay within himself or rely solely upon his own self-determination. Instead there was a whole range of complex social forces that bore heavily upon one's destiny. In Mills' words:

According to the old entrepreneur's ideology, success is always linked with the sober personal virtues of will-power and thrift, habits of order, neatness, and the constitutional inability to say Yes to the easy road. Now the stress is on agility rather than ability, on "getting along" in a context of associates, superiors, and rules, rather than "getting ahead" across an open market; on who you know rather than what you know; on techniques of self-display and the generalized knack of handling people, rather than on moral integrity, substantive accomplishments, and solidity of person; on loyalty to, or even identity with, one's own firm, rather than entrepreneurial virtuosity.[81]

Whether such conjectures were accurate has not been tested systematically. Surprisingly little empirical attention has been paid to individualism at all in light of the immense amount of speculation about it. There is no evidence to say for sure whether individualism has been declining in recent decades or not. The cross-sectional view that the Bay Area data provide suggests that in some respects

79. David Riesman, *The Lonely Crowd* (New Haven: Yale University Press, 1950); C. Wright Mills, *White Collar* (New York: Oxford University Press, 1951); William H. Whyte, Jr., *The Organization Man* (Garden City, N.Y.: Doubleday & Company, 1957).
80. Howard Leon, *Literature and the American Tradition* (Garden City, N.Y.: Doubleday & Company, 1960), p. 263.
81. Mills, *White Collar,* pp. 260–263.

individualism is still far from having disappeared. For instance, 87 percent believe their own willpower has a strong influence on their lives, 83 percent say "Whenever I fail, I have no one to blame but myself," and 73 percent believe "If one works hard enough, he can do anything he wants to."[82] But in another respect the more extreme manifestations of individualism so visible in the nineteenth century appear to remain common in only small minorities. Only 6 percent, for example, say that the main reason for poverty in this country is that "the poor simply aren't willing to work hard."

One crude method that has sometimes been relied on to assess whether or not cultural changes have taken place is to examine citations for certain topics listed in the *Reader's Guide to Periodical Literature*. Although these citations bear no necessary relation to the values and assumptions of the broader public, the fact that they are mostly from popular literature makes this connection somewhat tighter than if one were looking only, for example, at scholarly literature. Thus, one finds, for instance, that references listed under "God" show a decline over the past four decades much the same as suggested by other evidence on theism discussed earlier in this chapter. By the same token, an index of individualism (which enumerates entries listed under "individualism" divided by the total number of entries for the period covered and multiplied by a constant term such that index scores vary between 0 and 100) shows a steady decline over at least the past two decades: the index score for 1949–51 is 53; for 1959–61, 26; and for 1970–71, 15.

In the absence of more definitive data on trends in individualism, the literature of the nineteenth century is itself perhaps the most telling evidence of a cultural shift, at least over the long haul. In contrast with the social scientific views of society that have emerged in the twentieth century, the image of society portrayed in this literature is based upon entirely different premises. These premises, moreover, are ones which appear to discourage social experimentation whereas, as we shall see shortly, the more recent social scientific meaning system seems to encourage it. Although the more extreme formulations of nineteenth century individualism may no longer be common, it is still possible to hear arguments against social experimentation which follow the same logic; for example, that those who have been caught up in counter-cultural activities are at fault

82. Figures are from the total *weighted* sample.

above all for abandoning the quest for personal success, that they are thereby damaging the well-being of the whole economy, that social-reform efforts are misguided since individuals rather than social structures are at fault, and that social experiments represent a dangerous threat to the law and order necessary to protect the property and the interests of the more "respectable" members of society. If individualism has continued to decline over the last two decades, it seems reasonable, therefore, to suspect that this decline may have helped to legitimate the tendency for people to engage in social experimentation.

Proposition 3: The rise of social science as a meaning system has contributed to the rise of social experimentation.

Of the many belief systems that have competed for ascendency during the twentieth century, that which becomes apparent most clearly in the social sciences is one of the most significant. Its importance does not lie in the fact that a large proportion of people has been exposed to the teachings of social science, although this proportion has increased dramatically; rather, it stems from the fact that social science represents a view of reality that is distinctly contrary to both the theistic and the individualistic meaning systems and, as a result, conveys implications regarding social experimentation that also differ in a number of important respects.

Even though too much has been made of the so-called warfare between religion and science, it is clear that the two provide alternative answers to a number of the "ultimate" questions of life. Whereas a theistic mode of consciousness tends to place the construction and control of reality in the supernatural realm, science assumes it to be in the natural or empirical realm. While the one view assumes that some parts of reality are ultimately beyond man's control and knowledge, the latter, if only as a methodological rule, assumes that all parts of reality can conceivably be known. In the natural sciences this assumption has traditionally clashed with theism on such important matters as the motion of the planets and the evolution of life. But the social sciences have opened controversy on a whole range of fronts that had not been made problematic by the natural sciences alone. The social conditioning of belief, the cultural relativity of values, the biological roots of faith, the latent psychological needs served by myth and symbolism, all involve questions that bear upon the credibility of theistic arguments concerning the nature of reality. By the same token, social science is a distinct alternative to the individualistic mode of consciousness in a way in which science more generally is not. For it effectively turns the reality of the individualist upside down, making the individual a product of social forces. In the words of Auguste Comte: "Humanity alone is real; the individual is an abstraction." This is not to say that social science is totally contrary to individualism. In its early stages American social science, especially in the form of Social Darwinism, supplied new rationalizations for the dogged pursuit of individual self-interest, and, even yet, there is a strong sense of individual utilitarianism in theoretical orientations as diverse as symbolic interactionism, social behaviorism, and demography. While social science may be put to the service of self-gain, its fundamental mode of constructing reality is contrary to individualism, however, in that it emphasizes the primacy of the social environment over and against the personal will. In pursuing one's values, whatever they may be, and in orienting oneself to social and political issues, a whole different set of constraints have to be taken into account.

Social science also represents a particularly important alternative to the theistic and individualistic meaning systems because it contains within it its own unique expression of transcendence and wholeness. More than any concept in the physical sciences, the concept upon which the social sciences are based, the concept of society, is itself an important image of transcendence. Society transcends the here and now of everyday life. It reaches forward into the distant future and supplies a sense of immortality. Its collective goals can bestow meaning on individual activities and its collective needs can integrate discrete activities into meaningful systems of purposive behavior. Alfred Schutz has stated well the sense of transcendence the image of society conveys:

I know . . . the social world transcends the reality of my everyday life. I was born into a preorganized social world which will survive me, a world shared from the outset with fellow men who are organized in groups, a world which has its particular open horizons in time, in space, and also in what sociologists call social distance.[83]

83. Alfred Schutz, "Symbol, Reality and Society," pp. 287–356 in Lyman Bryson, Louis Finkelstein, Hudson Hoegland, and R.M. MacIver (eds.), *Symbols and Society: Fourteenth Symposium on Science, Philosophy, and Religion* (New York: Harper & Row, 1955); reprinted in Alfred Schutz, *Collected Papers, Vol. I: The Problem of Social Reality* (The Hague: Nijhoff, 1962).

Besides transcendence, the notion of society also conveys a sense of wholeness. It stands for the whole of which all individuals are a part. It expresses their mutual interdependence. Social forces influence all aspects of the individual's life and therefore provide a key for understanding oneself in that man is above all "social man."

The idea that society is prior to the individual and in a sense a more elemental dimension of reality did not have to await the development of modern social science, of course, or the advent of the twentieth century. Besides those like Comte, Saint-Simon, and ibn-Khaldun whom social science has now claimed as its forerunners, many others in the past have tended to see social forces as the central agents of reality; for example, the French scholar Bonald, writing in 1796, argued with a curiously modern ring that "Not only does man not constitute society, but it is society that constitutes man, that is, it forms him by social education. . . ."[84]

If the assumptions of social science, at least some of its more general assumptions, are not entirely recent, it is the case, however, that only within twentieth century culture in American society, and particularly only within the past three or four decades, is it possible to see these assumptions explicitly becoming diffused to a rather general audience. While there is no systematic evidence on the extent of this diffusion, enough evidence of a piecemeal sort has been accumulated to document the trend. Schneider and Dornbusch's study of inspirational religious literature in the United States from 1880 to 1955, for example, observes that in the 1920s general testimonials by scientists begin to appear, indicating an apparent tendency for science to be used to add prestige or legitimacy to religious ideas; then, in the thirties concepts from psychology begin to be used in this literature and a shift is observable toward emphasizing the social role of religion besides its personal role; and overall there is a trend toward an increasing emphasis upon faith *plus* reason rather than faith alone, also consistent with if not related to a diffusion of scientific principles.[85]

Other scattered evidence also suggests an increasing diffusion of social-scientific ideas during the thirties and forties. For example, a content analysis of third-grade readers showed a significant rise in 1953 as compared with the period of 1900 to 1920 in lessons concerning "how others live" in different cultures and concerning

84. Quoted in Lukes, *Individualism*, p. 78.
85. Louis Schneider and Sanford M. Dornbusch, *Popular Religion* (Chicago: University of Chicago Press, 1958).

various kinds of social activities.[86] An exploratory content-analysis of best-selling novels found evidence of an increasing tendency for psychological and sociological concepts to be employed in fiction when the years 1900, 1930, and 1965 were compared.[87] And studies of social science textbooks themselves have documented a shift during this period away from theories involving innate or individualistic traits to ones involving social and cultural factors.[88]

Since 1940 more systematic evidence is available on at least one aspect of the diffusion of social science understandings—the number of people actually receiving training in the social sciences. Between 1949 and 1967, for example, the number of bachelor's degrees granted in the social sciences (sociology, anthropology, political science, history, economics, social work, criminology, and general social science) increased by 160 percent, from 50,000 to nearly 130,000.[89] This increase was but part of a general tendency toward higher education; yet the rate of growth in the social sciences during this period was steeper than that in either the life sciences or the physical sciences. During the same time span the number of master's degrees in the social sciences also grew dramatically, from less than 6,000 to almost 20,000, as did the number of Ph.D. degrees, from less than 1,000 to nearly 4,000, both increases again being steeper than those in either the life or physical sciences.[90] By 1970 over 155,000 students were receiving their degrees in the social sciences annually, more than in the physical sciences, biological sciences, mathematics, and engineering *combined*.[91] Almost 50,000 students were enrolled in graduate programs in the social sciences, three times

86. Margaret P. Foster, *A Study of the Content of Selected Third Grade Readers Used in the United States from 1900 to 1953,* unpublished manuscript quoted by Kluckhohn, in Morison, *The American Style.*

87. Robert Wuthnow, "Toward a Historical Study of Explanatory Modes and the Black Revolution" (unpublished paper, Department of Sociology, University of California, Berkeley).

88. Dorothy P. Gary, "The Developing Study of Culture," pp. 172–220 in George A. Lundberg and Read Bain (eds.), *Trends in American Sociology* (New York: Harper & Row, 1929); Brewton Berry, "Concept of Race in Sociology Textbooks," *Social Forces* 18 (March 1940): 411–417; Chester L. Hunt, "The Treatment of 'Race' in Beginning Sociology Textbooks," *Sociology and Social Research* 35 (March-April 1951): 277–284.

89. Abbott L. Ferriss, *Indicators of Trends in American Education* (New York: Russell Sage Foundation, 1969), p. 134.

90. Ibid., pp. 137–140.

91. U.S. Bureau of the Census, *Statistical Abstract of the United States: 1972* (Washington, D.C.: Government Printing Office, 1972), p. 133.

as many as had been enrolled a decade before.[92] And the number of persons employed as social scientists was increasing at an equivalent rate: according to a 1969 Bureau of Labor Statistics estimate, the number of persons employed as social scientists, psychologists, or social workers was expected by 1975 to more than double the 1960 figure, a rate higher again than that for natural scientists, and considerably higher than the total labor force, which was expected to grow by only a third.[93] By 1970 the number of social scientists employed by the federal government was already one and one-half times what it had been in 1960 (7,113 as compared with 4,672), and the number of social scientists employed by colleges and universities had risen between 1965 and 1971 from 32,853 to 59,074 or 80 percent.[94]

Another indirect indication of the probable increase in recent years of social scientific understandings is the rate of expansion of funding of social scientific research. Before 1955 no grants had been given at all by the National Science Foundation to fund social-scientific research.[95] During the late fifties a few grants were given, and then in 1960 a Division of Social Sciences was established on a par with the divisions of Natural Science and Biological Science. Since 1960, federal obligations for research and development have grown steadily from 35 million dollars to 216 million dollars in 1972, a total increase of 517 percent, a rate higher than that for any of the other sciences.[96] Expenditures by institutions of higher education for research and training in the social sciences have also shown a similar increase, more than doubling between 1964 and 1970 alone (from $125 million to $273 million).[97] These trends in expenditures are perhaps also reflected in the fact that number of new books published in the social sciences mushroomed between 1950 and 1972 from 1,069 to 8,994.[98]

A small amount of direct evidence is also available on the extent

92. Ibid., p. 530.

93. Quoted in Daniel Bell, *The Coming of Post-Industrial Society: A Venture in Social Forecasting* (New York: Basic Books, 1973), p. 19.

94. U.S. Bureau of the Census, *Statistical Abstract of the United States: 1973,* (Washington, D.C.: Government Printing Office, 1973) pp. 525–526.

95. Robert W. Friedrichs, *A Sociology of Sociology* (New York: The Free Press, 1970), p. 87.

96. U.S. Bureau of the Census, *Statistical Abstract: 1973,* p. 522.

97. Ibid., p. 524.

98. UNESCO, *Statistical Yearbook: 1966* (Louvain: United Nations, 1968), p. 356; *Statistical Yearbook: 1971* (Louvain: United Nations, 1972), p. 694. This

to which social-scientific understandings have become increasingly diffused to the broader public. Ferriss reports some interesting evidence that shows that the average scores of Iowa high school seniors on the Iowa Tests of Educational Development, which are given annually, increased by 8.2 percent on the "basic social concepts" section between 1961 and 1967 and by 11.1 percent on "reading interpretation in social studies."[99] These increases apparently reflected a general upgrading in the quality of knowledge of these high school students, for their natural science scores increased at an equal rate. Nevertheless, they suggest that social-scientific ideas are becoming diffused to an audience considerably broader than that of social scientists themselves. Some evidence supporting this assertion is also provided by comparisons of achievement test scores among college seniors by the Educational Testing Service. While these scores generally tend to vary little over time, a comparison of 65 college samples showed that social science test scores were significantly higher in 31 of the samples in 1959 than they had been only four years before.[100]

While it is difficult to say, there has probably also been some increase in the extent to which ideas about society congruent with those espoused explicitly by social scientists are held in the broader culture which is only indirectly related to social science itself. On the one hand, there is some evidence that suggests a general upgrading of information about the character of society, probably due primarily to the expansion of the mass media. For example, surveys of the Detroit area at periodic intervals have shown some increase in the level of political information there over the last fifteen years, such as an increase from 35 percent in 1957 to 56 percent in 1971 in the proportion who could accurately identify one of Michigan's senators.[101] National studies of political attitudes conducted over the past twenty years by the University of Michigan also indicate that the public has become more informed about both domestic political matters and international affairs.[102] How much

---

was in comparison with an increase in religious books from 1104 to 2019 and an increase in pure science books from 1089 to 2519.

99. Ferriss, *Indicators of Trends in American Education*, p. 92.

100. Ibid., p. 96.

101. Duncan et al., *Social Change in a Metropolitan Community*, p. 78.

102. John P. Robinson, Harrold G. Rusk, and Kendra B. Head, *Measures of Political Attitudes* (Ann Arbor: Institute for Social Research, University of Michigan, 1968), pp. 25–27.

such information reflects only scattered bits of knowledge and how much it may indicate an increasing sophistication about the social conditioning of reality more generally is a matter for speculation. To the extent that broad constructions of reality develop a certain correspondence with existential situations themselves, it seems likely that simply the massification of modern society would lead to understandings that take into account the complex social and cultural forces impinging upon one's behavior. This, of course, is the idea expressed by many of the sociological studies that became popular in the 1950s, such as David Riesman's *The Lonely Crowd* and C. Wright Mills' *White Collar,* which suggested that the changing character of society itself, and especially the economy, was producing a new kind of personality or character that was much more socially oriented than its predecessors had been.[103]

In the Bay Area data, understandings consistent with social science are fairly prevalent. Fifty-five percent believe that a major cause of suffering in the world is "social arrangements that make people greedy for riches and power," 39 percent believe they can learn a lot about life from psychology, 57 percent agree with a statement designed to reflect one of the basic premises of Freudian psychology ("forgotten childhood experiences have an effect on me"), and 51 percent agree that man evolved from lower animals. While these figures do not document trends, they are consistent with the evidence above that suggests social-scientific assumptions have become widely diffused to the general public.

There is some evidence, then, both that traditional meaning systems have been eroded in recent decades and that the social scientific mode has become diffused, if not to a broad population segment, at least at a significantly increasing rate. But, apart from the question of how much actual impact social science may or may not have had, what is the basis for stating that it carries implications concerning social experimentation decidedly different from those of either the theistic or the individualistic meaning systems?

Different social scientific theories have been used, just as different forms of theism or individualism, in defense of virtually every kind of social norm. For instance, the first book by an American carrying the word "sociology" in its title was written in defense of the slave system. If any *predominant* tendency can be discerned, however,

103. Riesman, *The Lonely Crowd*; Mills, *White Collar.*

one that might be expected to be found even within the more general public, it would have to be that social science conveys what might be called a "libertarian" view of social organization. It tends to promote diversity more than conformity, deviance more than strict obedience to authority, change and reform more than static order; in brief, it tends to legitimate social experimentation. This is of course a hypothesis to be tested, although it is not at all a novel proposition.[104] There are several important threads in social science that make it plausible.

First, merely by emphasizing the role of social forces in reality social science tends to impute the blame for society's ills not to God, the individual, fate, or some other agent, but to the structure of society itself. While some broad understandings of life may help to reinforce existing social arrangements by rationalizing their shortcomings, the social-scientific understanding strips existing social arrangements of this kind of legitimacy.[105] Injustice, inequality, crime, alienation, become flaws attributable to the character of society itself. This understanding becomes a force for social experimentation, especially when it is coupled with views of man emerging out of the Enlightenment which perceive man as inherently good and ultimately perfectible rather than evil. Through gaining greater knowledge about society and experimenting with alternative social arrangements, a better society can be constructed. Man is not constrained to live with poverty forever, or crime, or repressive power, simply because of human nature, but can devise new social arrangements which will release human potential to achieve its

104. See Charles Y. Glock, "Images of 'God,' Images of Man, and the Organization of Social Life," pp. 297–311 in Charles Y. Glock (ed.), *Religion in Sociological Perspective: Essays in the Empirical Study of Religion* (Belmont, Calif.: Wadsworth Publishing Company, 1973); "Consciousness and Youth," chapter 17 in Charles Y. Glock and Robert N. Bellah (eds.), *The New Religious Consciousness* (Berkeley and Los Angeles: University of California Press, 1976). For an empirical examination of these relations among physicians, see Earl R. Babbie, *Science and Morality in Medicine: A Survey of Medical Educators* (Berkeley and Los Angeles: University of California Press, 1970), esp. p. 78.

105. With regard to the more general effects of science on the legitimacy of the social order, the following statement from the Marquis de Sade is particularly graphic: "What would become of your laws, your morality, your religion, your gallows, your Paradise, your Gods, your Hell, if it were shown that such and such fluids, such fibres, or a certain acridity in the blood, or in the animal spirits, alone suffice to make a man the object of your punishments or your rewards?"

capabilities. In fact, the idea that social ills can be blamed on structures tends to reinforce the idea that man himself is basically good.[106] Just as the notion of a totally good God is buttressed by theodicies that locate evil elsewhere, in the Devil for example, so the idea of the goodness of human nature is reinforced by an understanding that locates evil in social structures which are somehow realities in themselves. Men with good and just intentions create social structures, but these structures take on forms of their own, become hydra-headed monsters producing evil consequences which were never intended. That social structures are not reducible to the actions of individuals does not imply, however, that they cannot be changed. They operate according to their own laws, but these are laws that can be either changed or controlled to create "better" social arrangements. Thus, social scientists from Comte to Spencer to Durkheim to Parsons have tended to adopt at least an evolutionary view of social and cultural history and others have adopted an even more radical, apocalyptic view of social change.[107]

106. A statement by Clarence Darrow regarding the socially conditioned character of crime illustrates well this argument:

> There is no such thing as a crime as the word is generally understood. I do not believe there is any sort of distinction between the real moral conditions of the people in and out of jail. One is just as good as the other. The people here can no more help being here than the people outside can avoid being outside. I do not believe that people are in jail because they deserve to be. They are in jail simply because they cannot avoid it on account of circumstances which are entirely beyond their control and for which they are in no way responsible. . . . There are people who think that everything in this world is an accident. But really there is no such thing as an accident. . . . There are a great many people here who have done some of these things [murder, theft, etc.] who really do not know themselves why they did them. It looked to you at the time as if you had a chance to do them or not, as you saw fit; but still, after all you had no choice. . . . If you look at the question deeply enough and carefully enough you will see that there were circumstances that drove you to do exactly the thing which you did. You could not help it any more than we outside can help taking the positions that we take.

(A speech to prisoners in the Cook County Jail, quoted in Gerald Dworkin, *Determinism, Free Will, and Moral Responsibility*, Englewood Cliffs, N.J.: Prentice-Hall, 1970, p. 1.)

107. It is also the case, of course, that many social scientists do not share these understandings. But there is a strong common tendency to emphasize *social forces* of one kind or another that constrain individual behavior, whether they be the

The social-scientific perspective tends to "stir up" rather than solidify existing social institutions in an even more subtle way than simply identifying social problems, though, or calling for social reform. One of the central assumptions of social science is that ideas, values, and commitments are socially and culturally conditioned and therefore "relative" to particular social and cultural settings.[108] Thus, it is "all right," in one sense, for people to hold diverse values and to experiment with diverse styles of life. Diversity is not suspect as a possible flaw of character but is simply due to different environmental influences. In a deeper sense, diversity is not merely acceptable but is actually enjoined. All ideas and actions take the form they do because they fulfill certain social functions, often ones which are not obvious to the uninitiated observer. In this regard, the combined impact of Marx and Freud has undoubtedly been profound.[109] Religious beliefs of a certain kind may serve to rationalize economic interests, may be projections of the authority relations of one's community, or may grow out of early experiences in the family. In identifying these latent functions the social sciences tend to develop, as Peter Berger has argued, a debunking motif.[110] Any commitments become subject to question. One begins to wonder why he *really* thinks what he does or acts the way he does. Is he simply following the crowd, imitating his peers? Nonconformity, therefore, becomes a sign that one is not just a product of the social

socialized "me" of the symbolic interactionist, the socioeconomic variables of the demographer, or the social conditioning of the behavior modification theorist. Boulding has remarked that simply the concept of *system* in modern social science has probably helped to generate awareness of social interdependence and cultural relativism (Kenneth E. Boulding, *The Meaning of the Twentieth Century: A Great Transition,* New York: Harper & Row, 1964, p. 16).

108. Virtually all introductory sociology and anthropology texts stress the difference between cultural relativism and ethnocentrism, often in highly value-laden terms, as developed especially by William Graham Sumner (William Graham Sumner, *Folkways,* New York: New American Library, 1960).

109. For some general discussions of this impact, see Herbert Marcuse, *Eros and Civilization* (New York: Vintage Books, 1962); Norman O. Brown, *Life Against Death* (Middletown, Conn.: Wesleyan University Press, 1959); Theodore Roszak, *The Making of a Counter Culture* (Garden City, N.Y.: Doubleday & Company, 1969).

110. Peter L. Berger, *Invitation to Sociology: A Humanistic Perspective* (Garden City, N.Y.: Doubleday & Company, 1963).

milieu.[111] Instead of nonconformity being a sign of "bad" character it in effect becomes a sign of "good" character in that it shows one is a critical, self-aware person. Paradoxically the social-scientific perspective commands a greater degree of "individuality" in personal behavior than the traditional individualistic mode does.

Finally, social science has had an important impact on the notion of "character" itself.[112] Traditionally, the concept of character, which is perhaps most apropos to the individualistic meaning system, and such related concepts as the heart or soul in Judeo-Christian thought or the psyche in ancient Greek thought have nurtured a sense of internal consistency in personal behavior. Character was thought to be immutable. Every action was a sign of what one "really was" inside. To change or to be inconsistent in one's behavior was inevitably a mark of weak character. It was not possible simply to step into a different role momentarily and then return to more typical roles. Martyrdom was often more acceptable than such a betrayal of one's character. In post-Mead and especially post-Goffman thought, however, all this has changed.[113] Character has been replaced by "self." The self is neither immutable nor internally consistent. It can undergo change, different sides of it can be presented, internal discrepancies can be compartmentalized. All of which is to say, experimentation with all kinds of nonconventional activities can be conducted with much less cost to selves than to characters, or souls, or psyches. One can step out of one's usual role long enough to try drugs or to experiment with homosexuality, and

111. Waldmeir discusses this notion as a general theme in contemporary fiction (Joseph J. Waldmeir, "Quest Without Faith," pp. 53–62 in Joseph J. Waldmeir, ed., *Recent American Fiction: Some Critical Views*, Boston: Houghton Mifflin Company, 1963, see esp. pp. 53–54). This attitude as a source of student unrest has been discussed in Lewis S. Feuer, *The Conflict of Generations: The Character and Significance of Student Movements* (New York: Basic Books, 1969), see esp. p. 388; Mario Savio, "An End to History," pp. 239–243 in Michael V. Miller and Susan Gilmore (eds.), *Revolution at Berkeley* (New York: Dell Publishing Company, 1965), see esp. p. 242; and as a source of interest in experimentation with the occult in William Braden, *The Age of Aquarius: Technology and the Cultural Revolution* (New York: Pocket Books, 1970), p. 102, and John Charles Cooper, *Religion in the Age of Aquarius* (Philadelphia: The Westminster Press, 1971), p. 28.
112. I am grateful to Professor Bryan R. Wilson for first bringing this to my attention.
113. See George Herbert Mead, *On Social Psychology* (Chicago: University of Chicago Press, 1934); Erving Goffman, *The Presentation of Self in Everyday Life* (Garden City, N.Y.: Doubleday & Company, 1959).

then assume other roles if these activities are not to one's liking.[114] Indeed, the multifaceted nature of the self, to be quite complete, may require that some such experimentation be pursued.

To summarize, the social-scientific meaning system, whether it is acquired from social scientists themselves or more indirectly, is in certain respects not just a method of securing knowledge, but is an understanding of the forces governing life that bestows a distinct kind of meaning on experience and implies a view of society which is, on balance, conducive to social experimentation. The social-scientific mode in a sense rounds out the picture of the logically alternative ways in which reality can be constructed. There is a certain formal parallelism in suggesting that reality is constructed and controlled primarily by God in one instance, by the individual in another, and by society in another. And yet, to leave it at that misses a fourth, equally important way in which people construct reality.

Proposition 4: A rise in mystical meaning systems has contributed to the rise of social experimentation.

Over the entire course of American history it is possible to discern an alternative to more cognitively oriented modes of consciousness, a mode that emphasizes intense ecstatic experience as the primary way of constructing meaning out of reality. Like cognitive belief systems, such experiences have provided a means of resolving questions about meaning and purpose, although in an intuitive way. By creating a perception of a larger whole of which one is an integral part, they either resolve or "transvalue" questions about ultimate worth, about evil, about suffering. Pearl Buck, for example, has left a vivid description of such an experience which came upon her during the months of grief following her husband's death:

What did take place gradually as the days passed was a profound insurge of peace. No one became part of me, but I became part of the whole. The warm rock bed in which I lay, the wind rising cool from the sea, the sky intensely blue and the drifting white clouds, the gnarled pine tree bent above my head—of these I was a part, and beyond these, of the whole world. Myself ceased to be, at least for a time, a lonely creature with an aching heart. I was aware of healing pouring into me.[115]

114. The ability of American prisoners of war in North Vietnam to step into and out of different roles and for their behavior to be understood and regarded as legitimate by the American people is perhaps especially revealing.
115. Pearl S. Buck, *A Bridge for Passing* (New York: John Day Company, 1962), p. 235.

Like an arduously constructed philosophy of life, such an experience may suddenly produce an "understanding" of reality. Whereas cognitive modes of consciousness may consist of point-by-point arguments that address specific questions about meaning and purpose, the mystical mode is more likely to consist simply of a vague feeling that life does indeed make sense even though it may be impossible to put this conviction into precise language.

There is no systematic evidence showing that the mystical meaning system has become a major cultural phenomenon in recent years, yet every piece of impressionistic information that can be obtained suggests that it has become significant enough so that to disregard it would be amiss. An emphasis upon direct, intense personal experience is a common theme in such diverse activities as Zen meditation, body expression and massage classes, gatherings of mycological buffs, and groups of college students experiencing glossolalia for the first time. It is manifested in suburban church groups experimenting with folk-rock music, banners, colored balloons, and ritual chanting in worship services, in marathon encounter sessions, in scientific studies of *theta* states, hallucinogens, and biofeedback techniques. The quest for intense "peak" experiences has become expressed in a renaissance of interest in Hesse and Jung and in primitive folklore, mythology, and ritual. It has been popularized by Norman O. Brown, Herbert Marcuse, and Paul Goodman writing about Dionysian politics, by John Lilly experimenting with drugs and sensory deprivation effects, by George Leonard extolling the ecstatic dimensions of education, by Theodore Roszak molding an apocalyptic vision of social change from Blake's poetry, and by Carlos Castaneda experiencing extraordinary dimensions of reality in the desert of Mexico.[116] Still, the recent popularization of the mystical mode of consciousness should not mask its long tradition, its deep roots in American transcendentalism, in European romanticism, in medieval mysticism. The experiential mode has been expressed in broad and enduring cultural themes such as the American affinity for the wilderness, for natural beauty,

116. Norman O. Brown, *Love's Body* (New York: Vintage Books, 1966); Herbert Marcuse, *One-Dimensional Man: Studies in the Ideology of Advanced Industrial Society* (Boston: Beacon Press, 1964); Paul Goodman, *The Empire City* (New York: The Macmillan Company, 1964); John Lilly, *The Center of the Cyclone: An Autobiography of Inner Space* (New York: The Julian Press, 1972); George B. Leonard, *Education and Ecstasy* (New York: Delacorte Press, 1968), *The Transformation* (New York: Delacorte Press, 1972); Theodore Roszak, *Where the Wasteland Ends: Politics and Transcendence in Postindustrial Society* (Garden City,

for rural quietude, for innocence and simplicity.[117] And it has also been expressed in more concentrated form by the mystic, the visionary, and the poet.

Especially to those for whom cognitive belief systems have become so numerous, one philosophy of life sounding no better or no worse than another, or to those for whom ideas and beliefs have been made culturally and socially relative so that none remains convincing, the ecstatic personal experience seems to take on authority as the only "real" or reliable way to make sense out of one's world.[118] Wrote Wordsworth:

> One impulse from a vernal wood
> May teach you more of man,
> Of moral evil and of good,
> Than all the sages can.[119]

The ecstatic experience becomes a way of escaping the charge that all ideas and beliefs are simply the products of socialization. It makes reality a product of one's own experience, brings the construction of reality itself under one's own control. Whereas individualism made a person's individual fate a product of human action and the social-scientific mode brought social structures into the realm of humanly constructed reality, the mystical mode claims that the very definition of reality itself is subject to human control. Through the ecstatic experience, order is simply "projected" upon an otherwise incoherent reality. "What is implicit in every line of Whitman," for example, writes R.W.B. Lewis, "is the belief that the poet *projects* a world of order and meaning and identity into either a chaos or a sheer vacuum; he does not *discover* it. The poet may salute the chaos; but he creates the world."[120]

Poetry, metaphor, art, fantasy, and fiction become valued as the best way to talk about and make sense out of reality, for reality itself cannot be known or described directly but only approached

---

N.Y.: Doubleday & Company, 1972); Carlos Castaneda, *Journey to Ixtlan: The Lessons of Don Juan* (New York: Simon and Schuster, 1972).

117. For example see R.W.B. Lewis, *The American Adam: Innocence, Tragedy and Tradition in the Nineteenth Century* (Chicago: University of Chicago Press, 1955).

118. R.D. Laing has written, "If there are no meanings, no values, no source of sustenance or help, then man, as creator, must invent, conjure up meanings and values, sustenance and succor out of nothing" (R.D. Laing, *The Politics of Experience*, New York: Ballantine Books, 1967, p. 43).

119. Quoted in Perry Miller, *The Transcendentalists: An Anthology* (Cambridge, Mass.: Harvard University Press, 1960).

120. Lewis, *The American Adam*, p. 51.

asymptotically through the use of analogy.[121] Unlike the rationalist who, following Locke, says of poetry and fantasy, "'Tis a pleasant air but a barren soil," the person committed to the mystical mode is more likely to conclude that any kind of symbolic expression can illuminate some aspect of one's experience, making it more meaningful. But, and of considerable importance, such symbols are recognized simply as figurative ways of articulating reality rather than as actual descriptions of it.[122]

Whereas the theist regards God as the agent governing reality; the individualist, himself; and the social scientist, social forces, the mystic believes that the force responsible for governing reality is his own mind-set—the mental framework through which one filters events and symbolizes them to himself. As one writer within this tradition recently expressed it, "Every belief is a limit to be examined and transcended." Hence, the importance of the mystical experience is that it puts one in a different frame of mind, allows one to symbolically perceive an event in a different way and thereby gain control over it. In a sense, the mystic is very much an individualist and there are well-known examples of thinkers, such as Emerson, who combined both themes. But mysticism is a different kind of individualism than that described heretofore. The traditional rugged American individualist exerts his willpower within a matrix of fixed natural laws. The mystic denies or at least de-emphasizes such laws. He operates, instead, within a matrix of sensory and symbolic conditions that determine his ability to construct reality. These conditions are not entirely self-imposed; to an important extent they are socially imposed, which gives mysticism a certain resemblance

121. Of the importance of *nature* as a symbol to the transcendentalists, Loren Baritz has written: "Nature was the wordless analogy of the human mind, and its truths would not yield to the power of words. The wordlessness of truth and beauty required silent faith about which only the poet could sing" (Baritz, *City on a Hill*).

122. Robert Bellah has commented: ". . . there are nonobjective symbols that express the feelings, values, and hopes of subjects, or that organize and regulate the flow of interaction between subjects and objects, or that attempt to sum up the whole subject-object complex or even point to the context or ground of that whole. These symbols, too, express reality and are not reducible to empirical propositions" (Robert N. Bellah, *Beyond Belief*, New York: Harper & Row, 1970, p. 252). He further suggests that man is increasingly becoming aware that he is the creator of his symbols and can choose how he symbolizes reality to himself (see, for example, p. 42). See also Evelyn Underhill, *Mysticism* (New York: E. P. Dutton & Company, 1961) on the importance of symbolism in mysticism.

to social science. The important assumption, however, is that one need not be limited by the reality in which he lives, for by simply perceiving it differently he can change it.[123]

In the intense personal experience and in the figurative ways in which such experiences are expressed, normal, socially ingrained blinders to perception are thought to fall away and one sees things "fitting together" in a way they had not before. This is the literal meaning of ecstasy, *ekstasis,* things "stand outside" of their normal place; but in another sense, they "fall into place" in a new way.[124]

This sudden awareness of a larger coherence in reality tends to make everyday reality but one of a multiplex of realities. William James' account of his experimentation with such experiences, for example, is clear in this regard:

One conclusion was . . . that our normal waking consciousness, rational consciousness as we call it, is but one special type of consciousness, whilst all about it, parted from it by the filmiest of screens, there lie potential forms of consciousness entirely different.[125]

What are ordinarily defined as unrealities—fantasy, fiction, trances, dreams, myths—are elevated in the ecstatic experience, James observes, alongside the more "rational" dimensions of life and integrated into a broader picture of reality.

Like the other meaning systems, the mystical mode also contains implications concerning social experimentation. These implications have been hotly disputed, however, Consensus seems to exist only about the tendency for this meaning system to *devalue* established social expectations and social structures. The assumption that "what is really real" is to be found only in the ecstatic experience tends to make more ordinary experiences mere epiphenomena. This consequence can especially be seen in the attitudes of certain mystics, poets, and others toward suffering; indeed, the mystical meaning system contains a "theodicy" that copes with the problem of suffering just as more cognitive modes of consciousness do, although

123. For a related discussion, see Donald Stone, "The Human Potential Movement," in Glock and Bellah (eds.), *The New Religious Consciousness.*
124. Some vivid examples are provided in R.E.L. Masters and Jean Houston, *The Varieties of Psychedelic Experience* (New York: Dell Publishing Company, 1966), see, for example, pp. 220–221. See also Hermann Hesse, *Siddhartha* (New York: New Directions, 1951), pp. 110–111.
125. William James, *The Varieties of Religious Experience* (New York: New American Library, 1958), p. 298.

this theodicy tends more simply to devalue or transvalue the reality of suffering than to attempt a formal explanation for its existence. Thus, Emerson could transform himself into the "transparent eyeball" and make "swine, snakes, pests, madhouses, prisons, enemies" all vanish.[126] And Whitman could write with detachment:

> The sickness of one of my folks or of myself, or
>   ill-doing or loss or lack of money, or depressions
>   or exaltations,
> Battles, the horrors of fratricidal war, the fever of
>   doubtful news, the fitful events;
> These come to me days and nights and go from me again,
> But they are not the Me myself.[127]

The actual social implications of such a theodicy or more generally of the transvaluing character of the mystical orientation are ambiguous, however. One common conclusion has been that such an orientation leads to social and political apathy at minimum and in the extreme to antinomianism or anarchy. Dadaism, surrealism, monastic retreatism, visionary gnosticism, *wandervogelism,* mystical escapism, have all been cited as examples of the antinomian social consequences of this mode of consciousness.[128] Of mysticism, for example, Troeltsch concludes, its result is "a complete indifference, or impotence towards all social problems which lie outside the directly religious sphere. . . . Fundamentally, this school of thought has no idea at all of the way in which to deal with questions of the State or of economics; it only knows that everything ought to be altered and begun entirely afresh. When? And how? It is, indeed, hard to say."[129] In other words, the experiential emphasis that Troeltsch perceives to be at the core of mysticism creates disaffection with the world as it is, a desire for it to be something else, a different world in which love and harmony reign. But the experiential emphasis alone is incapable of producing a program for achieving such a transformation. Moreover, the radical personalism of the experiential mode reduces even the motivation to plan or experiment

126. See Baritz, *City on a Hill.*
127. See Lewis, *The American Adam,* p. 46; from "Song of Myself," section IV.
128. Nathan Adler, *The Underground Stream: New Life Styles and the Antinomian Personality* (New York: Harper & Row, 1972); see also Howard Becker, *German Youth: Bond or Free* (New York: Oxford University Press, 1946).
129. Ernst Troeltsch, *The Social Teaching of the Christian Churches* (New York: Harper & Row, 1960), II, p. 801.

with social arrangements or political policies for overcoming the problems of society.

In American transcendentalism, which is traditionally the most distinct expression of the experiential mode in American culture, this proclivity toward social disinterest and irresponsibility is clearly in evidence. Emerson, for example, even though he, like Marx, hoped for an age of "beneficent socialism," and even though his philosophy inspired others to engage in utopian social experiments, found it impossible to become personally interested in such activities. After listening to an evening of excited talk about Brook Farm, for example, he wrote in his diary: "Not once could I be inflamed but sat aloof and thoughtless; my voice faltered and fell."[130] In other matters he also shunned social concerns and obligations. "Do not tell me," he wrote, "of my obligation to put all poor men in good situations. Are they *my* poor? I tell thee, thou foolish philanthropist, that I grudge the dollar, the dime, the cent I give to such men as do not belong to me and to whom I do not belong."[131]

Yet, perhaps it was Emerson the rugged individualist more than Emerson the transcendentalist who penned such lines. For among Emerson's compatriots were such social activists as George Ripley, the leading spirit of Brook Farm, Orestes Brownson, who spent much of his time developing a sophisticated critique of the wage-labor system, and Henry David Thoreau, who felt that the corruption of the state places a special burden of responsibility on concerned citizens to act as its conscience and who, through his act of resistance against the Mexican War, for which he was jailed briefly, did much to formulate the idea of civil disobedience as a means of protest. And, in fact, Emerson himself had spoken out as one of the chief critics of the economic conditions that had led to the depression of 1837. Perhaps the experiential orientation of the transcendentalists, their euphoric adulation of nature, their quest for direct experiences of beauty and harmony, only loosened the bonds that tied others to established social conventions. But out of this detachment both moderate and utopian social experiments resulted.

The example of the transcendentalists, on the whole, indicates

130. Quoted in Albert Gilman and Roger Brown, "Personality and Style in Concord," pp. 87–122 in Myron Simon and Thornton H. Parsons (eds.), *Transcendentalism and Its Legacy* (Ann Arbor: University of Michigan Press, 1966), p. 89.
131. Quoted in Baritz, *City on a Hill*, p. 89.

that at minimum the mystical mode seems to produce attitudes toward social experimentation directly opposite those of theism and individualism, that is, a desire for major social change rather than a strict obedience to institutionalized authority and status systems. "Every actual state," Emerson declared, "is corrupt. Good men must not obey the laws too well."[132] Man was not understood to have been created in sin and therefore in need of strict laws and authorities to rule over him and protect him from himself, nor was he assumed to operate within an established "natural order" that inevitably rewarded certain kinds of virtue and punished certain kinds of vice, but he was thought to contain within him the seeds of perfection which both allowed and required him to set up his own laws and construct his own realities. The example set by the transcendentalists leaves inconclusive, however, whether or not the mystical meaning system leads only to antinomian retreatism or to active involvement in efforts to reform or transform society itself.

In more recent times, although much has been written about "peak" or ecstatic experiences as a result of a renewed interest especially among youth in drugs, meditation, body awareness, and the like, little additional insight has been provided into the social implications of experientially oriented forms of consciousness. Most that has been written has been devoted to the purely psychological and sometimes to the physiological characteristics of this orientation, reinforcing the conviction of some that it produces no social consequences but apathy. And yet, arguments have also been put forth suggesting reasons why this orientation has, or at least should have, more specific social implications.

Abraham Maslow, whose observations of peak experiences come from people in more ordinary walks of life than mystics or poets or communards, leans more toward the view that such experiences free people *for* social responsibilities rather than *from* these responsibilities, implying that mystics would be either active in or supportive of experiments designed to transform the social order.[133] While he warns that peak experiences can become an introspective obsession, he concludes that for many people they enhance personal security and meaning sufficiently to facilitate altruistic concerns of one form

132. Ibid., p. 244.
133. Abraham H. Maslow, *Toward a Psychology of Being* (Princeton, N.J.: D. Van Nostrand Company, 1962), *Religions, Values, and Peak-Experiences* (New York: The Viking Press, 1970).

or another and to reduce the value of such things as material possessions or self-aggrandizement. Maslow's observations are, of course, unsystematic and the prescriptive is often blended together with the actual.

Susanne Langer's philosophy of symbolism also contains an interesting theory concerning the conduciveness of mystical orientations to social experimentation.[134] In times of shifting and uncertain social circumstances, she suggests, ordinary cultural symbolism, ordinary language, becomes incapable of adequately capturing the meaning of events and of guiding individual and collective responses. It resonates with the more familiar experiences but is not designed to help people cope with new problems and actually limits their vision of potential solutions. In such circumstances, she believes, it is necessary to abandon the more cognitive, culturally available interpretations of events, immerse oneself personally in intense experiences where new symbolic meanings can be developed intuitively, and then make use of fantasy, metaphor, and analogy to express the new "understandings" one has developed. Major social transformations, she concludes, are almost always driven forward by the poet, the artist, the mystic, who is capable of gaining such insights and weaving new social visions from them. While the experientially oriented may be only the goad to social activism rather than the activist himself, he nevertheless performs a vital function in the process of social transformation. And to the person committed to more ordinary walks of life, the experiential orientation may at least be a facilitator of creative insights about social or personal concerns. Like Maslow's theory, Langer's has yet to be tested in a systematic fashion; still, it is a beguiling thesis and would appear to be worthy of such a test.

While there are arguments, therefore, suggesting both that the mystical meaning system leads to apathy and that it leads to more positive activity of one form or another to improve upon social arrangements, both arguments agree that this mode tends to be associated more with at least the desire for social *change* than with

134. Susanne K. Langer, *Philosophy in a New Key: A Study in the Symbolism of Reason, Rite, and Art* (New York: New American Library, 1948), *Feeling and Form: A Theory of Art* (New York: Charles Scribner's Sons, 1953), *Philosophical Sketches* (New York: New American Library, 1962). Kenneth Burke has described the value of metaphor in similar terms (Kenneth Burke, *Permanence and Change*, Los Altos, Calif.: Hermes Publications, 1954, see esp. p. 90).

loyalty to existing social structures. This consequence has also been observed for the particular life styles people adopt, apart from more macroscopic social concerns. Troeltsch notes that the mystic is particularly likely to experiment with nonconventional behavior in the realms of sex and family life, since these bear on him directly.[135] He may experiment with communes or other living arrangements which promise to live up to his desire for fellowship and harmony. And he is likely to reject conventional work careers to have more time to spend in nature, in meditation, or in other quests for ecstatic experiences. In general, the mystical meaning system seems to produce experimentation in life styles rather than conventionality, a quest for a diversity of nonconventional experiences rather than uniform patterns of conduct.

Part of the reason why this result is evident seems to lie in the assumption, usually accompanying this mode of consciousness, that human nature is basically good and ultimately perfectible. One is not likely, therefore, to destroy oneself if he does not follow time-tested styles of life but sets his own pattern of conduct. But there is also a more powerful motivating assumption implicit in this mode of consciousness, the assumption that each person must himself create whatever meaning he hopes to have in life through his own experiences. There are no absolute meanings that one can merely discover or learn about, for all such meanings are socially conditioned and culturally relative. Each person must create from his own experience that which is to have the most meaning for his own unique needs. The mark that one has discovered what is truly meaningful for himself, therefore, is that he lives in a unique way, not simply accepting what society says, but developing his own style of life. "Modern society," Paul Goodman has written, "does not let one be—it is too total—it forces one's hand."[136] If true reality can be discovered only through the intense personal experience, and if it can never be accurately captured in language but only approximated in poetry and metaphor, then the cultural systems and social structures that grow out of personal experiences become mere reifications, outdated modes of experiencing and thinking that must be broken down if one is again to experience reality in full. It becomes a short step from assuming that normal ideas about the

135. Troeltsch, *The Social Teaching of the Christian Churches.*
136. Paul Goodman, *Drawing the Line* (New York: Random House, 1962), pp. 8–9.

world have been socially constructed to assuming that they are also constraining. "The natural order is our construction, our constriction," says Norman O. Brown.[137] The person who has experienced reality in a deeper way, however, frees himself from these constrictions. He becomes a "seer," one who has, as Castaneda has put it, "stopped the world" as it usually presents itself.[138] He therefore becomes free to act differently, to violate social taboos; indeed, this is the way in which he demonstrates that he has seen reality in a deeper way. Maslow's summary of the marks of the peak-experiencer is that he is

more spontaneous, more expressive, more innocently behaving (guileless, naive, honest, candid, ingenuous, childlike, artless, unguarded, defenseless), more natural (simple, relaxed, unhesitant, plain, sincere, unaffected, primitive in a particular sense, immediate), more uncontrolled and freely flowing outward (automatic, impulsive, reflexlike, "instinctive," unrestrained, unselfconscious, thoughtless, unaware). . . . All this can be phrased in still another way as the aura of uniqueness, individuality, or idiosyncracy.[139]

The motivation for experimentation with nonconventional life styles, therefore, derives partly from the need to show that one has not just accepted things as they are but has found through his own experiences a deeper meaning in life that can only be vaguely expressed. But experimentation with a diversity of life styles is also motivated simply by the quest for personally meaningful experiences. Potentially, every new event that one experiences can illuminate some new aspect of reality for him, enhance his feeling of meaningfulness. And especially those experiences that are extraordinary enough to "blow one's mind," to cut through the haze of socially given understandings, are to be sought. Drugs, meditation, experience of nature's unadulterated simplicity, experiences that assert awareness of the body over mental processes, any experiences that short-circuit ordinary understandings, become valued.

The mystical meaning system, in sum, appears to contrast sharply with the theistic and the individualistic modes of consciousness in that it contains predominantly libertarian strains with respect both to personal life styles and to larger social experiments rather than values stressing conformity to authority and to strict moral standards.

137. Brown, *Love's Body*, p. 243.
138. Castaneda, *Journey to Ixtlan*.
139. Maslow, 1962, *Toward a Psychology of Being*, p. 101.

In a sense it is a variant of individualism in that it places emphasis upon the personal apparantly more than on the social. It, too, stresses notions of free choice and individual responsibility. But the individual's responsibility is not, as in more traditional forms of individualism, to follow laws of nature which are fairly obvious to all, but to cut through any such notions and experience a deeper form of reality, which cannot be reduced to such laws. In a number of respects the mystical mode, perhaps ironically, seems conducive to similar norms and expectations as the social-scientific mode, especially in perceiving faults in existing social arrangements and in stressing libertarian personal life styles. The two appear to differ, nevertheless, in the degree to which the one advocates specific social programs and activities while the other has a tendency to retreat from such involvements. Moreover, it seems that the diversity of life styles that the social-scientific mode tolerates because such things are supposed to be different in different cultural settings becomes more than simply tolerated in the experiential mode and is actually stressed as a way in which one can demonstrate that he is the maker of his own world rather than just the recipient of a socially given world.

Whether the mystical mode is gaining in ascendancy or whether it has only become more popularized in recent years is difficult to say without the benefit of hindsight. The witness of artists and mystics over the centuries suggests that it is not at all a new phenomenon; yet it has been argued that this mode has taken on a new character because of other cultural developments, such as theories about the socially constructed nature of reality, or studies of the effects of drugs, or new insights into the physiological functioning of the brain during such experiences. At minimum, this mode warrants systematic examination alongside and in comparison with the other, more cognitive modes of consciousness.

THE NEED FOR TESTING

By looking to various sources of unsystematic historical and theoretical evidence it is possible to discover in each of these meaning systems—the theistic, the individualistic, the social-scientific, and the mystical—a number of distinct implications concerning the propriety or impropriety of social experimentation. And these implications suggest ways in which society may become transformed if the long-range trends in meaning systems which have been postulated are in fact taking place and continue to take place. The various linkages between consciousness and social organization that have been discussed are merely hypotheses, however, which need to be tested now. How prevalent is each meaning system in contemporary culture? Does each affect specific values, attitudes, and involvements having to do with social experiments, or is this level of consciousness, whatever may be its psychological interest, largely irrelevant to the structuring of social life? Do the relations that appear to have been evident in the past between these modes and social experimentation still exist, or have circumstances changed them? Is there any evidence that the relative prominence of these meaning systems is now changing and may therefore produce changes in the character of society? These are the questions to which attention is now turned.

CHAPTER 4

Testing the Relations

With the use of the Bay Area data this chapter affords a partial test of the propositions we have just considered. It examines cross-sectionally the relations between social experimentation and theism, individualism, social science, and mysticism. To examine these relations we must first have at hand a measure of the four meaning systems. This measure is constructed in two steps. First, questionnaire items are combined to form a submeasure for each of the four meaning systems; then these submeasures are combined to form a single composite variable.

The items used to tap each of the four meaning systems were developed through a series of depth interviews and pretests with people in the Bay Area, selected to represent different walks of life (although not selected at random).[1] About a hundred such interviews were conducted in all. In the first round of these pretests, people were asked merely to talk in general terms about their understandings of the meaning and purpose of their lives. From this information, more specific questions were gradually developed, tested, and revised, resulting in a relatively small number of "fixed-response" items which were administered to the Bay Area sample.[2]

1. An easier method of developing these items would obviously have been to glean statements directly from historical or philosophical material. The items finally used were selected to be consistent with the historical material. It was feared, however, that items derived solely from historical or philosophical writings could easily fall prey to misinterpretation or, worse, be responded to in a superficial way without revealing much about how people nowadays actually understood their lives. For this reason, all of the questions eventually used were derived from and tested among people similar to those included in the survey.
2. It is worth noting that most of the impetus for focusing the present study on the four meaning systems described in the previous chapter actually came from these

The method devised for reaching the ways in which people in the sample understand their lives was to ask them, first, whether or not they had ever thought about various "ultimate" questions (Why is there suffering in the world? What happens after death? How did I come to be who I am? and so forth).[3] Overwhelmingly people said they had. On the average fewer than one person in ten said he had never thought about such questions and didn't consider them important.[4] Then people were asked what kinds of answers they found most useful for coping with these questions. The intention of this method was to get at the understandings that people actually use to make sense of their lives rather than beliefs or doctrines that might be ascribed to but not seen as particularly relevant to the actual problems of life.

The submeasures for the four meaning systems each consists of from three to five items which are used to classify respondents into four categories: those with a "high" likelihood of holding the particular meaning system in question, those with a "medium high" likelihood, those with a "medium low" likelihood, and those with a "low" likelihood.[5]

The items that were asked as indicators of the *theistic* meaning

---

depth interviews rather than from purely historical observations. Informal as well as formal interviews, conducted not only in connection with the present project but also with other projects with which the author had contact, suggested that these meaning systems are among the most common by which people understand their lives.

3. By "ultimate" questions is meant the kinds of questions that concern the boundary conditions of human existence or, more precisely, the limitations of human control over reality and the absolutes that are sought within reality. On a temporal dimension they include questions about the beginnings and endings of existence: Where did I come from? How did human life begin? What happens after death? How is the world going to end? Ultimate questions also concern boundaries between the natural and the supernatural; for example, questions about the existence of God or about God's control over reality. Other ultimate questions concern the limitations of man's ability to construct a world of his own choosing, a world without suffering, disappointment, and hatred: Why is there suffering in the world? Why is there injustice? Inequality? Ultimate questions are also reflected in the quest for limiting or unconditional qualities of good and bad: What is right and what is wrong? What is truth? What is love? What is the purpose of life? How can real happiness be found?

4. See Table C-3 in Appendix C.

5. The rationale underlying these submeasures differs from ordinary index construction logic. For further details see Appendix B.

system all focus in one way or another on *God as the agent who constructs reality and makes life meaningful, although they emphasize somewhat different aspects of God's role.*[6] For a respondent to be scored as having a "high" likelihood of being theistic he had to respond to three items as follows. First, he had to say he definitely believed in God. This choice was one of seven responses presented in connection with a question that asked "Which of these statements comes closest to expressing your belief about God?" The other responses included:

I don't believe in God.
I don't believe or disbelieve in God. I don't think it is possible to know if there is a God.
I am uncertain but lean toward *not* believing in God.
I am uncertain but lean toward believing in God.
I am uncomfortable about the word "God" but I do believe in something "more" or "beyond."
None of the above expresses my views.

Second, respondents were required to assert that God had an influence on their lives. To ascertain this, respondents were presented with a list of seven different forces, one of which was "God or some other supernatural force," and asked to say how strong an influence each had on their lives. Those who said at least a "strong" influence were considered to have met the requirement. Finally, to be considered theistic, respondents also had to assume God's activity in other parts of reality beyond their personal lives. One set of questions listed various reasons for the existence of suffering in the world, including "People suffer because they don't obey God." Of the various items in the data having to do with God's role in life, this was one of the more generally stated. Those who said not obeying God is a "major reason" for the existence of suffering were assumed to have met the requirement.

Altogether 24 percent of the sample met all three of these conditions. An additional 23 percent met two of them and were

6. It was assumed that most respondents would probably think of God in Biblical terms, but no attempt was made to impose any particular definition of God on them. In contrast to many empirical studies of conventional religious belief, no attempt was made to include beliefs about Christ, for example, or about the Bible or about Christian doctrine as part of this orientation. The intention was simply to devise a measure that would isolate respondents who definitely believe in a God and who feel that both their lives and life more generally are significantly influenced by this God.

classified as "medium high" in terms of the likelihood of their holding the theistic meaning system. The remaining 53 percent were divided among those who met only one condition, scored as "medium low" (19 percent), those that met none of the three conditions, scored as "low" (32 percent), and those who were unclassified because they failed to answer all three of the questions (2 percent).[7]

Individualism proved somewhat more complicated to construct a measure for than theism, partly because it was less clearly conceptualized when the survey instrument was written and partly because it has also been less precisely codified and communicated in the culture at large. It has clearly not been the subject of as much sermonizing, or as much explicit teaching, or as much conscious worship as theistic beliefs have been. All the items asked to assess *individualism* conveyed the idea that *individuals themselves are primarily in charge of their own destinies*. But the kind of individualism described in Chapter 3 is not one which just affirms that individuals are free to make their own choices. It is a more extreme form which, among other things, asserts that individuals themselves are chiefly to blame when they fail, that such things as social forces really do not limit persons in any significant way, and that even such problems as poverty and crime can be attributed mostly to the faults of individual character. The importance of distinguishing between this more pronounced form of individualism and simple assertions of free will can be seen in the data. Items which asked merely whether or not freedom of choice plays a part in persons' own lives were accepted by virtually everyone. As seen in Chapter 3, eight out of every nine respondents agreed that "your own willpower" has a strong influence on their lives. But there was a minority who also adhered to individualism in its more extreme forms. For example, 47 percent said that a major cause of suffering in the world is: "People usually bring suffering on themselves." And about one in four agreed that an important reason for inequality is that "the poor simply aren't willing to work hard." The data show that the

---

7. Obviously designations such as "high," "medium high," "medium low," and "low" are extremely arbitrary (they are set off in quotation marks to indicate this). More stringent or less stringent requirements could have been imposed for each of these categories. The purpose of these categories is simply to divide the sample into four relatively large units that can be compared to see if respondents who are *relatively more likely* to be theistic are any different from those who are *relatively less likely* to be theistic.

less extreme and the more extreme varieties of individualism are hardly related to one another at all. Of the people who think will-power has a strong influence on their lives, for example, 50 percent agree that "If someone does not succeed in life, you can be pretty sure it's his own fault." Of those who don't think willpower has a strong influence, exactly the same proportion agree with the latter item. The same kind of relation occurs between the item concerning willpower and the item stating that "the poor simply aren't willing to work hard."[8] The more extreme items, however, do cluster together. Six out of every ten people who think "people bringing suffering on themselves" is a major reason for suffering also agree that if someone doesn't succeed it's his own fault, while this proportion is only four out of ten for those who do not attribute suffering to people bringing it on themselves.[9]

Since the discussion of individualism in the last chapter was oriented toward its more extreme form, the measure developed to isolate this kind of meaning system is constructed from the more extreme rather than the less extreme items available in the data. The first item used as a criterion for categorizing respondents was "People usually bring suffering on themselves." As already seen, this is related to other items that reflect individualism in its more pronounced form. By itself, however, this item, it was discovered, does not seem to constitute a rejection of some of the other kinds of understandings that the extreme individualist would be expected to reject. For example, just as many people who accept this notion as who reject it also say that "Suffering is caused by social arrange-ments which make people greedy for riches and power."[10] Thus, to somewhat refine this item, respondents were given a point on the individualism measure only if they said the individualistic explana-tion was at least as important a reason for suffering as the social explanation. The second requirement that respondents had to meet if they were to be classified as having a "high" likelihood on the individualism measure was to agree with the statement, "The poor simply aren't willing to work hard." This item was included as part of the measure, even though it does not concern life in quite

8. The gamma is .022.
9. The gamma for this relation is .409. These observations are also warranted by the factor pattern discussed in Appendix B.
10. The gamma is .075.

as general a sense as most of the other items do, mainly because it loomed so clearly in the historical material and in the Bay Area data seemed to have greater validity and reliability than some of the other items.[11] Finally, so as to make the measure not entirely based on items concerning suffering and hardship, another item was used which read, "If one works hard enough, he can do anything he wants to." This belief was also seen clearly in the historical material. There, it was always tempered with the additional assumption, however, that hard work prevails because society doesn't interfere; that is, society guarantees equal opportunities to individuals so that they can make whatever they want of their lives. Therefore, respondents were required to not only agree that hard workers can do anything, but to also agree that the society gives people this opportunity. The best indication of this assumption in the data was *disagreement* with an item which read, "The poor are poor because the American way of life doesn't give all people an equal chance." Respondents meeting all three of these criteria (two of which involve appropriate answers to two items) were scored as having a "high" likelihood of being individualistic in the sense in which it was conceptualized in Chapter 3. Those meeting only two of the three requirements were scored as having a "medium high" likelihood. And scores of 1 and 0 were designated respectively as "medium low" and "low." The proportions receiving each score were: 11 percent, "high"; 25 percent, "medium high"; 42 percent, "medium low"; 19 percent, "low"; and 3 percent unclassifiable because they failed to answer at least one of the items.

The *social-scientific* meaning system also required several items to obtain a more accurate measure than any single item provided. The general intention of the items included in the data to tap this meaning system was to discover *whether or not people perceive reality to be significantly influenced by social, cultural, and social-psychological factors.* In addition, the desire was to isolate people who had a fairly sophisticated (i.e. a more scientific) understanding of these forces, as compared with people who merely felt some form of antagonism against the rich or against the government. Some of the items upon hindsight appeared to be measures only of this more

---

11. This observation is based partly on the fact that this item has been used on two other Bay Area surveys with relatively consistent results.

naive perspective and were not included in the final measure for this reason.[12]

For respondents to be categorized as having a "high" likelihood of holding a social-scientific meaning system, three requirements had to be met, which in combination suggested that they perceived social and social-psychological forces operating both in their own lives and in life more generally. First, they had to agree with an item that was designated to tap a Freudian kind of understanding of the factors influencing their own lives (although mention of Freud by name was intentionally avoided): "I believe forgotten childhood experiences have an influence on me." Second, to build in a more social structural understanding of life, respondents scoring "high" were required to say that "Suffering is caused by social arrangements which make people greedy for riches and power" is a major reason for suffering. And third, to emphasize the scientific orientation of this meaning system, respondents were required to agree that "Man evolved from lower animals." In combination these three conditions yielded 20 percent of the sample as having a "high" likelihood of being within the social-scientific perspective, 35 percent as having a "medium high" likelihood, 30 percent as having a "medium low" likelihood, 11 percent whose likelihood was "low," and 4 percent who were unclassifiable because they failed to answer one or more of the items included in the measure.

The last measure, the measure to tap the *mystical* meaning system, also combines several different kinds of items. The core of this meaning system, it will be recalled, is *the assumption that the meaning of life is grasped as much by intense peak experiences as it is by more cognitive understandings such as the other three meaning systems represent.* This orientation, it was suggested, manifests itself partly in the fact that some people not only have such experiences but also attribute lasting significance to them. Partly, it also seems to involve an appreciation of symbol, myth, and fantasy, that is, of figurative or metaphoric language that attempts to convey some of the intuitive understandings these experiences evoke.

Three items were included in the survey to discover how many people actually have intense peak or ecstatic experiences: "Have you

12. For example, items such as "People at the top keep those at the bottom from getting their share" and "The poor are poor because the wealthy and powerful keep them poor."

ever had the feeling that you were in close contact with something holy or sacred?'' ''Have you ever experienced the beauty of nature in a deeply moving way?'' ''How about the feeling that you were in harmony with the universe?'' For each of the questions, the following options were provided:

No, and I really don't care whether I ever do.
No, but I would like to.
Yes, but it has not had a deep and lasting influence on my life.
Yes, and it has had a lasting influence on my life.

Since most of those who had had any of these experiences had also had an experience of the beauty of nature, this experience was used as one ingredient in the mysticism measure.[13] The second requirement respondents who were classified as ''high'' on mysticism had to meet was to agree that ''It is good to live in a fantasy world every now and then.'' The purpose of this item was to emphasize that part of the mystical meaning system. which, as suggested in Chapter 3, is oriented toward the value of myth, symbolism, and fantasy. Finally, to further specify the measure, making it sensitive to the ideas of ''illumination'' or ''intuitive insights'' which have generally been associated with the mystical orientation, respondents receiving ''high'' scores were required to say that ''new insights'' about themselves have at least a strong influence on their lives. In all, 25 percent of the sample was classified as having a ''high'' likelihood of being oriented to the mystical meaning system. Another 38 percent was classed as ''medium high,'' 26 percent as ''medium low,'' 8 percent as ''low,'' and 3 percent remained unclassifiable.[14]

These four measures could be used separately. But to do so would lead to unnecessary repetition as well as some problems of interpretation. Consequently, a composite measure based on these submeasures is used instead.

The logic for constructing this variable is to have a way of classifying people according to which meaning system they are most *likely* to hold, judging from the available information. For many people, the likelihood of their holding one of the four meaning systems is

13. Ninety-eight percent of those deeply affected by an experience of harmony with the universe and 90 percent of those deeply affected by the holy or sacred had also been deeply moved by the beauty of nature.
14. For details concerning the validity of each submeasure, see Appendix B.

greater than the likelihood of their holding any of the other three meaning systems. Some persons, for instance, were categorized as having a "high" likelihood on the theism measure, but only a "medium high," "medium low," or "low" likelihood on the individualistic, social-scientific, and mystical measures. But other people were equally likely to hold two or more of the meaning systems. This is to say, the four meaning systems are not entirely mutually exclusive.[15] The procedure for developing a single composite measure, therefore, is to classify people according to the single meaning system or combination of meaning systems on which the likelihood is greatest for them.[16]

Since each of the four measures was constructed in such a way that it had four categories ("high," "medium high," "medium low," and "low"), respondents who received a "high" designation on one or more of the measures were categorized first, then those with no "high" scores but at least one "medium high" score, and, finally, those with no "medium high" scores but at least one "medium low" score. There were none with "low" scores on all four of the measures. This procedure yielded 15 percent for whom the likelihood of being theistic was greater than the likelihood of their holding any of the other three meaning systems; 8 percent scored this way on individualism; 14 percent on social science; and 13 percent on the mystical meaning system.[17] Thus, 50 percent of the sample in all was classified as adhering to only one of the four meaning systems with a greater degree of likelihood than any of the other three. The remainder was divided into three categories. First, since there was a moderately positive relation between theism and individualism, a separate category was created for people holding both of these meaning systems with an equal degree of likelihood. Four percent fell into this category. For want of a better label it is referred to

15. See Appendix B.
16. The logic behind the development of this measure is somewhat akin to that which might be used to determine which church affiliations people hold if direct information were not available, but only various pieces of information about theological views, etc. The present measure is simply a "nominal variable," according to standard terminology; it is not a "typology" in the strict sense of the word (see, for example, Morris Rosenberg, *The Logic of Survey Analysis,* New York: Basic Books, 1968).
17. Figures cited are based on weighted cases to compensate for the oversampling of youth.

subsequently as "traditional," since it contains people who adhere to both of the meaning systems which were suggested in Chapter 3 as being historically more traditional. For similar reasons, a separate category was also established for people for whom there was equal likelihood of holding the social scientific and mystical meaning systems. Twelve percent fell into this category. It will be referred to as "modern," since it is a blend of the two meaning systems of supposedly more recent prominence. Finally, a "transitional" category was established to allow for the possibility of people adhering simultaneously to one of the more traditional and one of the more modern meaning systems.[18] Twenty-five percent fit into this category.[19]

A measure such as this, like any empirical measure, has certain strengths and certain limitations and these need to be kept clearly in mind throughout the subsequent inquiry. One of its main advantages, of course, is that it provides a simple summary of much of the information contained in the four separate measures (see Appendix B). The limitation of this measure is that its categories are not entirely "pure," that is, they do not consist of people who adhere to one system of meaning and who reject all the others. This is because people themselves do not simply adhere to one meaning system at the exclusion of all others. But this measure does have an advantage over four separate measures in that it attempts to determine which meaning system or set of meaning systems is most likely to be *dominant*.[20]

18. The label "transitional," of course, presumes some cultural shift from the more traditional to the more modern meaning systems, a proposition that will have to wait until Chapter 5 to be examined insofar as it can be examined at all with cross-sectional data.

19. An analysis of the transitional category revealed no clear subcategories within it. Ten percent of those answering in the sample, it should be noted, were not assigned to any category, since they failed to answer at least one item included in at least one of the four original measures.

20. To isolate effects resulting solely from individualism, for example, and not theism or the other meaning systems, relations with the former would have to be examined while "holding constant" all of the latter. The present measure sacrifices some of the precision that would be obtained from examining the relations between each meaning system and other variables and at the same time controlling for all the other meaning systems. To maintain the general readability of the subsequent analysis, an examination of the independent effects of each meaning system on social experimentation is reserved for Appendix B.

Table 8. **ITEMS IN EXPERIMENTATION INDEXES**

Political experimentation:

    Taken part in a demonstration
    Personally favor or tolerate the activities of a revolutionary
    Our form of government needs a major overhaul
    Probably would not admire an anti-Communist
    Mostly oppose giving the police more power
    Political position is radical or liberal
    Value working for major social change

Economic experimentation:

    Would vote for a candidate supporting affirmative action
    Value helping women get equal rights
    Favor new tax laws that would keep people from becoming wealthy
    Favor a guaranteed minimum wage plan for the poor

Religious experimentation:

    Attracted to at least one Eastern religious movement
    Value taking part in church little or none
    Attend church less than several times a month
    Pray less than several times a month

Family experimentation:

    Mostly favor an unmarried couple living together
    Mostly favor more freedom for homosexuals
    Would like to live in a commune

Leisure experimentation:

    Been high on drugs
    Like to smoke dope a lot
    Mostly favor legalizing marijuana
    Value getting to know your inner self
    Value becoming more aware of your body
    Value living close to nature
    Value having lots of free time
    Admire someone who goes to the wilderness to live
    Have been in an encounter group
    Attracted to at least one personal growth group

MEANING SYSTEMS AND EXPERIMENTATION

As in Chapter 1, we shall consider five kinds of social experimentation: political, economic, religious, family or sexual, and leisure. A summary index of each, using the items discussed in Chapter 1, will serve for examining the relations between dominant meaning systems and experimentation. Table 8 lists the items comprised in each index. In each case, acceptance of more than half the items is deemed tantamount to being supportive of social experimentation of the kind described in Chapter 1. An overall experimentation index that summarizes how many kinds of experimentation are supported is also considered. Details on the construction and validation of these indexes are presented in Appendix B.

From the historical material our expectation is that people holding theistic or individualistic meaning systems should be relatively nonsupportive of all kinds of social experimentation, although for different reasons, and that people holding social-scientific or mystical meaning systems should be more supportive of experimentation, but again for different reasons. Theism, as defined in Chapter 3, was hypothesized to legitimate opposition to social experiments because of, among other reasons, its traditionally pessimistic view regarding the potential for human betterment, its other-worldly reliance, and its tendency to be associated with Biblical literalism. In general, American theism appears historically to have reinforced an image of society *ordained and governed by God,* a society assumed to have little hope of being improved upon by human effort, especially experimentation with nonconventional social experiments. Individualism, in its more extreme form, was predicted to discourage experimentation because of its strong emphasis upon *individual willpower,* self-determination, and virtue, and because of its tendency to blame individuals for their own misfortunes. The social-scientific meaning system, in contrast, was hypothesized to encourage social experimentation, because of its attribution of human problems to *social forces.* The mystical meaning system was predicted to reinforce social experimentation because of its emphasis upon the need to *transcend* ordinary social influences and *experience* deeper, more meaningful levels of reality.

Table 9 reports the proportions supporting each kind of social experimentation among those holding each of the four meaning systems and among those holding each of the three combinations

Table 9. **EXPERIMENTATION BY MEANING SYSTEMS*** (Total Weighted Sample)

Percent scoring high on each kind of experimentation listed at the left among those whose dominant meaning system is:

Experimentation	Tradi- tional	Theistic	Individ- ualistic	Transi- tional	Social	Mystical	Modern
Political	0%	13%	11%	23%	48%	50%	61%
Economic	19%	34%	34%	39%	52%	48%	58%
Religious	16%	12%	53%	37%	70%	69%	85%
Family	10%	12%	27%	35%	61%	63%	77%
Leisure	11%	17%	17%	42%	51%	71%	72%
Summary	1%	8%	20%	25%	58%	65%	72%
Number	(43)	(145)	(80)	(250)	(139)	(127)	(118)

*All relations significant at or beyond the .05 level (chi square).

of meaning systems.[21] The relations shown give strong and consistent support to each of the hypotheses. On all five kinds of experimentation the theistic and individualistic types are relatively disinclined to be experimenters while the social and mystical types are much more so inclined.[22] The traditional type (more likely to hold theism and individualism than either social science or mysticism) is as resistant as, if not more resistant than, the theistic and the individualistic types. The transitional type (who holds some combination of either theism or individualism *and* social science or mysticism) is usually more supportive of experimentation than the theists or the individualists but is less supportive than the social or mystical types. The modern type (who holds both social science and mysticism with greater likelihood than either theism or individualism) is in all cases the most supportive of experimentation. Thus, on the summary experimentation index the proportion who support at least three or more kinds of experimentation ranges all the way from only 1 percent among the traditional types to 72 percent among the modern types.[23]

Those readers who have accepted the bulk of the argument thus far will find these results hardly surprising. We have attempted to argue that each meaning system should be related to social experimentation in a certain way, at least in contemporary American culture. And this is what we have found. But we might also have argued that high-level meaning systems that deal with questions about God, suffering, personal identity, and so forth should have little bearing on such mundane issues as political or economic or leisure experiments. Certainly it seems unlikely that most people consciously think through the implications of their tacit assumptions about life to this degree. What the present results suggest, nonetheless, is that specific orientations toward politics or toward sexual

21. A complete report of the relations between the dominant meaning system measure and the 28 items comprising the various experimentation indexes is given in Table C-4 in Appendix C.

22. For an examination of the relations between each separate meaning system and experimentation holding constant the effects of all the other meaning systems, see Appendix B.

23. Since these proportions turn out to be ordered along an ordinal continuum, an estimate of the strength of this relation can be obtained with Goodman's gamma. The gamma is a powerful .669. These relations hold among both the young and the old, females and males, and whites and nonwhites. See Table C-5 in Appendix C.

experiments or toward the use of drugs are very deeply imbedded in and influenced by more general understandings of life.

Unfortunately the present data afford no means of testing in detail the specific linkages that were posited between each meaning system and experimentation. The arguments developed in Chapter 3 have given ample cause to predict the relations just examined. But the details of these arguments must remain largely speculative. Some crude indications of the validity of some of these arguments can be obtained, nevertheless, by looking at the relations between the different meaning systems and some of the more specific items in the questionnaire.[24]

One inference that can be drawn from some of the more specific items in the data is that theists may resist social experimentation primarily on moralistic grounds while individualists may resist it more because of materialistic values. For instance, 53 percent of the theists compared with only 35 percent of the individualists attach great importance to "living up to strict moral standards." These same differences are also evident with regard to items having to do with specific moral questions such as receiving stolen goods, playing hooky, or engaging in deviant sexual behavior. In contrast, the individualists score higher than the theists on economic values. For example, 34 percent of the individualists compared with 24 percent of the theists choose "job security" as one of their three most important values. These findings seem consistent with the historical material.

Another empirical pattern that seems consistent with the material in Chapter 3 is that the mystics seem to desire radical social change as greatly as the social-scientific types, but they are not as interested in more concrete or serious proposals for actually reforming society. For instance, the mystics are just as likely as the social-scientific types to value major social change, to be tolerant of an avowed revolutionary, and even to have taken part in demonstrations. But they are less likely to value helping solve problems such as poverty or air polution, are less likely to favor new tax laws, and less likely to favor a guaranteed minimum wage program.[25]

---

24. The following results must be regarded as extremely tentative since it is difficult to determine statistical significance. As a rule of thumb, the results discussed here all involve at least 8 to 10 percentage point differences between the meaning systems compared.

25. See Table C-4 in Appendix C.

Just the opposite pattern is shown with regard to the more personal forms of experimentation. The social-scientific types are just as likely as the mystics to be involved with some of the more superficial forms of personal experimentation, such as taking drugs, but they are less likely to display serious involvement with personal experimentation, such as being interested in growth groups or encounter groups, or valuing body awareness, or admiring a life spent in the wilderness.[26]

These kinds of differences support the claim that the four meaning systems are at least partially different ways of understanding life rather than simply reducible to some more general underlying themes. Even though the theistic and the individualistic meaning systems appear to have much the same *general* implications regarding experimentation, as do the social-scientific and the mystical meaning systems, there are also some important differences.

CONCLUSIONS

The data thus far have demonstrated that people who use different meaning systems to understand the forces governing their lives take very different positions regarding the various social experiments that have appeared in recent years. People who believe God governs their lives and people who believe their lives are governed by sheer determination and who think failure is their own fault are generally much less likely to look favorably upon these experiments than people who think social forces govern their lives or people who believe their own perceptions and experiences govern their lives, regardless of whether the experiment at issue is a new political arrangement, a new economic policy, a new family structure, a new way of spending one's leisure time, or a new form of religious commitment.

These findings imply that one reason for the rise of social experimentation in recent decades may be that more and more Americans are coming to hold meaning systems that are conducive to these experiments, i.e. social scientific or mystical rather than theistic or individualistic meaning systems (as defined and operationalized in the foregoing). To suggest this possibility is not to suggest that a shift in meaning systems has *caused* the rise of

26. See Table C-4 in Appendix C.

social experimentation. It is more reasonable to assume a mutually reinforcing pattern. Interest in social experiments may have nourished a shift toward meaning systems more compatible with such experimentation. But then the shift in meaning systems also nourished social experimentation by making it more meaningful or reasonable, that is, by legitimating it. We have already considered historical material that suggests that such a shift may have been taking place and that indicates some of the possible reasons behind it. We turn now to the question of whether there is any evidence in the present data that such a shift may be taking place.

CHAPTER 5

Is a Shift in Meaning
Systems Taking Place?

The Bay Area data, collected in only one short span of time, do not provide a way to discover directly or conclusively whether or not a shift in meaning systems is occurring. An accurate appraisal of trends, if any exist, would require a series of systematic surveys or comparable data-collection procedures conducted at periodic intervals in the past, a source of evidence that obviously can no longer be obtained, or else a series of systematic studies in the future, which hopefully will be initiated but whose prospect reveals nothing about possible trends in the meantime. It seems worthwhile to examine the Bay Area data, in spite of their limitations, to discover what clues about possible trends or the lack of trends they may contain. This chapter investigates two areas in which such clues would seem likely to manifest themselves.

The first area involves differences between the meaning systems of the young and the old. The existence of a "generation gap" always arouses suspicion that some form of change may be occurring. Today's youths, as the adage has it, are tomorrow's leaders. And if they have ideas markedly different from their parents', there is a strong possibility that these ideas will come to play a more and more prominent role as time progresses. If Bay Area young people are no different from their elders in the systems of meaning they hold, little credence would be lent to the notion that some sort of cultural shift is taking place. But if they are noticeably *more* likely than their elders to hold, for instance, social-scientific and mystical meaning systems and *less* likely to adopt theistic and individualistic meaning systems, a cultural shift in the direction of the former and away from the latter is one logical possibility.

If differences exist between younger and older people, they may, of course, be more the products of maturation than harbingers of a generational drift. Young people may revert to more traditional understandings as they grow older, get married, have children, take jobs, and assume the other responsibilities that come with age. It will prove useful, therefore, to probe age differences, to the extent that they exist, to discover whether they are largely a function of life-cycle differences or whether they are indicative of a more lasting cultural trend.

The other source of clues in the present data about a possible shift in meaning systems involves comparisons between relatively well-educated, culturally sophisticated people and people with relatively less education and cultural sophistication. One of the most profound developments in American history has been a gradual upgrading of its educational level. People with college educations and other forms of professional training have become a larger and larger segment of the population.[1] If this trend continues, the ways in which these people understand their lives will undoubtedly occupy an increasingly prominent place in the culture. A second test of the notion that a shift in the direction of social-scientific and mystical meaning systems may be taking place, therefore, is to see if these meaning systems tend to be located among the relatively better educated, more culturally sophisticated.

AGE DIFFERENCES: GENERATIONAL OR MATURATIONAL?

Young people in the Bay Area tend to hold social-scientific and mystical systems of meaning, while older people assume theistic and individualistic meaning systems (see Table 10). Fifty percent of the social-scientific types and 48 percent of the mystical types are between the ages of 16 and 30, while only 25 percent of the theists and 16 percent of the individualists fall within this age bracket. The modern types also tend to be young (49 percent age 16 through 30) and the traditional types tend to be old (only 11 percent age 16 through 30), while the transitional types fall in between (29 percent under 30).

Does this generation gap signal that the social-scientific and

1. Between 1940 and 1970, for example, the median years of school completed rose from 8.6 years to 12.2 years (U.S. Bureau of the Census, *Statistical Abstract of the United States: 1971,* Washington, D.C.: Government Printing Office, 1971, p. xv).

Table 10. **AGE BY MEANING SYSTEMS** * (Total Weighted Sample)

| | Percent recruited from each age category listed at the left among those whose dominant meaning system is: | | | | | | |
Age	Tradi-tional	Theistic	Individ-ualistic	Transi-tional	Social	Mystical	Modern
16-20	4%	10%	7%	14%	19%	18%	15%
21-25	3	8	5	9	15	17	19
26-30	4	7	4	6	16	13	15
Total	11	25	16	29	50	48	49
31-40	29	24	17	22	18	15	22
41-50	14	16	10	16	16	18	9
Over 50	46	35	56	33	17	19	20
Number	(43)	(145)	(80)	(250)	(139)	(127)	(118)

*Numbers may not add to 100 percent due to rounding; the relation shown is significant at or beyond the .05 level (chi square).

mystical meaning systems may be the wave of the future? Or are the young likely to reject these meaning systems and return to theistic and individualistic meaning systems as they become more mature? No one can say which will happen for sure. But a clue to what may happen can be obtained by imagining for a moment that young people and older people were the same in every respect except their ages. Suppose that young people were just as likely as older people to have completed their educations, to have jobs, to be married, to have children, and to be stable community residents. Suppose they had the same worries and responsibilities as older people. Would they then be just as likely as older people to believe that God controls their lives or that willpower determines their destiny? Or would they still be more likely to believe in social forces and in their own mystical experiences?

There are ample reasons to suspect that younger people and older people would hold the same kinds of understandings of life if they were the same on such simple things as their likelihood of being married, having children, having a job, or being a stable member of the community. For one, marriage and parenthood bring with them the responsibility of socializing children into the generally accepted norms and values of the society. As a result, society puts greater pressure on persons in these roles to conform to its traditions than it does on people who are not performing a socializing function.[2] Young people "on the loose" can "get away with" more than people who should be "setting a proper example" for their children. The same has been suggested with regard to assuming job responsibilities.[3] Whereas a student or an apprentice does no harm in voicing novel ideas, persons with jobs—especially those in positions of authority—are expected to conform more to the "tried and true" ways of thinking and behaving. If God-oriented and individualistic understandings have been more familiar throughout American history than social-scientific and mystical views, older people might espouse the former simply because, as parents and breadwinners, they feel a greater responsibility to uphold these traditions.

2. Sidney L. Pressey and Raymond G. Kuhlen, *Psychological Development Through the Life Span* (New York: Harper & Row, 1957), pp. 494 et seq.
3. For example, see Ludwig Von Mises, *Bureaucracy* (New Haven, Conn.: Yale University Press, 1946), p. 97; Ely Chinoy, *Automobile Workers and the American Dream* (Boston: Beacon Press, 1955), p. 117.

That people are more willing to dabble in novel philosophies when only themselves are involved than when children or a job are at stake has, in fact, been noticed regarding beliefs about God and other traditional tenets of the church. While young people have long tended to abandon the church during their school years, they have also tended to return to it with the onset of parenthood.[4] One respondent in the Bay Area, for example, commented that religious beliefs had become totally meaningless to her; yet "just in case," she had baptized her son (at home in the bathtub) and was planning to send him to catechism class.

Another reason why differences in meaning systems may have more to do with maturation than with a cultural trend is that young people's ideas may be seriously affected by their marginality to the larger society.[5] Typically, young people are isolated in high schools or on college campuses rather than being an integral part of the labor force. They are often geographical itinerants rather than stable community members. They may find themselves on the fringes of church and other community organizations or even alienated from their families. Feelings of meaninglessness and powerlessness may be the result. Thus, social-scientific notions may be endorsed simply as a way of expressing one's feeling of being victim, rather than master, of the society in which he lives. By the same token, mysticism may be held as an ideologically comforting escape from society.

There is another reason to suspect that the theistic meaning system in particular may be found more among older people than among younger people because of maturational differences rather than because it is declining in prominence. Scholars have often pointed out that the churches, and Christian theology itself, are very much

4. See Michael Argyle, "Religious Observance," pp. 421–428 in David L. Sills (ed.), *International Encyclopedia of the Social Sciences* (New York: The Macmillan Company and The Free Press, 1968), vol. 13, p. 426; Joseph H. Fichter, *Social Relations in an Urban Parish* (Chicago: University of Chicago Press, 1954); Yoshio Fukuyama, "The Major Dimensions of Church Membership," *Review of Religious Research* 2 (1961): 154–161.

5. For intellectual foundations of this argument, see Erich Fromm, *The Sane Society* (New York: Holt, Rinehart & Winston, 1955), p. 124; Robert Nisbet, *Community and Power* (New York: Oxford University Press, 1962), p. 54; and William Kornhauser, *The Politics of Mass Society* (New York: The Free Press, 1959), pp. 90–93. For a related argument, see Harold Wilensky, "Work, Careers, and Social Integration," *International Social Science Journal* 12 (Fall 1960): 543–560, especially p. 551.

oriented to the family.[6] For instance, church school classes are often concerned with family problems; classes are provided for the training of young people and children; social activities are often designed with the couple or the family in mind. Biblical teachings themselves are replete with events involving the family. It is possible, therefore, that older people, because they have marital and family responsibilities, find the churches more relevant to their interests than those without such ties and, consequently, are also more likely to hold God-centered understandings about their lives.

Which of these notions is most consistent with the data? Do the young espouse certain meaning systems and the old others because they are simply at different points in the life cycle or because there is a generational trend afoot? To see what the effect of life cycle factors is, respondents were asked a series of questions about their marital status, parental status, employment status, and about their status with respect to more subjective concerns, such as the kinds of problems they worry about. Since some older people and some younger people are at the same stage in their life cycle with regard to these factors, it is possible to see what has the most important effect on meaning systems—one's age or being at a certain place in one's life cycle.[7]

Five of the factors that differentiate most strongly young people and older people (arbitrarily defined here as age 16 through 30 versus over age 30) were chosen to be analyzed simultaneously to determine their effect on the relation between age and the various meaning systems: being a student versus being out of school, being unresolved about one's self-identity in the sense of "wondering about the meaning and purpose of life" versus having resolved this question, being single versus having been married at least once, having no children versus having some children, and being unsettled in the sense of having moved at least once in the past two years versus being a more stable member of a community (see Table 11).

Table 12 shows the relation between age and meaning systems,

6. See for example, Charles Y. Glock, Benjamin Ringer, and Earl Babbie, *To Comfort and To Challenge: A Dilemma of the Contemporary Church* (Berkeley and Los Angeles: University of California Press, 1967), especially chapter 3.
7. For a discussion of the dangers of drawing inferences about social trends from age cohorts, see Matilda White Riley, "Aging and Cohort Succession: Interpretations and Misinterpretations," *Public Opinion Quarterly* 37 (Spring 1973): 35–49.

Table 11. **MATURATION CHARACTERISTICS BY AGE***
(Total Unweighted Sample)

	Percent having each of the characteristics listed at the left among those whose age is:	
	16-30	*Over 30*
Full-time students	36%	2%
Bothered a lot or some wondering about the meaning and purpose of life	42%	27%
Never married	89%	11%
No children	76%	25%
Moved during past two years	58%	22%
Number	(565)	(435)

*All relations significant at or beyond the .05 level (chi square).

first separately and then taking into account the effects of these five life cycle factors. The table expresses these relations in terminology that must be explained before the results are interpreted. Since the simultaneous relations among this many variables become exceedingly complex and therefore difficult to assess accurately, a computerized statistical system recently developed by Leo Goodman at the University of Chicago was used.[8] Instead of being based on

8. Leo Goodman, "A Modified Multiple Regression Approach to the Analysis of Dichotomous Variables," *American Sociological Review* 37 (February 1972): 28–46. For an introduction to the logic of the Goodman system, see James A. Davis, "Hierarchical Models for Significance Tests in Multivariate Contingency Tables: An Exegesis of Goodman's Recent Papers," pp. 189–231 in Herbert L. Costner (ed.), *Sociological Methodology 1973-1974* (San Francisco: Jossey-Bass Publishers, 1974); James A. Davis, "The Goodman Log Linear System for Assessing Effects in Multivariate Contingency Tables," mimeo (Chicago: National Opinion Research Center, June 1972); James A. Davis and Susan R. Schooler, "The Multivariate Logic of Log Linear Effects," mimeo (Chicago: National Opinion Research Center, January 1973); James A. Davis, "Survey Replications, The Log Linear Model, and Theories of Social Change," mimeo (Chicago: National Opinion Research Center, November 1972). For more recent extensions of this analytic system, see Leo A.

percentages this system uses *odds,* for example, the odds that
someone who is a mystical type will be young rather than old.
Thus in Table 12 it can be seen that the odds of being a youth if one
is traditional are 5 to 24 or .21; the odds of being a youth if one is
transitional, in contrast, are 120 to 111 or 1.08, and the odds of
being a youth if one is modern are 96 to 39 or 2.46. The statistics
that the Goodman system relies upon most are not the odds themselves, however, but *ratios* between different pairs of odds. Thus, it
can also be seen in Table 12 that the odds of being a youth if one
is a modern type are 11.7 times greater than if one is a traditional
type (2.46 divided by .21) or, as Goodman prefers to put it, the
"odds-ratio" is 11.7. By the same logic it can be seen that the odds
of being a youth are 11.6 times greater if one is a mystical type than
if one is a traditional type, 12.3 times greater if one is a social-
scientific type than if one is a traditional type, and so forth.[9]

The results shown in Table 12 demonstrate that the relation
between age and the different types of meaning systems is partly a
function of life cycle differences, but that young people and older
people still differ considerably even when these life cycle differences
are taken into account. Modern types are initially 11.2 times more
likely than traditional types to be young; 5.1 times more likely after
taking into account the effects of the five life cycle variables. Mystical
types are initially 11.0 times more likely than traditional types to be
young, 5.7 times more likely when the life cycle factors are held
constant.[10] Of the three modern types, the social-scientific type
appears to be most clearly associated with being young after the life
cycle effects are taken into account. But in all comparisons the three

---

Goodman, "Causal Analysis of Data from Panel Studies and Other Kinds of
Surveys," *American Journal of Sociology* 78 (March 1973): 1135–1191, "The
Analysis of Systems of Qualitative Variables When Some of the Variables Are
Unobservable. Part I—A Modified Latent Structure Approach," *American Journal
of Sociology* 79 (March 1974): 1179–1259.
9. Ratios can, of course, be computed between any pair of odds. In the present
case we have computed the ratios between the odds for each category of the
meaning system variable and the "traditional" category, chiefly because this yields
odds-ratios greater than 1 in all instances. Put differently, the "traditional"
category is used as the base line for comparisons. Any other category could be used
as well.
10. The odds-ratios cited here differ slightly from those cited in the previous
paragraph because of missing data incurred by introducing the five control variables.

Table 12. AGE, MEANING SYSTEMS, AND MATURATIONAL FACTORS (Total Unweighted Sample)

	Dominant meaning system						
	Tradi-tional	Theistic	Individ-ualistic	Transi-tional	Social	Mystical	Modern
Number of people:							
Under 30	5	55	23	120	114	102	96
Over 30	24	69	42	111	44	42	39
Odds of being young	.21	.80	.55	1.08	2.59	2.43	2.46
Ratios of odds (using traditional category as base)	1.0	3.8	2.6	5.1	12.3	11.6	11.7
Ratios controlling for maturational factors*	1.0	2.8	2.1	3.5	8.2	5.7	5.1

*Based on model [ABCDEF] [AG] [BG] [CG] [DG] [EG] [FG], where A = student status, B = meaning problems, C = marital status, D = have children, E = moved in past two years, F = age, and G = meaning systems. Chi square = 194.55, df = 342, p greater than .99.

modern types are still considerably more likely to be young than the three more traditional types.[11]

Table 13 shows in somewhat greater detail how age and the various life cycle factors affect one's choice of meaning systems. What it does, in effect, is follow two hypothetical groups of people—one under age 30, the other over 30—as they advance through a "typical" life cycle, showing how likely it is for them to be modern types rather than traditional types.[12] In the first phase, both groups are students, worry about problems of meaning and purpose, are single, have no children, and are geographically mobile. In this phase the young people are 65 times more likely to be modern types than traditional types (there are too few older people in this phase to compare); that is, if there were 10 traditional types in this group, there would be 650 modern types. Phase two is the same as phase one except that everyone has gotten out of school. This reduces the odds of being a modern type somewhat (568 moderns to every 10 traditionals among the youth). But note that the young people are still much more likely than the older people to be modern types. In phase three, everyone in the two hypothetical groups now resolves his or her worries about meaning and purpose, apparently becoming more settled about identities and goals in life. Accomplishing this feat is associated with another decline in the odds of being a modern type (195 now for every 10 traditional types among the youth). But again the youths are still much more likely than their elders to espouse modern rather than traditional meaning systems. In the next phases they all get married, then they have children, and finally they settle down as stable community residents. Marriage, it turns out, increases the odds of being a modern type somewhat. But each of the other developmental stages is associated with a reduction in the odds of espousing a modern meaning system, so that by the last phase there would be only 40 modern types for every 10 traditional types among the youth. Nevertheless, in each phase modern meaning systems are still about

11. It is important to note that all figures cited in Table 12 and Table 13 are based, not on *actual* frequencies (i.e. on actual numbers as previous tables have been), but on *estimated* frequencies derived from a hypothetical model produced by Goodman's statistical system. As the subscript to Table 12 notes, the probability that the differences between the estimated frequencies and the actual frequencies did *not* happen by chance is less than .01.

12. The choice of modern and traditional types is purely incidental; any other pair of meaning-system types could also be compared.

Table 13. **MODERN VERSUS TRADITIONAL
MEANING SYSTEMS, AGE, AND PHASE OF
LIFE CYCLE**
(Based on Total Unweighted Sample)

	Phase of Life Cycle					
	1	*2*	*3*	*4*	*5*	*6*
	Student Nonstudent ⟶					
	Meaning problems ⟶ Resolved ⟶					
	Single ⟶ Married ⟶					
	No kids ⟶ Kids ⟶					
	Mobile ⟶ Stable					
	Odds of being modern rather than traditional					
Under 30	65.0	56.8	19.5	22.8	11.1	4.0
Over 30	*	11.1	3.9	4.5	2.2	0.8

*Too few cases.

five times more likely among the young people than among the older group.[13]

It is risky to infer too much from these results since these are only *hypothetical* people who have been traced through their life cycles rather than actual people. What is suggested, however, is that people do gradually become more traditional as they grow older. Yet the fact that young people are still more likely than older people to hold modern meaning systems when both groups are the same with respect to maturation suggests that there may be some historical trend toward the more modern meaning systems too. Put differently, as young people mature, it seems doubtful that they will become as "traditional" in their meaning systems as previous generations.

Several other cautions are also in order. These comparisons were made by looking only at five maturational factors. Dozens of others might have been considered. If they were, it might be that maturational differences would explain away all the differences between the meaning systems of the young and the old. The age breakdown

13. It is important to note that there are no significant "interaction" effects in these relations, that is, the *relation* between maturation factors and choice of meaning systems does not vary, for example, by age.

used was also extremely crude, since a more refined one would have yielded too few people of any particular kind to compare. It seems safe to conclude, nonetheless, that these results are at present more consistent with the theory that a historical shift in meaning systems is taking place than with the notion that no shift at all is happening.

EDUCATION AND RELATED FACTORS

If there is a cultural trend away from theistic and individualistic meaning systems toward social-scientific and mystical meaning systems, this trend should also be reflected in differences between the better educated, more cognitively sophisticated, and the less educated, less cognitively sophisticated. New ideas never reach all parts of a society at once.[14] Some people are close to major arteries of communication, others more distant. In a modern society such as the United States these arteries consist largely of educational institutions and the mass media.[15] If social-scientific and mystical understandings are currently in the process of being diffused to wider and wider audiences, then it is reasonable to expect that a greater proportion of the educated and otherwise more exposed would already subscribe to these meaning systems than of the less educated, less exposed.[16] By the same token, more of the relatively unsophisticated than the sophisticated would probably still cling to the presumably more traditional theistic and individualistic views.

To find that the more sophisticated hold different kinds of meaning systems than the less sophisticated also suggests that the meaning systems of the more sophisticated will continue gradually to assume greater significance in the future. As social-scientific and mystical meaning systems come to be more accepted among the more

14. James S. Coleman, Elihu Katz, and Herbert Menzel, "The Diffusion of Innovation Among Physicians," *Sociometry* 20 (December 1957): 253–269; Everett M. Rogers, *The Diffusion of Innovations,* rev. ed. (New York: The Free Press, 1971); Robert L. Hamblin, R. Brooke Jacobsen, and Jerry L.L. Miller, *A Mathematical Theory of Social Change* (New York: John Wiley & Sons, 1973).

15. See Harold L. Wilensky, "Mass Society and Mass Culture: Interdependence or Independence?" *American Sociological Review* 29 (April 1964): 173–197.

16. Studies of prejudice tend to imply that the better educated pick up new ideas more quickly than the less educated and that their differential exposure to more modern ideas has important consequences for other attitudes. See, for example, Gertrude J. Selznick and Stephen Steinberg, *The Tenacity of Prejudice* (New York: Harper & Row, 1969); Charles Y. Glock, Robert Wuthnow, Jane Piliavin, and Metta Spencer, *Adolescent Prejudice* (New York: Harper & Row, 1975).

informed, they are likely to be diffused via other channels until the less informed gradually become exposed to them as well. There is no guarantee, of course, that exposure will lead to acceptance. But it will certainly not hinder it. And even if the less informed never accept the newer meaning systems, their numbers have been steadily diminishing. So, for this reason alone, their meaning systems should gradually lose importance relative to the culture at large.[17]

Table 14 shows that there are indeed rather marked differences between the kinds of meaning systems held by the better informed and the less well informed. Nearly two-thirds of the modern types are college graduates compared to only a sixth of the traditional types; about half of both the social-scientific and mystical types are, compared with only about a quarter of the theistic and individualistic types. And while only 6 percent of the traditionals have been to graduate school, nearly half of the moderns have been.[18]

The same kinds of differences show up regardless of what indicator is used to judge relative levels of cultural sophistication (see Table 15). About two-thirds of the three modern types come from homes where the parents were at least high school graduates, compared with about one-third of the three traditional types. The proportion who like to go to concerts and plays a lot varies from 44 percent among the most modern types down to 13 percent among the individualists. The proportion whose general intelligence or awareness was rated as above average by the interviewer varies from 68 percent of the moderns to only 28 percent of the traditionals.[19] And among those

17. This is not to say that each person's ideas have equal weight in shaping a culture and, therefore, that numbers are a measure of influence. The better educated undoubtedly have greater influence relative to their numbers than the less educated. This is another indication that the meaning systems of the better educated may come to have greater cultural importance in the future.

18. The education measure used is adjusted to compensate for the impossibility of the younger members of the sample to have completed as much education as the older members. For persons age 16 through 30, expected level of education is substituted for actual education; for persons age 31 through 35, expected education is substituted if the person has at least a high school education already. Virtually no one over age 35 expected to achieve a higher level of education than he had already attained. It should also be observed that the relations between education and meaning systems hold controlling for occupational status and controlling for family income (see Table C-6 in Appendix C).

19. No claim is made as to the validity of this item as a measure of IQ. It is perhaps more accurately to be regarded as the interviewer's assessment of the respondent's overall cognitive sophistication.

Table 14. EDUCATION AND MEANING SYSTEMS* (Total Weighted Sample)

	Percent recruited from each of the educational categories listed at the left among those whose dominant meaning system is:						
Education	Tradi-tional	Theistic	Individ-ualistic	Transi-tional	Social	Mystical	Modern
Postgraduate	6%	10%	14%	18%	29%	32%	46%
College graduate	10	12	14	17	22	21	17
Total	16	22	28	35	51	53	63
Some college or less	84	78	72	65	49	47	37
Number	(43)	(145)	(80)	(250)	(139)	(127)	(118)

*The relation is significant at or beyond the .05 level (chi square).

Table 15. **CULTURAL SOPHISTICATION AND MEANING SYSTEMS*** (Total Weighted Sample)

	Percent having each characteristic listed at the left among those whose dominant meaning system is:						
	Tradi-tional	Theistic	Individ-ualistic	Transi-tional	Social	Mystical	Modern
Mother a high school graduate	34%	38%	42%	48%	70%	61%	71%
Father a high school graduate	23%	29%	39%	46%	66%	59%	62%
Like to go to concerts and plays a lot	25%	23%	13%	27%	30%	43%	44%
IQ rated above average by interviewer	28%	41%	36%	44%	57%	59%	68%
Number	(43)	(145)	(80)	(250)	(139)	(127)	(118)
Majored in science or humanities (persons with some college only)	25%	29%	42%	42%	53%	46%	56%
Number	(12)	(45)	(24)	(120)	(81)	(79)	(86)

*All relations significant at or beyond the .05 level (chi square).

who have been to college, those who have majored in the pure sciences or humanities and, therefore, are probably most likely to have been exposed to new theories and philosophies are more concentrated among the modern types than the traditional types.

It might be noted that these results are consistent with those obtained earlier regarding age in that they both suggest that a gradual shift in cultural meaning systems may be occurring. Before speculating further on their implications, however, it is well to consider some of the other characteristics that distinguish people who adhere to the different meaning systems.

OTHER BACKGROUND CHARACTERISTICS

Thus far, this investigation indicates that the social-scientific and the mystical meaning systems seem to attract pretty much the same kinds of people (the young and the better educated). The theistic and the individualistic meaning systems also seem to attract similar kinds of people (the old and the less well educated). The social-scientific types seem to come from a somewhat better educated background than the mystics. And the individualists show some signs of more educational exposure than the theistic types. But these differences are relatively small. The reasons people choose one or the other modern or one or the other more traditional meaning system appear to lie in other background characteristics.

It was assumed that sex would be a major factor in channeling people into different meaning systems. Studies of religious belief and practice have tended to find women more committed than men, suggesting that here they would probably be more theistic while men would be more individualistic.[20] As between the social-scientific and the mystical types, it seemed, in the absence of any previous data, that women might tend toward the latter and men the former since conventional wisdom has it that women are more "intuitive" and men more "rational." Neither of these expectations is confirmed, however (see Table 16). Except for the traditional category, which has a disproportionate number of women, all the types comprise remarkably similar proportions of women and men.

Race appears to be one of the most important determinants of whether someone adopts theism or individualism. While only a sixth

20. For example, Glock et al., *To Comfort and to Challenge.*

Table 16. BACKGROUND CHARACTERISTICS AND MEANING SYSTEMS* (Total Weighted Sample)

Percent having each characteristic listed at the left among those whose dominant meaning system is:

	Tradi-tional	Theistic	Individ-ualistic	Transi-tional	Social	Mystical	Modern
Female	70%	58%	56%	57%	50%	54%	51%
Nonwhite	15%	37%	14%	18%	17%	18%	17%
Mother's religion:**							
Protestant	70%	51%	52%	44%	46%	39%	48%
Catholic	25	40	27	36	30	44	28
Jewish	0	1	4	4	7	3	8
None	1	1	3	5	10	9	7
Father's religion:**							
Protestant	67%	51%	40%	41%	45%	36%	38%
Catholic	20	37	28	33	24	36	25
Jewish	0	1	4	4	7	3	8
None	6	2	11	10	14	19	18
Politically liberal:							
Mother	10%	9%	9%	16%	21%	11%	20%
Father	10%	10%	11%	14%	25%	14%	23%
Number	(43)	(145)	(80)	(250)	(139)	(127)	(118)

*Overall relations are not significant at .05 level (chi square).
**Remainder = "other" religions.

of the sample is nonwhite, over a third of the theists are.[21] This finding is consistent with other studies that have found nonwhites to be more committed to traditional religious practices than whites. The tendency for nonwhites to espouse theism appears to be as much a function of their rejection of individualism as their specific orientation toward God, however. Even when individualism is mixed with theism (the traditional category), nonwhites are no more likely to choose it than in its more pure form.

Political background is another factor that seems to help explain why people come to hold different meaning systems, at least why some come to be more social scientific and others more mystical. Only 14 percent of the respondents' mothers and 15 percent of their fathers were politically liberal. But the social-scientific types are substantially more likely than the other types to have come from liberal backgrounds. Twenty-one percent had liberal mothers and 25 percent had liberal fathers. This finding seems consistent with the foregoing conclusions. If there is a relation, as seen in Chapter 4, between liberalism and the kind of social awareness that is part of the social-scientific meaning system, then liberal parents should be more likely than conservative parents to pass on this kind of social awareness to their children. The modern types who combine both social science and mysticism are also likely to have come from politically liberal backgrounds. But the mystics are no more likely than any of the more traditional types to have come from liberal homes. This difference suggests that even though the social-scientific types and the mystical types both now hold many of the same kinds of values and attitudes, the process by which they have come to their present positions is somewhat different.

Religious background seems to be another factor important in channeling people toward different meaning systems. It was not anticipated that crude religious differences—such as Protestant, Catholic, Jew—would be very helpful in predicting why people choose different meaning systems. From the results of other studies it was assumed that specific religious denominations might encourage different meaning systems (for example, fundamentalists being more theistic while traditional carriers of ascetic Protestantism, such as Congregationalism, might be more individualistic), but too few respondents belonged to the various denominations to make such comparisons possible. Contrary to expectations, however, simply

21. Nonwhite includes Black, Oriental, Mexican-American, and other Spanish-American.

knowing whether someone came from a Protestant, Catholic, or Jewish background shows some interesting differences in relative tendencies to choose different meaning systems. People whose parents were Protestants are disproportionately likely to be traditionals while those from Catholic backgrounds are more likely to be theists, consistent with long-held notions that Protestantism is more individualistic than Catholicism. A Jewish background seems most conducive to either social-scientific assumptions or a mixture of social-scientific and mystical assumptions, consistent with the image of Jews as especially oriented toward academic and, therefore, presumably more modern ideas.

These relations must be regarded as rather tentative since they are based on relatively crude indicators. Other background factors, it should be noted, were only weakly related to these meaning systems.[22] Overall, the choice between the more modern and the more traditional meaning systems seems highly influenced by educational and maturational variables and by age. The choice between the two modern or between the two traditional meaning systems is partly a function of racial, religious, and political background. But there are undoubtedly other factors involved, perhaps more psychological than social, which we have been unable to examine.

CONCLUSIONS

The present data have not enabled a test of the longer range historical trends discussed in Chapter 3. They have provided an indirect assessment of the possibility that trends may now be under way or

22. Using the factor-score coefficient scales for each of the four meaning systems (see Appendix B), the total fraction of variance explained by 28 background variables (age in years, sex, education, family income, college major, geographical mobility, church attendance as a youth, rural background, estimated IQ, feeling lonely, money problems, work problems, sexual problems, meaning problems, reading books a lot, liking concerts and plays a lot, attending school, number of children, father's education, mother's education, race, marital status, mother nonreligious, father nonreligious, mother's political position, father's political position, number of close friends, and keeping up on the news) is .262 for theism, .095 for individualism, .213 for social science (using the Factor III scale), and .152 for mysticism. That meaning systems are not related more strongly to background variables is congruent with the independence theory developed by Wilensky regarding the relations between mass society and mass culture (Wilensky, "Mass Society and Mass Culture").

that they have been taking place during the past generation. On this score, the results seem to be relatively consistent with the evidence cited in Chapter 3 suggesting that theistic and individualistic understandings have witnessed a noticeable decline in the past several decades while social-scientific and mystical ideas have shown an equal increase in importance. Thus, during the same period in which various forms of social unrest and experimentation have increased, there has apparently been at least a gradual shift in the systems of meaning by which Americans make sense of their lives. This historical parallel, combined with the close relations seen in Chapter 4 between meaning systems and social experimentation, suggests that the rise of the latter may have been significantly nurtured by the changing character of the former.

While the direction of change in meaning systems seems clear, the *rate* of change is more ambiguous. Some of the evidence presented in Chapter 3 suggested rather phenomenal developments (e.g., as in the growth of social science), but most of it argued more for an extremely gradual shift. The present data, to the extent that they suggest trends, also seem to lend more support to the notion of gradual than of climactic change. For all the differences between youths and their elders, the likelihood of youths returning to the views of their parents as they grow older seems great enough to suggest that whatever long-range changes remain will be relatively small. Similarly, the effects on the culture due to people becoming more and more educated have been exceedingly gradual thus far and appear likely to remain that way in the future. Certainly, a cataclysmic shift in beliefs and values such as many predicted during the height of the counter-culture of the late sixties seems remote.

CHAPTER 6

Alternative Theories of
Social Experimentation

The foregoing chapters have shown that people's general understandings of the forces governing their lives are strongly related to their views regarding social experiments. *Why* this relation exists, however, is still subject to question. Do these different forms of consciousness actually have important effects of their own? Or are there some other factors that actually lie at the bottom of both people's general understandings of life and their more specific views toward social experimentation?

The reason for examining the role of consciousness in the first place, it will be recalled, is that, theoretically, general interpretations of life seem capable of influencing attitudes and actions just as much as the actual character of people's worlds. There is good cause to suspect that this may not be entirely true, however, given the findings just discussed in Chapter 5. Some of the background factors, notably age and education, that seem to determine most strongly which kind of meaning system a person will hold are also the very factors one would expect to determine a person's views toward experimentation. It may be that these are the factors that should be focused upon rather than different forms of consciousness.

There are many existing theories of social experimentation, but generally the main ones have been of the following types, each of which is relevant to the relations observed here between meaning systems and experimentation. One is the "marginality" theory of social experimentation; that is, people engage in social experimentation because they find themselves marginal to more established social arrangements. The second suggests that cognitive sophistication or its absence is the key determinant of social experimentation. The third suggests that experimentation stems more than anything else from early socialization into a certain kind of value set. These theories are not just straw men; each has found considerable empirical support in previous studies. It is well to examine them to discover if they modify the interpretation of the present data.

SOCIAL MARGINALITY AS AN ALTERNATIVE THEORY

The finding that young, single, geographically mobile students are likely to espouse social-scientific and mystical meaning systems suggests an especially compelling explanation for the positive relation between these meaning systems and social experimentation. Perhaps people who hold these meaning systems favor social experiments, not because of their meaning systems at all, but simply because of their marginal social position. People are likely to throw stones, an old saying has it, when they feel left out of things. Revolutionaries foment revolutions because they feel left out of political decision-making processes. New religious movements start when people find themselves left on the fringes of established religious institutions. People join communes to salve their ache for a more conventional family life.[1]

Students of contemporary social experiments have been wont to point out that the progenitors of these experiments occupy a marginal position when it comes to many of the things that people generally value in life.[2] Although they tend to be privileged in some ways

1. For some general theoretical treatments of the nexus between marginality and social experimentation, see Robert K. Merton, "Social Structure and Anomie," pp. 131–160 in Robert K. Merton, *Social Theory and Social Structure* (New York: The Free Press, 1957); Talcott Parsons, *The Social System* (New York: The Free Press, 1951), pp. 249–325; Max Scheler, *Ressentiment* (New York: Schocken Books, 1961); with regard to the rise of religious expierments, see especially Charles Y. Glock, "The Role of Deprivation in the Origin and Evolution of Religious Groups," pp. 242–260 in Charles Y. Glock and Rodney Stark, *Religion and Society in Tension* (Chicago: Rand McNally, 1965); with regard to the rise of political experiments, see especially Ted Robert Gurr, *Why Men Rebel* (Princeton: Princeton University Press, 1970).

2. Talcott Parsons, "Youth in the Context of American Society," pp. 93–119 in Erik H. Erikson (ed.), *Youth: Change and Challenge* (New York: Basic Books, 1963); Kenneth Keniston, *Youth and Dissent: The Rise of a New Opposition* (New York: Harcourt Brace Jovanovich, 1971); William Braden, *The Age of Aquarius: Technology and the Cultural Revolution* (New York: Pocket Books, 1970), p. 52. Yablonsky's study of hippies indicates they tend to be marginal to friendship networks (Lewis Yablonsky, *The Hippie Trip,* New York: Pegasus, 1968). Block and her colleagues found a low level of integration with parents and family among student dissenters (Jeanne H. Block, Norma Haan, and M. Brewster Smith,

(young, educated, affluent backgrounds), they are typically marginal in other significant respects. Since many of them are still in school, they are marginal to the labor force and the larger economy. Since many of them are neither married yet nor parents, they are marginal to the dominant pattern of family life. They are likely to be marginal to other social institutions as well, such as churches, political parties, and community organizations, since the programs of such institutions are typically orchestrated toward the interests of older, more established residents of the community. The conclusion that has been drawn from these observations is that people in such marginal positions come to be interested in alternative social arrangements as a substitute for the conventional style of life they would actually prefer to have but have not yet been able to attain. The opposite conclusion—that people of marginal status are there by choice and would not pursue more conventional life styles if they could—has also been proposed.[3] But given the tremendous pressure that most people feel to conform to generally accepted styles of life, scholars tend to believe that there is characteristically some degree of longing among the marginal to occupy a more central or conventional position within the established society.[4]

"Socialization Correlates of Student Activism," *Journal of Social Issues* 25, Autumn 1969: 143–177). Feuer stresses the psychological importance of young people feeling they have no voice in political affairs (Lewis S. Feuer, *The Conflict of Generations: The Character and Significance of Student Movements*, New York: Basic Books, 1969, esp. p. 388). Peterson and Mauss rely on Glock's typology of deprivations in their analysis of Jesus People. Donald W. Peterson and Armand L. Mauss, "The Cross and the Commune: An Interpretation of the Jesus People," pp. 261–279 in Charles Y. Glock (ed.), *Religion in Sociological Perspective: Essays in the Empirical Study of Religion* (Belmont, Calif.: Wadsworth Publishing Company, 1973). Ryder stresses the *opportunities* marginality creates for the young to engage in social experiments (Norman B. Ryder, "The Cohort as a Concept in the Study of Social Change," *American Sociological Review* 30, December 1965: 843–861.

3. For example, Charles A. Reich, *The Greening of America* (New York: Bantam Books, 1970).

4. Bennett M. Berger has remarked that people typically attempt to make "moral capital" out of bad situations (Bennett M. Berger, *Looking for America: Essays on Youth, Suburbia, and Other American Obsessions*, Englewood Cliffs, N.J.: Prentice-Hall, 1971). In this regard it is especially relevant that one of the values frequently identified among marginal young people engaged in social experimentation is the value of *autonomy* (Yablonsky, *The Hippie Trip*; Nathan Adler, *The Underground Stream: New Life Styles and the Antinomian Personality*, New York: Harper & Row, 1972; Robert Jay Lifton, "Protean Man," *Partisan Review*, Winter 1968: 13–27).

The theory that social experiments are nourished by those who find themselves excluded from full participation in more traditional social arrangements also explains why social experiments have flourished in recent years. Because of various developments in the economy, chief of which is probably the need for more and more people to obtain extensive educations, an increasing number of young people have had to postpone entry into the labor market, marriage, and parenthood, and have had to stay isolated on the nations's college campuses, where overcrowded conditions often prevail and where they are given little voice in the decisions affecting their lives. The concomitant frustrations incurred, the theory argues, have been one of the main reasons for nonconventional life styles becoming so appealing.[5]

If this theory is correct, it is conceivable that the rise of social experiments has not been nourished at all by a shift in the consciousness of the American people, but simply by certain developments in the economy or in the broader social structure. Socially marginal people come to hold certain kinds of meaning systems, as indicated in Chapter 5, and they also come to be interested in social experiments, but their meaning systems are not the cause of their proclivity for social experiments.

Fortunately, this theory can be rather easily put to the test. The items used in Chapter 5 as indicators of immaturity or maturity summarize well the characteristics of the marginal person who has been thought to be most interested in social experiments: in school rather than in the labor force, not married, no children, not a stable resident of a community, and subjectively bothered about life goals. This measure is, in fact, a strong predictor of whether or not someone will be favorable toward social experiments. The odds of receiving a high score on the summary social experimentation index are six times greater among persons who exhibit all five of these traits of marginality than among those who exhibit none of them, even after the effects of age (over versus under 30) are taken into account. It is also the case that the more ways in which a person is marginal, the more likely he is to be a social experimenter. Thus, the odds of being an experimenter are 1.9 times greater if a person is marginal in one way than in none (age-controlled), 3.4 times greater if he is

5. See especially Parsons, ''Youth in the Context of American Society''; Keniston, *Youth and Dissent*; see also Daniel Bell, *The Coming of Post-Industrial Society* (New York: Basic Books, 1973).

marginal in two ways, 4.0 times greater if marginal in three ways, 5.5 times if four ways, and 6.1 times if five ways.[6] The proposition that marginality explains away the relation between meaning systems and social experimentation can be examined, therefore, by simply considering simultaneously the relations among these three variables.

Since more modern meaning systems have been seen to be more common among the marginal and since experimentation has also been seen to be more characteristic of the marginal, it is not un-reasonable to expect that the relation between modern meaning systems and social experimentation will vanish once the effects of marginality are controlled. If the relation does *not* vanish, the argument that meaning systems have an independent effect on people's attitudes toward social experimentation will be enhanced.

Table 17 shows the relation between the different kinds of meaning systems and the summary social experimentation scale, first, without the effects of marginality being taken into account, then with them taken into account. Since age appears to have an independent effect of its own on experimentation, it is also held constant in both cases. The relations are presented in terms of Goodman's odds-ratio statistic, which was discussed in the last chapter.[7] As was done there, the traditional category is used as a base line for these figures. The "62.4" in the first row indicates that the odds of being a social experimenter are 62.4 times greater if one espouses a modern meaning system than if one espouses a traditional meaning system; the "44.4" indicates that the odds of being an experimenter are 44.4 times greater if one is a mystical type rather than a traditional type, and so on.

The table demonstrates that when the effects of marginality are taken into account, the likelihood of being an experimenter still varies dramatically among people espousing different meaning systems. Modern types are still over fifty times as likely to be exper-imenters as traditional types; mystical types are still forty times more likely; and social-scientific types are almost thirty times more likely. In other words, the relation between the more modern meaning systems and attraction to social experiments is not just an

6. See Table 18. These figures are not based on actual cases but on *estimated* frequencies from the Goodman models; see Table C-7 in Appendix C.
7. The models tested using these variables are listed in Table C-7 in Appendix C. *Unweighted* figures are used in the calculations of these and subsequent tables, since age is controlled.

Table 17. EXPERIMENTATION BY MEANING SYSTEMS, CONTROLLING FOR AGE AND MARGINALITY
(Based on Total Unweighted Sample)

				Dominant meaning system:			
	Tradi-tional	Theistic	Individ-ualistic	Transi-tional	Social	Mystical	Modern
Experimentation (odds-ratios)*							
Controlling for age	1.0	2.7	8.0	9.0	31.2	44.4	62.4
Controlling for age and marginality	1.0	2.4	7.9	8.4	29.9	40.3	54.9

*Ratios between the odds of scoring high on the summary experimentation index if one's dominant meaning system is as listed and the odds of scoring high if one's dominant meaning system is traditional.

artifact of both being more common among the socially marginal. The various meaning systems bear a strong relation to social experimentation *independently* of marginality.

It might be added that even though marginality does not explain away the relation between meaning systems and experimentation, it does have an independent effect of its own on experimentation (see Table 18). For example, people scoring 4 (relatively high) on the marginality index are about five times as likely to be experimenters as those scoring 0 (low). Overall, the effects of marginality are not nearly as strong as those of the different meaning systems, however.

Table 18. **EXPERIMENTATION BY MARGINALITY, CONTROLLING FOR AGE AND MEANING SYSTEMS** (Based on Total Unweighted Sample)

	Marginality Index					
	Low 0	1	2	3	4	High 5
Experimentation (odds-ratios)*						
Controlling for age	1.0	1.9	3.4	4.0	5.5	6.1
Controlling for age and meaning systems	1.0	1.6	3.1	3.4	4.9	3.5

*Ratios between the odds of scoring high on the summary experimentation index if one's score on the marginality index is as listed and the odds of scoring high if one's score on the marginality index is 0.

COGNITIVE SOPHISTICATION AS AN ALTERNATIVE THEORY

Another compelling theory of why some people experiment with nonconventional styles of life and others don't is that the experimenters may be better informed than the nonexperimenters. One can't join a new group he hasn't heard of; he isn't likely to favor a new policy he doesn't understand. The relation between cognitive sophistication and social experimentation has, in fact, been one of the more noticeable aspects of the recent counter-culture.[8] College students have been observed in virtually every kind of experiment considerably more often than noncollege young people. And among college students, studies have consistently found the most active experimenters to be the better students. In the general population, higher education has also consistently been a correlate of support for alternative life styles and social policies.[9] It is not surprising, therefore, that people in the Bay Area sample who are college graduates, whose fathers are college graduates, who have majored in the pure sciences or humanities, and who enjoy going to cultural events are over five times as likely to be experimenters as those who manifest none of these traits.[10]

Cognitive sophistication theory also offers a plausible explanation of why social experiments have taken place with such magnitude at this particular time in history. Never before have so many people obtained a higher education or, for that matter, been as exposed to sources of new information through the mass media. In 1970 there were over 7 million college students; just twenty-five years before there were only 1.6 million.[11] During the same period the median level of education climbed steadily from 8.6 to 12.2 years.[12] One

8. Keniston's review of the literature on student political activists concludes that they tend to be outstanding students from the homes of the better educated, students at the best colleges, and students in academic rather than vocational majors (Kenneth Keniston, *Young Radicals: Notes on Committed Youth,* New York: Harcourt, Brace & World, 1968, appendix B). His more recent review of the literature on casual drug experimentation shows the same correlates (Keniston, *Youth and Dissent,* pp. 230–252). Regarding religious experimentation, see Robert Wuthnow and Charles Y. Glock, "Religious Loyalty, Defection, and Experimentation Among College Youth," *Journal for the Scientific Study of Religion* 12 (June 1973): 157–180, and "The Shifting Focus of Faith: A Survey Report," *Psychology Today* 8 (November 1974): 131–136. More generally, higher IQs have been found related to lower degrees of conformism (Read D. Tuddenham, "Correlates of Yielding to a Distorted Group Norm," *Journal of Personality* 27, 1959: 272–284).

9. Gallup polls such as those cited in Chapter 1 typically find the better educated more supportive of social experimentation.

10. See Table 20.

11. Seymour Martin Lipset, *Rebellion in the University* (Boston: Little, Brown & Company, 1972), p. xvi.

12. U.S. Bureau of the Census, *Statistical Abstract of the United States: 1971* (Washington, D.C.: Government Printing Office, 1971), p. xv. The proportion of young adults (age 25 through 29) with college degrees has almost tripled since 1940, from 6 percent to 16 percent in 1970. Since 1940 the proportion in this age

likely consequence of this increase is that more and more people have become aware of such things as communes, alternative political systems, Eastern religions, and the like. An equally important result is that higher levels of cognitive sophistication may have heightened the public's general willingness to tolerate differences in life styles and in opinions. While the vast majority of the better informed may not practice nonconventional life styles, they may be substantially more willing than the less informed to stand for others practicing them.

Cognitive sophistication varies considerably, as was seen in Chapter 5, among people with different meaning systems. Those meaning systems most conducive to experimentation are also most likely to be associated with cognitive sophistication. It may be argued, therefore, that cognitive sophistication is actually what causes people to experiment, not the particular kind of meaning system they hold. The case for this alternative explanation can be put in the following way. The cognitively sophisticated are more likely both to espouse social scientific and mystical meaning systems and to be experimenters. But their experimentation does not stem from their particular understanding of life; rather, both are a product of their being more exposed to modern ideas. Many readers, indeed, will likely have already been wondering if this might not be the case or even perhaps that the measure used to tap the different meaning systems may not actually just be tapping some underlying continuum of sophistication-unsophistication. Statistically, the implication of this alternative explanation is that if levels of cognitive sophistication were controlled, the relationship between meaning systems and experimentation would vanish.

Table 19 puts this explanation to the test. The first row of figures shows the original relation between the different meaning systems and the summary social experimentation index, controlling only for the effects of age. The second row shows this relation again taking into account the effects of a five-category cognitive sophistication index that gives respondents a point each for being a college graduate, for having majored in the pure sciences or humanities, for liking to attend cultural events, and for having a college-educated

bracket with high school diplomas has risen from 38 percent to 72 percent. Rosenthal has pointed out that the fathers of nearly two-thirds of the college students today never went beyond high school themselves (Jack Rosenthal, "Census Study Finds an 'Education Gap,' " *New York Times,* February 4, 1971).

Table 19. **EXPERIMENTATION BY MEANING SYSTEMS, CONTROLLING FOR AGE AND COGNITIVE SOPHISTICATION** (Based on Total Unweighted Sample)

	Dominant meaning system:					
	Tradi-tional	Theistic	Individ-ualistic	Transi-tional	Social	Mystical	Modern
Experimentation (odds-ratios)*							
Controlling for age	1.0	3.2	7.2	9.2	33.2	46.0	69.9
Controlling for age and cognitive sophistication	1.0	3.2	7.2	8.7	28.6	41.8	62.0

*Ratios between the odds of scoring high on the summary experimentation index if one's dominant meaning system is as listed and the odds of scoring high if one's dominant meaning system is traditional.

father. The figures are again derived from Goodman's statistical system for analyzing complex tables.[13] They indicate how many times more likely it is to be an experimenter for those who hold each type of meaning system than it is for those who are traditional types. The table shows that the relation between meaning systems and experimentation is reduced when cognitive sophistication is controlled, but this reduction is only a slight fraction of the original relation. Overall the tendency to be an experimenter still varies dramatically when cognitive sophistication is controlled. For instance, modern types are about seventy times more likely than traditional types to be experimenters with only age controlled, and they are still about sixty times more likely with both age and cognitive sophistication controlled. Likewise, mystical types are still about forty times as likely as traditional types to be experimenters and social-scientific types are still about thirty times as likely.

Table 20. **EXPERIMENTATION BY COGNITIVE SOPHISTICATION, CONTROLLING FOR AGE AND MEANING SYSTEMS**
(Based on Total Unweighted Sample)

	Cognitive Sophistication Index				
	Low 0	*1*	*2*	*3*	*High* 4
Experimentation (odds-ratios)*					
Controlling for age	1.0	.9	1.9	3.2	5.3
Controlling for age and meaning systems	1.0	.7	1.4	2.1	2.7

*Ratios between the odds of scoring high on the summary experimentation index if one's cognitive sophistication score is as listed and the odds of scoring high if one's cognitive sophistication score is 0.

A further look at the joint relations among meaning systems, cognitive sophistication, and experimentation (see Table 20) suggests that both the cognitive sophistication theory and the meaning systems theory may be true, rather than being alternative explanations of the same thing. The relation between cognitive sophistication

13. See Table C-8 in Appendix C for the model upon which these figures are based.

and experimentation also holds up when the effects of meaning systems are controlled. Those with scores of 4 are still about three times as likely as those with scores of 0 to be experimenters.[14] Again, as with the effects of marginality, it appears that meaning systems are much more powerfully related to experimentation than cognitive sophistication, although it is difficult to know absolutely whether or not this is the case since the present meaning-systems measure is considerably more refined than the present measure of cognitive sophistication.

The present data, of course, do not afford a direct test of the view that social experimentation has arisen because of an upgrading of general cognitive sophistication rather than a shift in meaning systems. To the extent that both developments have occurred, as the historical evidence suggests they have, it seems safe to conclude, nevertheless, that each has contributed to the emergence of non-conventional life styles and social arrangements.

LIBERAL BACKGROUND AS AN ALTERNATIVE THEORY

The third alternative theory to be tested is also compelling both by its logic and by the empirical evidence which supports it. The reason some people get involved with alternative social experiments while others don't, it suggests, is simply that they have been reared in more liberal environments. Those with more modern meaning systems, therefore, would be experimenters more often than those with more traditional meaning systems simply because they grew up in more liberal homes. The psychologist Kenneth Keniston has aptly termed this the "red diaper baby" theory in connection with radical politics.[15] People engaged in political dissent today, according to this theory, are generally the offspring of parents who engaged in similar forms of dissent a generation ago. In support of this theory the sociologist Seymour Martin Lipset has gathered an im-

14. The Goodman models indicate that there is an interactive effect among age, cognitive sophistication, and experimentation, i.e. the relation between cognitive sophistication and experimentation is different for young and for old people (see Table C-8 in Appendix C). The effects of this interaction are slight; consequently, for purposes of simplicity, it has been ignored in Table 20. For the results taking into account the interactive effects, see Table C-9 in Appendix C.
15. Keniston, *Young Radicals*, p. 47.

pressive mass of poll data which suggest that, even at the height of campus rebellions in the late sixties, young people tended largely to reflect the political views of their parents.[16] Other data have been collected showing that campus radicalism appears to reflect not only the political views of parents, but their views on other matters as well; for instance, liberally religious and nonreligious parents seem to generate politically radical youth much more often than conservatively religious parents.[17]

The present data tend to confirm these findings and suggest that liberal backgrounds are conducive not only to political experiments but to other kinds of experimentation as well. While the vast majority of respondents, according to their own report, came from conservative or moderate homes, a minority said that either their father or mother (or both) were politically liberal or radical. A somewhat smaller minority also said their parents were religiously liberal or, perhaps more accurately, religiously nonconventional, by describing their parents as having no religious beliefs, as being atheists or agnostics, or as being humanists. The tendency is for each kind of liberalism reported about parents to be associated with a greater likelihood of being an experimenter. Thus, on a 0–4 scale giving respondents a point for each parent who was politically liberal and each parent who was religiously nonconventional, those with scores of 1 are 1.5 times as likely to be experimenters (controlling for age) as those with scores of 0, those with scores of 2 are 3 times more likely, and those with scores of 3 or 4 are 7.2 times more likely. But, regardless of how

16. Lipset, *Rebellion in the University.*
17. Keniston, *Young Radicals;* Seymour Martin Lipset and Sheldon S. Wolin (eds.), *The Berkeley Student Revolt: Facts and Interpretations* (Garden City, N.Y.: Doubleday & Company, 1965), see esp. pp. 472–473, 509, 523; Wuthnow and Glock, "Religious Loyalty, Defection, and Experimentation Among College Youth." Other studies indicate that social experimenters come from homes characterized by a general climate of libertarianism or permissiveness. See Richard Flacks, "The Liberated Generation: An Exploration of the Roots of Student Protest," pp. 104–126 in Richard Flacks (ed.), *Conformity, Resistance, and Self Determination: The Individual and Authority* (Boston: Little Brown & Company, 1973); Henry Malcolm, *Generation of Narcissus* (Boston: Little Brown & Company, 1971); Keniston, *Youth and Dissent,* p. 278. For more general results concerning the converse relation, see Paul H. Mussen and Jerome Kagan, "Group Conformity and Perceptions of Parents," *Child Development* 29 (1958): 57–60. Berger, *Looking for America,* discusses these relations in terms of a more general theory of social change.

Table 21. **EXPERIMENTATION BY MEANING SYSTEMS, CONTROLLING FOR AGE AND LIBERAL BACKGROUND** (Based on Total Unweighted Sample)

				Dominant meaning system:			
	Tradi-tional	Theistic	Individ-ualistic	Transi-tional	Social	Mystical	Modern
Experimentation (odds-ratios)*							
Controlling for age	1.0	3.2	10.3	10.0	35.1	50.4	66.7
Controlling for age and liberal background	1.0	3.8	12.2	11.2	37.9	59.1	74.7

*Ratios between the odds of scoring high on the summary experimentation index if one's dominant meaning system is as listed and the odds of scoring high if one's dominant meaning system is traditional.

conducive a liberal background is to experimentation, the question remains whether liberal backgrounds account for the relations between meaning systems and experimentation.

Looking at Table 21, it is clear that controlling for liberal background does not reduce the relation between meaning systems and experimentation. Someone from a totally "nonliberal" background is still much more likely to be an experimenter if he subscribes to a more modern meaning system than if he subscribes to a more traditional meaning system, just like someone whose parents were liberal both in politics and in religion. The ratio for both is for modern types to be over seventy times as likely as traditional types to be experimenters, mystical types to be almost sixty times as likely, and social-scientific types to be over thirty times as likely.[18]

The fact that liberal background in no way explains away the relation between meaning systems and experimentation suggests another interesting possibility: perhaps the meaning system measure is really just another way of measuring liberalism. Since it has shown an almost linear relation with experimentation, it may be just a measure of some underlying conservatism-liberalism dimension which is even more basic than the specific meaning systems on which so much emphasis has been placed in the foregoing pages. Perhaps the true interpretation of the data is that a liberal background produces a liberal world view which, in turn, causes people to support social experimentation. Statistically, this interpretation would be indicated if the relation between liberal background and experimentation were to vanish when controlling for the meaning-system measure. That is, the meaning-system measure, as a measure of liberalism, would "interpret" the relation between liberal background and experimentation.

This explanation is not consistent with the data (see Table 22). The original relation between liberal background and experimentation is scarcely affected at all by the introduction of the meaning-system measure into the relation. The most plausible interpretation of the data seems to be simply that the meaning-system measure is indeed tapping something other than just a simple liberalism-conservatism

18. It is interesting to note that the relation is somewhat stronger when liberal background is controlled than when it is not. This appears to result mainly from the traditional category's odds being disproportionately small in the former case. For the models upon which Tables 21 and 22 are based, see Table C-10 in Appendix C.

Table 22. **EXPERIMENTATION BY LIBERAL BACKGROUND,
CONTROLLING FOR AGE AND MEANING SYSTEMS**
(Based on Total Unweighted Sample)

	Liberal Background Index			
	Low 0	1	2	High 3
Experimentation (odds-ratios)*				
Controlling for age	1.0	1.5	3.0	7.2
Controlling for age and meaning systems	1.0	1.2	2.8	7.1

*Ratios between the odds of scoring high on the summary experimentation index if
one's "liberal background" score is as listed and the odds of scoring high if one's
"liberal background" score is 0.

dimension and/or that it bears a strong relation to experimentation
entirely apart from the effects of having been reared in a liberal
rather than a conservative background.

CONCLUSIONS

The three theories tested in this chapter by no means exhaust the
possible alternative theories that could be proposed. But they do
cover the theories that have been most widely agreed upon by social
scientists concerned with contemporary unrest. Considering this
agreement, their inability to do damage to the relations between
meaning systems and experimentation is especially significant.[19]

19. Although the properties of the present data do not meet the necessary
requirements, a path analysis that includes all the variables discussed in this
chapter tends to confirm these conclusions. Meaning systems still have a strong
direct relation to experimentation, taking into account the effects of age, marginality, cognitive sophistication, and liberal background. Indeed the direct effects of
the meaning system variable (used only because it has consistently shown relatively
linear relations with experimentation) are substantially more powerful than those
of any of the other variables. The path model also suggests that the meaning system
variable is largely *not* an intervening variable between the other variables and
experimentation. See Table C-11 in Appendix C. The strength of the meaning
systems is also indicated by multiple regression analysis of the data. The fraction of
total variance explained by the 28 background variables (see Chapter 5, note 22)
is .378. Introducing the four factor-score coefficient scales for the four meaning
systems increases this fraction to .513.

There are several other kinds of theories that have purposely not been examined and that, therefore, deserve some comment.

One alternative to the model developed in the foregoing chapters is to suggest that meaning systems really have no effect on experimentation because the path of influence is the other way around—a person's meaning system is a by-product of his involvement with and attitudes toward contemporary social experiments. The present discussion has in no way been meant to imply that involvement in social experiments might not have a strong influence on one's meaning system. Devotion to an Eastern religious experiment could very well turn one in the direction of a mystical meaning system, just as involvement in a radical political experiment could heighten one's commitment to a social-scientific meaning system. To suggest that meaning systems have no influence on one's attitudes regarding experimentation, however, seems as absurd as to suggest the converse. The path of influence is undoubtedly two-directional. Meaning systems influence more specific attitudes and activities by making them seem sensible or not sensible; more specific involvements reinforce particular meaning systems by verifying or falsifying them. To sift out the more specific directions of influence between the two would require much more extensive data, including panel data and experimental data over time, than what has been available here. The reason for emphasizing the influence of meaning systems upon experimentation in the present study more than the opposite relation is partly that experimentation has aroused a great deal more attention than meaning systems have and, thus, has appeared to be more the matter requiring explanation than are the meaning systems people hold. Beyond that, the historical evidence also suggests that the current shift in meaning systems was probably under way well before the advent of the recent social experiments. But the latter have undoubtedly nourished the former as well.

A second kind of alternative explanation that does not seem to warrant serious testing is the suggestion that the link between meaning systems and experimentation is merely an artifact of some genetic trait or deep-seated psychological process. While this may be entirely the case, such an explanation is at an entirely different level of analysis than is involved in the present study. It would reveal little about the *cultural* processes themselves that have been taking place during recent American history.

Finally, another alternative explanation likely to find some supporters is one that concludes that the present theory has ordered the data entirely wrong. It might be concluded, from a factor analysis of the data, for example, that the simplest way to reduce the data to some easily manipulable variables is to combine all the items having to do with religion, all the items having to do with social issues, and analyze the relations between the two. Or it might be concluded that the distinction made between highly general understandings of life and more specific attitudes and opinions is not important and that the two kinds of items should simply be lumped together and then analyzed in relation to some set of background variables. But such possibilities are really not alternatives to the present theory. They are suggestions for an entirely different study.

To review briefly, the general proposition with which we began is that the unrest and social experimentation of recent years has been reinforced by a shift in cultural meaning systems. While it has not been possible to test this proposition fully or even directly, the bulk of the evidence examined has tended to support it.

The overall argument can be divided into three parts. First, the results of national polls and other surveys over the past two decades indicate that unrest and experimentation of numerous kinds, but especially of a *liberal* nature, have been gradually, but steadily, increasing: political alienation, toleration of radical groups, favorability toward the full inclusion of racial and sexual minorities, defection from traditional religious institutions and experimentation with new groups, libertarianism in standards of sexual conduct, experimentation with alternatives to the family, and experimentation with alternative ways of spending leisure time. Although there is still a high degree of commitment to more conventional social forms, the unrest and experimentation of recent years are far from limited to their more visible manifestations. The past two decades may be merely a temporary disruption of a more general commitment to the traditional. But at this writing, at least, there are few signs that the more general shifts in attitudes and life styles of the past twenty years are being reversed.

Second, evidence has been examined that suggests that the cultural meaning systems with which people make sense of their lives at the highest level of generality have been changing at least during the past generation if not over a longer period. Scattered evidence on religious belief gathered over time consistently shows a gradual erosion of the theistic meaning system as we have defined it. Some quantitative evidence plus a great deal of more speculative observation suggest that traditional American individualism in its more extreme forms has also been declining. A variety of evidence was cited that suggests that the kind of meaning system espoused by social scientists has been gradually becoming more prominent. What has been called the "mystical" meaning system also appears to have been gaining acceptance, although there is no systematic evidence to back up this impression; certainly, there are clear precedents of this meaning system in American history. The Bay Area data have also been seen to be *consistent* with these notions regarding cultural change, even though they have afforded no direct information on trends. Differences between the younger generation and the older generation, which do not seem explicable entirely on the basis of maturation alone, reflect a possible shift in meaning systems. This shift is also reflected in differences between the more culturally sophisticated and the less culturally sophisticated respondents in the Bay Area. None of this evidence is conclusive. The expenditures required to document definitively the presence or absence of such a cultural shift would be vast. But the evidence currently available lends itself much more to the conclusion that a cultural trend, albeit extremely gradual, is present than to the conclusion that no such trend at all exists.

Third, our effort to establish a link between a shift in cultural meaning systems and the apparent increase of social unrest and experimentation took the form primarily of a cross-sectional comparison of the attitudes and life styles of people in the Bay Area who adhere to different meaning systems. The differences expected from considering each meaning system in its historical context were strongly substantiated by the data. Theists and individualists, as operationally defined in Chapter 4, are much less likely to support counter-culture experimentation than those with social-scientific or mystical meaning systems. By and large, those with the most "modern" meaning systems are at least fifty times more likely to be supportive of experimentation than those with the most "traditional" meaning systems, even after taking into account the effects of such things as social marginality, cognitive sophistication, and liberal background. The Bay Area findings cannot be generalized directly to the nation at large. The frequency of experimentation and of the several meaning systems is undoubtedly different in the Bay Area than it would be in American society at large. But there seems to be no reason why the *relations* found should be substantially different elsewhere. These relations, of course, do not illuminate the actual processes by which meaning systems have nurtured or resisted social experimentation. That would require an investigation in itself. It seemed more important to establish the connection in the first place before attempting to explicate its details.

Apart from what the present findings imply about the course of American society, which will be taken up in the next chapter, there are several theoretical implications that should be mentioned. First, the foregoing has demonstrated the feasibility of conducting empirical research on highly general cultural meaning systems.[20] By no means were the complexities of each meaning system tapped nor were the many variations of each meaning system investigated. The data suggested, for example, that attention might also have been paid to a different kind of individualism or to a different kind of social determinism. Thus, we have maintained throughout that we were attempting to formulate and test hypotheses only about particular forms or manifestations of each meaning system. But enough of the crucial assumptions of each meaning system as conceptualized seem to have been tapped to produce strong relations with a variety of other variables. In this regard, it is critical to bear in mind that the differentiating factor in our choice of meaning systems was their *content,* more specifically, different forces identified as controlling and ordering reality. Although attention could be, and has been, paid to the purely "formal" characteristics of meaning systems, their content also appears to have important ramifications.[21]

As illustrative of these ramifications, two avenues for further research might be proposed. First, the possibility of comparing alternative meaning systems suggests that sociologists of religion might well expand their empirical investigations beyond the study of how much or how little religious faith people have or how conservative or how liberal their theology is to the comparative analysis

20. This is not to deny the need for paying attention to the meanings that develop in and become specific to particular situations, as emphasized in the symbolic interactionist and ethnomethodological traditions. But it does suggest the existence of more general, situationally transcendent systems of meaning which can also be identified and which have a strong influence on behavior and attitudes.

21. For instance, inquiries into the nature of meaning systems regarding the question of suffering have tended to emphasize formal characteristics, such as optimism-pessimism and rationality-irrationality, more than substantive characteristics. Weber's initial work on this problem, of course, suggested the need to do both.

of wholly different belief systems, using empirical and even quantitative methods. The theoretical groundwork has already been laid. Construction of the empirical edifice itself could also begin.[22] Second, the study of meaning as a problem relating to political alienation might effectively be enlarged. Besides giving attention simply to how much or how little meaning people have, attention might also be fruitfully directed, as the foregoing has shown, toward the *kinds* of meaning people have and the effects of these different meaning systems on their political activity. In this regard, we have attempted to argue that interpretations of what ultimately governs life are probably most decisive.

Another general implication of this inquiry pertains to the study of values. There has traditionally been a tendency to define cultures primarily in terms of their values, i.e. the kinds of goal-orientations represented. While this perspective has been useful, it has tended to be somewhat less than satisfactory. In particular, it has tended to render culture somewhat superfluous to the study of actual social behavior. To explain social experimentation, for example, by saying that people value social change verges on tautology. The obvious question is *why* they value change. The study of meaning systems helps to answer this question. The reason certain values are held and certain behaviors are engaged in lies partly in the way in which events, or the forces governing one's life more generally, are *understood.*[23] Given one understanding of the forces governing life it "makes sense" to want and to do some things to change or improve one's life; given a different understanding it "makes sense" to want and to do other things. Of course, it then can be asked in turn why different meaning systems become held. This question, too, is crucial and needs investigation. But the mere act of introducing meaning systems into the causal analysis of behavior goes

22. Especially the work of Peter L. Berger and Thomas Luckmann has established a theoretical basis for the comparative study of alternative meaning systems, or what they would probably prefer to call "symbolic universes." As yet, empirical sociology has done little to translate their general formulations into specific research problems.

23. The basis for looking at general understandings rather than just at values can, in fact, be found in some of the more generally accepted discussions of culture, for example, in Clyde Kluckhohn, "Values and Value-Orientations in the Theory of Action: An Exploration in Definition and Classification," pp. 388–433 in Talcott Parsons and Edward A. Shils (eds.), *Toward a General Theory of Action* (New York: Harper & Row, 1951). What Kluckhohn referred to as "existential propositions" have thus far been relatively neglected in empirical research.

a long way toward overcoming the circularity of focusing only upon values, that is, of explaining action simply by a voluntaristic approach that says "they did it" because "they wanted to."

Finally, the foregoing seems to argue once again, as Weber originally argued, for the importance of the subjective element in social life. If two people, both relatively the same in terms of age, marital status, and occupational status or in terms of educational level and educational background, can still differ by a factor of fifty times in their willingness to support social experimentation, just because of the meaning systems they hold, this should suggest that meaning systems may have powerful implications for other issues as well. Attitudes toward crime or propensities to engage in crime, for example, might be found to differ markedly between people having different understandings of the forces governing their lives. And to the extent that these understandings could be identified, they might afford an especially useful lever for combating crime. This is not to say that subjective understandings are unrelated to social, psychological, and biological antecedents. But it may be more strategic to focus on the subjective understandings themselves than the many antecedents that determine them.

CHAPTER 7

The Politics of
Diversification

In this concluding chapter I wish to turn to the more general questions of "What does it all mean?" and "Where do we go from here?" In looking for answers it will be necessary to go beyond what can be inferred directly from the foregoing data. We shall have to enter quite consciously and deliberately upon speculative ground. If such speculation raises new questions that provoke further inquiry, it will have served its purpose.

Some observers of the social experimentation of recent years have concluded that it may eventually culminate in a radically new kind of society. Although many of the alternative life styles and social arrangements experimented with in recent years may be destined to fail, in their very failure lies also the hope, as witnessed by every past period of social transformation, that one such experiment will lead to a better or at least a more viable future. For example, the simple communalism of the counter-culture may foreshadow a much-needed corrective to the devastating individualism that has been advanced to such extremes by modern industrial capitalism. Those who have discovered new states of consciousness through the experiences of mysticism and drugs may help to initiate a welcome addition to the stark rationalism that has dominated the post-Renaissance period of Western civilization. Even the failures of the political experiments that have been loosely associated with the New Left have proven to be more abrasive than established policy-makers were sometimes able to withstand.

As likely as it may seem to some that the pendulum of current events will swing toward major social transformation, it appears just as likely, however, that it will swing in the opposite direction. The uncertainties inherent in times of unrest and experimentation and the costs inevitably associated with bringing about social improvements provide powerful incentives to the emergence of reactionary nostalgia and to compulsive loyalty to any symbol of strong unifying leadership, no matter how retrogressive such leadership may prove in the long run.

It is perhaps incumbent upon those who find themselves in the midst of a period of turmoil and change to speculate about the prospects of revolution on the one hand and of reactionary traditionalism on the other. The unfortunate aspect of speculating in such a dualistic manner about the future is that it tends to obscure what may in fact be the most important transformation of our time, a shift in the character of society that is already well under way.

McLuhan has reminded us that the medium of communication may actually be the message itself. By the same token, we would do well to consider the possibility that the medium of social transformation has in fact become the transformation.

Efforts to bring about social change during the past few years have resulted in what might well be called a process of "social diversification." Signs of this process, as seen in Chapter 1, are evident in virtually every area of American society. Whereas there was once a normative standard that allowed only one or several kinds of family or economic or religious structures, the normative order appears to have become elastic to the point where a variety of diverse social forms can now be countenanced. While marriage and children were once virtually the only form of family life considered acceptable to the vast majority of the public, a whole range of family styles—trial marriages, group marriages, homosexuality, childless marriages, serial monogamy, communes—have come to be widely accepted. While the Judeo-Christian tradition was once virtually co-extensive with the span of American religion, now dozens of Eastern and quasi-religious movements have become readily available alternatives.

Rather than looking upon the experimentation and diversity of our time only as a harbinger of change, it would appear more fruitful to consider the process of diversification as itself a form of social change. For the prospects of a society characterized by increasing structural diversity appear greater than the prospects for either total revolution or total social stagnation.[1]

1. Philip Rieff has written, "Our cultural revolution does not aim, like its predecessors, at victory for some rival commitment, but rather at a way of using all commitments, which amounts to loyalty toward none" (*The Triumph of the Therapeutic*, New York: Harper & Row, 1966, p. 21).

Diversification represents a fundamental shift in the character of social evolution from that which has been dominant heretofore. During the era of modernization the most sweeping form of structural transformation was a process called "institutional differentiation." This process, as in the classic example of economic functions becoming differentiated from the family, typically was characterized by the development of two or more social institutions, each performing a unique social function, each of which had formerly been carried out by a single institution.[2] In contrast, the diversification process now evident in the post-modern era is typified by the development of two or more social institutions each performing basically the *same* social function as the others (albeit in different ways), the same function that previously had been performed by a single social institution.[3] Rather than there simply being a shift toward a more distinguishable economy or a more distinguishable family, multiple forms of economic relations and multiple means of fulfilling family functions are developing.

In some respects, of course, diversification and differentiation are not entirely separate processes. At the same time that more specialized institutions (in terms of the uniqueness of the functions they fulfilled) were developing, a greater variety of competing institutions might also emerge. However, some of the current diversity in social arrangements represents a conscious attempt either to halt or to reverse the process of differentiation. The agrarian commune reflects an interest in reuniting economic and familial functions in one institution. The political militancy of some of the new mystical religious cults stands in sharp contrast to the differentiation that Ernst Troeltsch, for example, believed would be manifested between the two and even in contrast to the circum-

2. See Emile Durkheim, *The Division of Labor in Society* (New York: The Free Press, 1933); Talcott Parsons, *The System of Modern Societies* (Englewood Cliffs, N.J.: Prentice-Hall, 1971); Neil J. Smelser, *Social Change in the Industrial Revolution* (Chicago: University of Chicago Press, 1959).

3. The current diversification process may eventually result in a condition of pluralism, i.e. a system where there is a balance of power among different economic, regional, racial and ethnic, and religious groups (William E. Connally, "The Challenge to Pluralist Theory," pp. 3–34 in William E. Connally, ed., *The Bias of Pluralism*, New York: Atherton Press, 1969). As yet, such a balance of power has by no means been achieved (one that would include the new religious, political, and economic experiments of recent years), thus making the term "pluralism" somewhat misleading for what would be better described simply as "diversity."

spection that established churches have practiced with regard to politics.[4] Such examples may not be typical of other recent social experiments, but their significance is enhanced by the indication they give that differentiation may be reaching the point at which it becomes humanly counterproductive. The limits of ever greater specialization have long been reached in industry, where the efficiency gained thereby has had to be weighed against the human costs incurred. It would not be surprising, therefore, if such a point of diminishing returns were not also present with respect to differentiation at a societal level. Thus, diversification may be replacing differentiation as the major process of social evolution of our time.

Diversification is obviously not an entirely recent development, as the great diversity that has characterized American religion throughout its history attests. Especially during periods of social strain, as in the early nineteenth century, diverse social experiments have appeared in virtually every realm of society. But the present range of diversity appears to be greater than at any previous point in history and the level of normative support for diverse social experiments, as the evidence considered in Chapter 1 indicates, appears to be at a point higher currently than at any time previously, at least since systematic attitudinal data have been collected. This normative support also appears to be integrally rooted in broader cultural meaning systems, which give it legitimacy to a greater extent, if our larger thesis is correct, than has been the case in the past.

The advent of diversification on a relatively widespread scale suggests that new metaphors may be necessary to describe this process adequately. The concept of differentiation has been based on a biological analogy and more specifically on biological concepts that found their way into social science through the writings of Herbert Spencer and his contemporaries before the turn of the century. Just as there are biological structures which perform special physiological functions, so it was assumed there are social structures which perform special social functions. The biological analogy breaks down, however, if there are multiple structures all performing essentially the same functions but in different ways. Furthermore, the concept of structure itself ceases to be central. As the variety of structures performing the same social functions proliferates, the

4. Ernst Troeltsch, *The Social Teaching of the Christian Churches,* 2 vols. (New York: Harper & Row, 1960).

relations between these structures become more interesting than
the structures themselves.[5] The nature of communication and
coordination between structures (of circulation and of the transfer
of energy) become more crucial than the nature of commitment to
or the organization of separate social structures. In brief, synergy
replaces structure as the concept of most concern.[6]

In microcosm a useful model of the synergistic society is the
small, free-wheeling, task-force groups that have come to be known
as "synectics" groups.[7] Designed to maximize the serendipitous
benefits of diversity, the synectics group is consciously constituted
with members of widely varying skills and perspectives whose
energies are coordinated toward resolving difficult problems, such
as inventing new kinds of pipeline valves or new sources of food,
in ways that would likely not occur to the members of the group
were they working individually. The nature of the interaction in such
a group is readily seen in the following transcript, which describes
a synectics group attempting to invent a new kind of can opener:

D: How about having the unit automatic? Just put in the can and the
    top is off.
A: That wouldn't be a basic invention. It would just be putting the thing
    on wheels.
B: We aren't going to get anywhere if we limit our thinking to improve-
    ments. My understanding is that the client wants a radically new
    can opener . . . not a slightly better one.
A: I think you're right. Let's back way off from the problem . . . What
    does "open" mean?
E: In nature there are things that are completely closed, then open
    up . . . a clam for instance.
B: But with a clam the process is reversible. We don't need that for our
    problem. We don't need to close the can up again.
E: I guess not . . . How about a pea pod? That really opens up along a
    line . . . it's got a built-in weakness and splits along the line.
A: Has a can got a built-in weakness? A weakness we can take advantage
    of?

5. This is, in fact, one of the reasons I have chosen to focus in this chapter on the
fact of diversity rather than the nature of the diversity.
6. Metaphors from modern physics may be especially appropriate in this regard.
Heisenberg, for example, has argued that the world can no longer be divided into
different groups of objects but has to be divided into different groups of *connections*
(John Lukacs, *Historical Consciousness: or, the Remembered Past,* New York:
Harper & Row, 1968, pp. 278–289).
7. William J.J. Gordon, *Synectics: The Development of Creative Capacity* (New
York: Collier Books, 1961).

E:	Let's see. The seam in a can looks like this . . . double where the two layers of metal are rolled over. If we just cut into the first layer and peeled it back . . .

B:	You know, that's not bad. If you did that then you'd have a top that could be put back on. It would be larger than the diameter of the can itself.[8]

The necessary precondition for the successful functioning of such a group is an ethos that tolerates and, in fact, encourages diverse points of view and novel ideas. In the above example the group members include an engineer, a psychologist, a biologist, and a philosopher, each reflecting his own unique experience in the comments he makes. Without such an ethos of toleration, the group would be more effectively constituted by homogeneous than by heterogeneous elements. Once diversity is regarded as a positive value, however, much effort is still required to coordinate the group toward an optimum solution of its task-problem. Unlike a homogeneous group where little coordination might be needed and unlike a group who shared no common problem and could simply go their separate ways, a delicate equilibrium must be achieved between too much and too little coordination. If so much control is exercised over the group that diversity is molded into uniformity, the potential creative strength that lies in diversity is lost. If too little control is exercised, the group is likely to disintegrate into its component parts. For the most creative products to emerge from the group, the essential diversity of the members has to be protected, but at the same time each member has to be responsive to the ideas of the other members as well.

Although the analogy should not be pushed too far, a highly diversified society appears to manifest some of the same dynamics as the small synectics group. On the one hand, it contains the promise of more creative adaptive potential than that of a more homogeneous society. This is partly because of the dialectic by-products likely to emerge from the interchange between diverse social and cultural elements. These by-products have often been noted in industries that have diversified their product lines.[9] Sometimes through conscious deliberation and sometimes through pure serendipity,

8. Ibid., pp. 123–124.
9. Richard Duane Herring, *Product Diversification as a Business Policy with a Case Study of Crown Zellerbach Corporation* (unpublished master's thesis, University of California, Berkeley, 1956).

the technology developed in one division has led to vital innovations in other divisions. The application of railroad technology to the development of the disc brake for automobiles is one example. With regard to contemporary social experiments, it is conceivable that the presence of parallel institutions will result in mutual benefits, as in the case of established churches learning from the recruitment methods of the new religious groups, for example, or the new groups learning from the organizational strengths of the established churches. Partly the adaptive potential of the diversified society also lies in its capacity to secure the energies of a greater variety of people than would be the case under more monolithic conditions, as is especially evident in the attempts to diversify the reward structure of American society so that women and blacks and other minority groups can be more fully included in fulfilling the functions of the society.

On the other hand, the diversified society contains the peril of disintegration just as does the small synectics group. The meaning systems that appear to be ascendant rationalize diversity and thereby contribute to greater freedom of choice, but they do not seem to afford a basis for consensus on the pursuit of specific social ends. "Do your own thing" is a liberating experience at the individual level, but at a social level is an insufficient directive for organized action. As in the synectics group, therefore, the crucial issue under conditions of increasing societal diversity becomes one of coordination. The traditional Hobbsean problem of order must be raised once again but with perhaps even more serious implications than in the past. The benefits of free choice from a novel menu of life styles and social forms must be protected. But at the same time the competition among these alternative forms needs to be regulated. Even more so than under conditions of differentiation, once a variety of structures exists, each competing to perform the same social functions, a delicate degree of coordination must be instituted.

Before considering this problem of social order, it is well to consider further for a moment whether a problem, indeed, exists. At one level it may be argued that there is currently no crisis of social order at all. The everyday definitions of reality without which no society could function seem to be well in place. Ask a businessman and a street person to drive from San Francisco to Los Angeles and both will exhibit an amazing degree of consensus about traffic regulations, distance, temporal measures, and so forth. But a society cannot be maintained on everyday definitions of reality alone. Such definitions may be effective at telling how to get to Los Angeles, but they offer little help in deciding whether or not to go in the first place or in rationalizing why one should or should not go.

Traditionally, the "whether to" and the "why" questions of daily life have been answered by broad cultural meaning systems. At this level, the crisis of social order is clearly in evidence. The emergent social-scientific and mystical meaning systems appear to be greatly more adaptable to diversity pushed to its extremes than either traditional American theism or individualism. The newer forms of consciousness make diversity respectable. But they offer little help in maintaining order in the midst of such diversity. The authoritative do's and don'ts of theism and individualism that formed a highly rationalized system of means and ends are replaced in the social-scientific and the mystical meaning systems by libertarian views that give ultimate legitimacy to nothing except the values of freedom and pluralism.[10]

In the long run some new meaning systems may again be constructed that will serve to maintain the social order. In the meantime, however, other mechanisms have rushed in to fulfill this function. The social order is not simply dissolving as traditional meaning systems undergo challenge and change. Society has proven considerably more capable of coping with diversity than many had predicted. And yet, the delicate relations that must be maintained under optimum conditions in a diversified society place a heavy and complex burden on these mechanisms. The viability of society itself may well depend on the manner in which they function. The patterns that are being established in this regard, therefore, warrant examination. To set the stage, we shall begin by considering *repressive* mechanisms of social control.

Traditionally one of the most common means of maintaining social order has been to nip deviant behavior in the bud by various means of repression or punishment or by simply giving it labels that strip it of any legitimacy, for example, labeling homosexuality as a

10. In part the social-scientific and the mystical meaning systems may be said to rationalize specific social ends as clearly as theism and individualism did. The value of equality for all may be as decisive a rallying cry as the notion of a covenant people, for example. What the social-scientific and mystical meaning systems fail to do, however, is to grant legitimacy to any one source of institutionalized authority, which is always necessary to translate collective ends into collective action.

sign of madness, premarital sex as a form of moral degeneration, radicalism as un-American, mysticism as heresy, and so on.[11] Increasingly, as the data have shown, fewer people are willing to support such harsh sanctions against nonconventional behavior whatever it may be or to define it as deviant and illegitimate. Psychological space is created in which such forms can develop and flourish. This is not to say that they will necessarily grow until they choke out more established forms of behavior. But for those who wish to try them, there is less risk than formerly of having to face repressive mechanisms of social control. The newer meaning systems make nonconventional behavior seem as reasonable as conventional behavior. The result is that it is much more difficult to punish or to label negatively behavior that makes sense than it was to do so to behavior that seemed foolish or illogical in the first place.

There is also a more social "structural" reason why repression of nonconventional behavior seems less likely in the future than it has been in the past. Nonconventional behavior clearly has its social costs, but it also is of strategic social value. On the negative side, experimentation with diverse social forms is inefficient and "expensive." It presupposes a minimal degree of overall economic well-being.[12] Such experiments inevitably must be performed on a trial-and-error basis. A few communes may prove viable while countless others fail. The key to happy alternative sexual styles may be found by some but at the cost of considerable mental and emotional distress to others. Certainly the experimentation with drugs over the last decades has given evidence to the risks associated with discovery. This is to say, in some respects a shift toward greater structual diversity is likely to be a drain on the overall resources of the society at least in the short run.[13] Under conditions of affluence such as have existed in the postwar period these costs can be borne with little difficulty. But given some less prosperous social conditions, it is conceivable that strong resistance to experimentation will

11. Talcott Parsons, *The Social System* (New York: The Free Press, 1951), pp. 297–321.
12. For a discussion of the relations between affluence and social experimentation, see Daniel Bell, *The Coming of Post Industrial Society* (New York: Basic Books, 1973).
13. Studies of disaster victims provide a parallel case. In the aftermath of crisis the experiments engaged in as means of coping tend to be done on a purely trial-and-error basis and are often more costly than beneficial until an effective means of coping is discovered.

emerge. Under adverse conditions the society would find itself either unable or unwilling to pay for the casualties incurred in the uncertain quest for hopefully better social arrangements. On the positive side, balanced against the costs of structural diversification, must be considered the gains this process affords. If established institutions perform their social functions in so circumscribed a way as to fail to secure commitment from a substantial portion of the society's members, a shift to more diversified institutional forms may provide a means of reintegrating these members into the society. If, for instance, the shackles of bureaucracy become so constraining that large numbers of young people choose to not work at all rather than submit themselves to the bureaucratic life, alternative means of production, like agrarian communes or small-scale artisan trades, may be functionally positive for the overall well-being of the society. The data in this volume point to the danger that opting for an alternative social form in one area of life may simply reinforce such opting-out in other areas of life as well. Finding an alternative way of fulfilling one need does not seem to maintain commitment to other established institutions. If the choice for the alienated is simply to remain uncommitted to any social forms or to become committed to alternative social forms, the latter may nevertheless be the most functional for the larger society. Especially as long as alternative social forms remain relatively small, as at present, they may serve to institutionalize and thereby curb alienation more than to foster unrest and change.

It needs to be added that the positive consequences of structural diversification may be especially crucial to the viability of an advanced capitalistic economy where the problem of meeting supply with demand becomes greater than the problem of meeting demand with supply.[14] Although the scarcity of natural resources may operate to limit supply as it already has in certain areas, the overall functioning of the economy may be such as to require a degree of constant unemployment as well as the perpetual creation of new demands through advertising and other means. If this is the case, siphoning off substantial numbers of people into essentially nonproductive (as far as the overall economy is concerned) roles may be more supportive than debilitating to the economic system. This may be so

14. A general discussion of post-scarcity economic conditions is found in Bell, *The Coming of Post-Industrial Society*.

in spite of the more manifest criticism which such people become subject to, just as the presence of a large body of welfare recipients may be an inevitable by-product of advanced capitalism in spite of the negative sentiments expressed against it. Perhaps more clearly evident has been the economic utility of the counter-culture in creating new markets, for everything from "natural" shampoos to tarot cards, toward which the productive capacity of the economy can be directed. While a minor share of this demand has been filled by the small-scale artisans of the counter-culture themselves, the established industrial order has undoubtedly benefited most from the new markets that have been created. Increased diversification of life styles may be inefficient as far as certain personal costs and certain political entanglements are concerned, but it may become a vital outlet for the productive capacity of the economy. In this regard, the emphasis in many of the contemporary social experiments on the self and its need for gratification as opposed to more traditional self-negating attitudes may be of special significance.

While repressive mechanisms of social control are not entirely absent or unlikely, therefore, it seems that increasingly the kind of control mechanism deployed will be the *regulatory* mechanism. These mechanisms become useful once a modicum of legitimacy has been granted to nonconventional social forms, in that they allow such forms to be perpetuated but limit the extent to which they are likely to spread and facilitate the relations that must develop between these forms and more established social institutions. These regulatory mechanisms are extremely important because the manner in which they function is decisive as to whether new, nonconventional forms of life will contribute successfully to the betterment of the larger society, whether they will simply be used inadvertently to buttress conventional social arrangements, or whether they will in effect be rendered superfluous as far as the larger society is concerned.

One of these regulatory mechanisms is the commercialization of nonconventional behavior. Commercialization is the act of transforming goods into commodities. Goods initially having little market potential (either because they are too costly or too esoteric to have much appeal) are processed, packaged, and priced, making them readily marketable and exchangeable on a wide scale. The genius of American technology has come to tailor, advertise, and distribute everything from organic foods to mystical experiences.[15] They can be bought, sold, traded in, or simply taken out on approval. What for St. Catherine of Siena may have taken twenty years to attain is now marketed to mass audiences in easy weekend seminars and ready-to-swallow capsules. Alternative states of awareness or alternative living arrangements can be experienced with virtually no sacrifice and virtually no risk of becoming involved too deeply.

Commercialization greatly facilitates the task of maintaining order amidst diversity by minimizing the problem of choice. In a society where multiple ways of fulfilling virtually every human wish are available and where the cultural meaning systems make any of the available options equally reasonable, the obvious question is: How does one choose? Traditionally this question has lain at the heart of the problem of order. On the one hand, the problem of choice may become so perplexing in the absence of effective guidelines that anxiety and uncertainty build up until they have paralyzing effects. On the other hand, the problem of choice may be resolved, but in the manner both Hobbes and Locke feared, each person committing himself wholeheartedly to ends entirely at odds with those of his fellows. But commercialization minimizes the problem of choice by making choice inconsequential. Choice exists only where sacrifice is involved. The effect of commercialization is to minimize these sacrifices. Liability is always limited. There are no irreversible decisions. Flexibility rather than immutability is the hallmark of such transactions. The problem of choice need not be paralyzing, for any number of choices can be made on a purely temporary basis. Nor does freedom of choice need to result in the antagonism of each against all because no choice need become a true commitment. The costs of one choice are not so great as to obviate other choices. One may practice zazen and be a businessman too. One can opt for communal living today but leave open the possibility of marriage tomorrow. As one considers the variety of available options, it soon becomes evident that which one is chosen actually makes little difference because it can readily be traded in for another if it is not to one's liking.

The commercialization of nonconventional activities helps regulate them by ensuring that people do not become so heavily involved that they cannot return again to more conventional patterns of life.

15. See Herbert Marcuse, *One-Dimensional Man* (Boston: Beacon Press, 1964), p. 57.

As nonconventional activities have themselves become more institutionalized, successive layers of involvement have become defined so that at all but the very deepest layers avenues of withdrawal remain open. Even a totally involving movement such as Hare Krishna provides levels of commitment at which the elemental rites of the movement can be experienced without any obligation to become more deeply involved or to give up other involvements.[16] The benefits of limited involvement accrue to the stability of society in that they minimize the need to give up (either in the short- or the long-run) conventional commitment to experiment with the less conventional. At the same time, limited involvement obviously facilitates the ability of alternative social movements to reach and influence larger audiences than would otherwise be the case. Easy withdrawal means easy entry too. Therein may lie the real challenge of these movements to the established society rather than in their ability to secure total commitment to their causes. Indeed, much of the symbolism that has developed regarding the counter-culture has characterized it more in terms of networks of people who *flow through* various groups and activities rather than those who are caught up with any of them. Unlike the gurus of the East, those of the West have been less concerned with recruiting full-time disciples than with making available their basic principles on a relatively wide scale. This is not to say that large numbers of deeply committed converts would not pose an even greater challenge to the society. It is to say, however, that commercialization as a regulatory mechanism works both against and in favor of alternative social arrangements, which is another indication of the likelihood that social diversification is a process that will continue.

Another regulatory mechanism that has operated in tandem with commercialization is privatization. Although experimentation has been evident in all areas of social life, it has been most pronounced in the more private realms, namely, family, leisure, and religion, than in the political or economic realms. This has been even more the case in the seventies than it was in the late sixties. Privatization has been decried by some, but it is extremely functional as far as the problem of maintaining order in the midst of diversity is con-

16. Gregory Johnson, "A Counter-Culture in Microcosm: Sources of Commitment to the Hari Krisna," chapter 2 in Charles Y. Glock and Robert N. Bellah (eds.), *The New Religious Consciousness* (Berkeley and Los Angeles: University of California Press, 1976).

cerned. Political and economic structures, because of their functions of distributing wealth and power, link people together in such a way that changes in one sector inevitably influence those in other sectors as well. The women's liberation movement has ramifications for the entire economy. Reforms in campaign spending affect the entire electoral process. Even a small fringe cult such as the SLA calls forth widespread political and legislative action. In contrast, the voluntaristic character of leisure, religion, and even the family make it possible to experiment without much immediate effect on the larger society. Some can opt for cohabitation and others for marriage in a way in which some could not choose socialism while others chose capitalism. The current interest in yoga has emerged with little direct expense to the sports industry or even to the churches. Participation in encounter groups may enrich but not necessarily replace going hiking and camping. What this means is not that experimentation in the private spheres is inconsequential. If yoga came to replace Christianity, there would most certainly be sweeping ramifications for the entire society. In the short run, however, it is considerably easier for social diversity to be permitted if it is limited mostly to free-time activities and to activities that individuals can participate in without affecting the organizational structure of the society.

A third regulatory mechanism is the ritualization of nonconventional behavior. There is a striking similarity between many contemporary forms of alternative behavior and the rituals known in past societies as "festivals of misrule." These festivals involve the deliberate violation of social norms, for example, ritually ingesting the totemic animal, which is otherwise strictly taboo. In American culture the Mardi Gras is perhaps the clearest example of a festival of misrule. Paradoxically, such festivals safeguard the sanctity of the very taboos that are violated. They do so by establishing the conditions under which the taboo may be violated. Especially where there is a likelihood of the taboo being violated anyway, these festivals help the society to retain control over the nature and the extent of the violations. They afford a safety-valve mechanism for frustrations which may be engendered by the observance of the taboos. At the same time, they demonstrate that the society is in control of things. It is the society that decides that the taboo can be broken, not the individual deviant. The society sets the temporal and spatial bounds within which deviance can occur and thereby is able to make sure that it spreads no further than is planned.

Nonconventional behavior in contemporary society tends to be ritualized to the extent that it fulfills order-maintaining functions in much the same way as a festival of misrule. Among other functions, the weekend encounter marathon institutionalizes non-conventional modes of expressing oneself and relating to others so that it does not break out in random and more disruptive times and places. The less extreme elements of the New Left have been regarded by some within the movement as a way of keeping the lid on "crazies" who might express their discontent in more disruptive ways were it not for the more institutionalized avenues available within the New Left. The development of the extremely disruptive SLA has been attributed, in fact, to the disintegration of the New Left in the wake of the Vietnam war. The ritual character of much of the counter-culture can be seen especially clearly in comparison with more established social institutions. Rather than being long-term and even life-long commitments such as church membership or marriage have been, the new commitments tend to be limited to short-term periods of engagement, after which termination is expected. Sensitivity groups run for a fixed number of sessions and then end, unlike traditional forms of community which they seek to replicate. Involvement in tantric yoga classes is initiated with the clear understanding that it will also end on a given date, unlike involvement in a conventional church. Experimentation with communal living is likely to be ventured upon with a one- or two-year maximum limit in mind, unlike conventional marriage. Participation in a demonstration can be readily engaged in and disengaged from, in contrast to the more permanent commitments required by the established political parties.[17] Even forms of behavior that ostensibly require total, long-term commitment are often engaged in with the implicit assumption that one will be graduating or moving on in a few months or years. These temporal boundaries tend to make many of these activities more like celebrations that are engaged in from time to time as outlets, as temporary forms of dropping out before entering again into the more conventional affairs of the society. Festivals such as Woodstock and Altamont serve as chief examples. Undoubtedly most of those who attended simply went home afterward and resumed the normal life they had temporarily abandoned.

The purpose of the festival of misrule is to inoculate. But the

17. The consternation of those detained by the police for hours or days after the cessation of demonstrations takes on added meaning when such demonstrations are seen as temporary festivals of misrule.

danger is that it may infect instead. Woodstock undoubtedly satisfied the secret fascination of drugs and rock and nudity for some (and if it did not, Altamont did). Once revealed, the mysteries of the taboo became less enchanting. For others, though, it was simply an initiation rite into a whole new realm of activity. While encounter groups "drain off" some of the energy that might be invested in more permanent attempts to form community, they also infuse communitarian and expressive ideals into other areas of life. Thus, the delicate equilibrium that must obtain in a diversified society is again in evidence; as a regulatory mechanism, ritualization tends to circumscribe the novel, but in doing so it also allows the novel to inform the conventional.

A final regulatory mechanism that must be mentioned is isolation. For all the publicity social experiments have received, the vast majority of the public has been effectively shielded from getting close enough to them to be seriously tempted. The major share of the commune movement, largely for economic reasons, has taken place in remote rural areas.[18] Most of the political experimentation of the past decade has been isolated on college campuses and has been met with extreme resistance when it has attempted to move out of this "ghetto," as it did in Chicago in 1968. More generally, the tendency for social experimentation to be most common among the educated young is especially significant in this regard. With the exception of the sick and the aged, young people are perhaps the most isolated segment of the entire population. Probably the majority have very little day-to-day contact with the labor market, with the church, or even with their families. Many are effectively isolated within their own peer group, often encapsulated spatially in a campus community that attempts to serve not only their educational interests but also to fulfill the political, religious, familial, and leisure functions an adult would pursue in a whole range of different settings.[19] Consequently, much of the experimentation that grows in campus communities and among young people in similar situations never permeates directly into the larger society.

In much the same way in which geographic isolation has permitted diversity to exist in the past, social isolation permits it to exist at

18. There is a growing commune movement in the cities as well, as forthcoming work by Rosabeth Kanter indicates.
19. Talcott Parsons, "Youth in the Context of American Society," pp. 110–141 in Erik H. Erikson (ed.), *The Challenge of Youth* (Garden City, N.Y.: Doubleday & Company, 1965).

present. Such isolation keeps social experiments from becoming a threat to the established order. At the same time, it also permits nonconventionality "space" in which to grow without being threatened either by repression or cooptation. The functionality of isolation can be seen in the explicit attempts of social movements to build social (if not geographical) barriers around themselves. The saffron robes and shaved heads of the Krishna Consciousness Society or the white clothing and turbans of the Sikh-influenced Happy-Healthy-Holy Organization are excellent examples of mechanisms that tend to set their members apart from the rest of the world.[20] On the one hand, such apparel undoubtedly restricts the number who become involved in these movements. On the other hand, it allows these movements to be in the society without losing their identity to the society. The ease with which nonconventional behavior has become commercialized and ritualized makes this especially important. To develop proleptic models of conduct that may actually inform and not just reflect the broader society, it is necessary to withdraw at least temporarily from its immediate involvements.[21] Groups such as 3HO, The Seedlings, and the Ecumenical Institute have come to follow this principle quite consciously; others do so less deliberately but in effect follow the same pattern. The number involved in working out such models need not be large; size may even be a negative factor. If there is a cadre sufficiently isolated to pursue its objectives much as it wishes, then those who filter in and out of experimental activities at lesser levels of commitment may provide the conduits for influencing the larger society.

These regulatory mechanisms appear to be functioning effectively, at least in the short run, to maintain social diversity with minimal degrees of abrasiveness or disorganization. Whether they can bind the society together in the long run is another matter. In the past, purely mechanical means of social control have usually been augmented by overarching meaning systems which specified what was good and proper and what was evil. The social-scientific and the mystical meaning systems appear to sanction freedom and diversity. But thus far at least, they seem to provide little basis for concerted action, for action that requires coordination and cooperation rather

20. Gregory Johnson, "A Counter-Culture in Microcosm"; Alan Tobey, "New Errand into the Wilderness: The Summer Solstice of the Happy-Healthy-Holy Organization," chapter 1 in Glock and Bellah, *The New Religious Consciousness.*
21. For a discussion of the proleptic ethic, see Tobey, "New Errand into the Wilderness."

than mere toleration. This is somewhat ironic in light of the supreme emphasis placed upon *community* by those in the counter-culture who, the foregoing has indicated, are precisely those most likely to hold social-scientific and/or mystical meaning systems. But even though community has been emphasized, it has usually meant community of a rather limited scope, for example, among members of the same commune, among friends, in a church, in a neighborhood. The grand vision of community at a national or even international level that was so important to the early Puritans or even the Social Darwinists is not a part of the current counter-culture, except perhaps in some vague notions of a miraculous Aquarian Age. There is a sense of cosmic interdependence that might provide a basis for such a vision, but there is a total lack of clarity about the ends that might be pursued collectively or the means by which people might be bound together to pursue such ends.

It should be recognized, however, that even though American meaning systems appear to be in a time of transition, the traditional meaning systems are still far from being ineffective. Both theism and individualism are still sufficiently strong to exert an influence on the direction the society takes. After more than a century Congress has again set aside an official Day of Prayer and Humiliation much as was observed regularly in the colonial period. Billy Graham still calls people to repentance, sobriety, and hard work in the name of God's commands. The individualistic creed continues to pervade the economic system, the courts, and the penal institutions. It is by no means adequate, therefore, to suggest that social order has come to be maintained entirely by purely mechanical regulatory methods. High values are still espoused which direct and integrate social activity. The meaning systems that sanction these values may be eroding, but the erosion process appears to be extremely gradual.

Even if social science and mysticism were to continue growing and gradually become more and more pervasive, it does not seem likely that they would come to simply replace theism and individualism. Modernity does not replace tradition; it simply builds on top of it. The shape of the new is powerfully influenced by the old. But in the process, the old is often revitalized by the new. Misplaced emphases and ideals gone sour often become corrected from the vantage of new perspectives.

The strength of traditional theism and traditional individualism has rested partly on their capacity to bind together contradictory ideas and assumptions. Calvinism carefully incorporated the determinism of an all-powerful God with the free will of totally accountable mankind. American Puritanism held within it the tensions of a revolutionary ethic on the one hand and rigid authoritarianism on the other. It stressed personal liberty and community loyalty at the same time. Individualism held within it the paradox of fatalistic natural laws and complete personal self-determination. Rugged nonconformity and rigid overconformity were both conceivable within its inner logic. The foregoing data have shown that typically one side of these paradoxes has become dominant to the extent that both theism and individualism currently legitimate certain kinds of values almost to the exclusion of others that might also be conceivable.

There is a chance that the new meaning systems will not so much replace the old ones as provide the basis for them to be reorganized. If there is indeed an upsurge of social science and mysticism, two vital themes in the American tradition, in particular, seem capable of being revitalized. First, the collectivist character of theism, which was manifested most clearly in the covenant notion of the Puritans but which soon faded into the background as the individualism of the Enlightenment came more and more to the fore, may again be rediscovered as social science makes us more aware of our interdependence and mutual responsibility.[22] Second, the high value that was placed on being an individual as an end in itself by the founders of American culture, but which became subverted into the crassest kind of utilitarianism during the nineteenth and twentieth centuries, may find new expression in the mystical emphasis of simply being and experiencing rather than doing. The potential for such revitalization is there. Whether in the long run it will be realized is, of course, another matter.

It has become fashionable to be either pessimistic or uncertain about the future. The optimistic end of the continuum has been lopped off. But the future seems neither as uncertain nor as grim as many have come to portray it. In the midst of unparalleled social experimentation the society has adapted quickly and in highly effective ways to maintain order. Business as usual is far more the order of the day than social disintegration. Mechanisms have developed that regulate diversity but do not annihilate it. In the

22. See Robert N. Bellah, *The Broken Covenant* (New York: The Seabury Press, 1975).

short run these mechanisms of control seem sufficiently adaptable to allow some of the creative fruits of diversity to be enjoyed. Whether a viable long run order that is not only viable but healthy can be attained is more open to question. Given the opportunities available in the short run, perhaps America's third century can be a time of rebuilding for a more livable world in the long run.

APPENDIX A

The Bay Area as a Cultural Seedbed

Residents of the San Francisco Bay Area pride themselves more on their uniqueness than on their similarity to people in other parts of the country. Legend has it that the clamoring spirit of '49 still prevails, that the Bay Area is a modern day El Dorado, a beautiful Venice of the West, an experiment in novelty and deviance. It was for its uniqueness that the Bay Area was chosen as the locus of the present study. Far from being a mere parochial obsession with one's backyard, this choice was made on the belief that some processes of social transformation were happening here which were probably not as concentrated in any other part of America. Yet, it was also assumed that what was happening here was not entirely unique and might be suggestive of developments to come later in other areas.

In this appendix some of the ways in which the Bay Area differs from the norm in America and in other metropolitan areas are considered as are some of the ways in which it is similar. The purpose of these comments is to illuminate the degree to which the Bay Area may be considered a laboratory for the study of social and cultural experimentation.

It is beyond question that the Bay Area contrasts sharply with the average social situation in the United States. Per capita income in the Bay Area is $5,009 (1969 figures), while for the United States it is $3,688. In the Bay Area 34 percent of the population has at least some college education (1970 figures), while for the United States as a whole the proportion is 21 percent. Both the proportion of nonwhite citizens and residents of foreign stock is considerably higher in the Bay Area than in other parts of the country (in 1970,

33 percent compared to 22 percent and 29 versus 13 percent respectively). Statistics on growth in population, political preference, religious preference, crime, divorce, suicide, and other characteristics also differ markedly between the Bay Area and the national average.

If the Bay Area deviates from American society at large, it must be recognized, however, that the same holds true for all large metropolitan areas. The question remains, then, to what extent is the Bay Area, if not representative of social conditions nationally, different from other large metropolitan areas and to what extent is it similar?

When the Bay Area, which ranks sixth in size (according to 1970 figures) among all Standard Metropolitan Statistical Areas, is compared with the other SMSAs ranking in the top ten (New York, Los Angeles, Chicago, Philadelphia, Detroit, Washington, Boston, Pittsburgh, and St. Louis), similarities outweigh differences on a number of characteristics. The average proportion of nonwhite residents in the ten largest areas, for example, is 34 percent. In the Bay Area it is virtually the same, 33 percent. Proportion of foreign stock on the average is 25 percent. In the Bay Area it is only slightly higher, 29 percent. In terms of ethnic composition, the Bay Area differs little from cities such as Boston, Chicago, Los Angeles, and New York. Employment figures also reveal strong similarities between the Bay Area and other large metropolitan areas, except that employment in the Bay Area is less likely to be concentrated in heavy industry, as in Detroit, Philadelphia, and Pittsburgh, and is more heavily concentrated in shipping and transportation than average. By industry, employment for the Bay Area and for the ten largest SMSAs (averaged) breaks down as follows: manufacturing, 16 and 25 percent; wholesale and retail trade, 21 and 21 percent; services 18 and 19 percent; transportation and public utilities, 11 and 7 percent; finance, insurance, and real estate, 8 and 6 percent; and government, 21 and 17 percent.

But on other characteristics the Bay Area contrasts markedly with other metropolitan areas. In particular, it seems to stand out on characteristics conducive to social experimentation and innovation.

Although social and cultural innovation is not yet well understood by social scientists, a brief and hopefully not too simplistic theory of the conditions necessary for it to emerge can be presented. Leaving aside extreme cases of revolution or dictatorship, there are at least four conditions necessary for spontaneous, evolutionary social experimentation and innovation to take place, whether it be in an organization, in one sector of society, or in a whole society. In combination these conditions may not be sufficient to produce social changes, but for change to take place each condition seems to be a necessary ingredient. First, there must be a minimum amount of cultural pluralism. Some diversity of opinion must exist, and this diversity must be tolerated by those in power rather than being suppressed and having uniform cultural standards imposed.[1] In the presence of diverse opinion, ideas and values are likely to clash or at least be questioned and compared. Such mutual criticism encourages the dialectic production of new ideas. Second, legitimating beliefs are necessary to stimulate the anticipation of cultural experimentation and innovation and to validate its desirability. H.G. Barnett in his classic study of innovation has written: "Innovation flourishes in an atmosphere of anticipation of it. If the members of a society expect something new it is more likely to appear than if it is unforeseen and unheralded. The chance of frequency will be augmented in proportion to the number of expectant individuals. It is like seeing ghosts at midnight. The greater the number of people who expect to see them, the more frequently they will be seen."[2] Third, cultural innovation is influenced by the presence or absence of creative leadership and the resources which the leaders have at their disposal. And fourth, there has to be a minimum amount of social strain present to motivate interest in change, to create a constituency for new ideas.[3] The Bay Area seems to be relatively strong in all of these conditions.

Cultural pluralism is generally considered to be a pronounced trait of American society as a whole. But it is more salient in some areas than others. Cities such as New York and Boston, for example, which are composed of highly diverse ethnic groups and which serve as cosmopolitan centers of trade and communication, illustrate higher levels of cultural pluralism than average. The Bay Area is also one of the areas that manifests a high degree of pluralism, much of which must be attributed to its unique history.

San Francisco and other early towns in the Bay Area blossomed almost overnight in the mid-nineteenth century as a result of the Gold Rush. Between 1848 and 1850 the population of San Francisco

1. This is one of the elements of "structural conduciveness" discussed by Neil Smelser (*A Theory of Collective Behavior*, New York: The Free Press, 1962).
2. H. G. Barnett, *Innovation: The Basis of Cultural Change* (New York: McGraw-Hill, 1953), p. 56.
3. Smelser, *A Theory of Collective Behavior*.

grew from 800 to nearly 35,000. This influx was highly diverse ethnically. The Gold Rush brought, among others, Chilean peasants, destitute survivors of the potato famine of 1846–1847 in Ireland, dissidents from France following the revolution in 1848, and thousands of farmers from China who had been uprooted by the Taiping Rebellion after 1850. Such ethnic heterogeneity has been more usual than unusual in the history of the United States. What was unusual about the Bay Area experience, however, was that all of these different groups arrived simultaneously in an area that had virtually no existing culture laid down by earlier immigrants.[4] Immigration did not follow the typical ''serial'' pattern of, for example, first Anglo-Saxon groups, then Irish, then Italian, and finally Eastern Europeans. A greater degree of cultural pluralism was made possible by this simultaneous infusion of ethnic groups. Although ethnic rivalries and discrimination have by no means been absent in the Bay Area, it was more difficult here than in many other places for one ethnic group to impose its culture uniformly on others merely by virtue of prior residency.

Besides reinforcing cultural pluralism, it might be added, the rapid influx of immigrants during the Gold Rush was also conducive to the development of new, experimental social arrangements. Rapid migration, such as that associated not only with gold rushes, but also with oil booms, land rushes, and wars, tends to overload existing social structures and necessitates improvising new customs and institutions to solve the problems of collective life. It seems likely that this need, coupled with the ethnic diversity of the early Bay Area populace, tended to guarantee a higher inclusion of diverse ideas, not only in the cultural life of the area, but in the institutional life as well.

Cultural pluralism was also fostered by the events which took place during the decades following the initial settlement of the Bay Area. The ''boom town'' spirit that flourished throughout the latter half of the nineteenth century, first from the Gold Rush, then from the completion of the transcontinental railroad, and throughout from expanding fortunes in real estate, trade, and shipping, created an unusually dynamic situation which is difficult to imagine in more stable times. Especially the economic structure of the Bay Area was affected by this situation. Fortunes were won overnight, but they

4. This is not to say, of course, that there was no indigenous culture.

were also lost just as rapidly. One historian, for example, has written of the erratic economic climate of San Francisco in the 1860s: "The sand-shoveler and the millionnaire may change places tomorrow, and they know it; so the former does not usually cringe nor the other strut when they meet."[5] A few names, such as Charles Crocker, Leland Stanford, and Mark Hopkins, survive as wealthy beneficiaries of this era, but for the most part the rapid fluctuations in economic conditions made it difficult for an aristocratic elite to develop. Consequently, the Bay Area was spared to some extent the imposition of cultural standards by an old-line ruling establishment such as that prevailing in many of the cities along the Eastern seaboard.

The difficulty encountered in attempting to gain control over the early culture of the Bay Area is readily seen, for example, in the outcome of the efforts by conservative religious and business leaders from New England to import their cultural norms. Early in the settlement of the Bay Area a movement was led by New Englanders to impose Puritan religious and moral standards upon the Bay Area community. At first, their efforts culminated in the Know-Nothing Party's defeat of the Irish machine in San Francisco in 1854 and in the capture of the state governorship in 1855. Their success was short-lived, however, for the ethnic diversity of the area was too great, and by 1857 the Puritan establishment had lost its power. Attempts in 1858 and again in 1861 to pass blue laws also failed.[6]

Today cultural pluralism continues to survive in the Bay Area at least in myth if not in reality. A high level of official tolerance for deviance is frequently noted by modern observers of the area. And although such tolerance is difficult to measure objectively, there are numerous signs that suggest its presence. Not only is the crime rate higher in the Bay Area than in any of the other ten largest metropolitan areas, but other forms of nonconventional behavior also prevail. Among other things, the Bay Area boasts a large homosexual population (90,000 in San Francisco alone); it is reputed to have more bars and taverns per square mile than any other city; its alcoholism and suicide rates are among the highest in the country; and recently it has developed a booming business in pornography and the so-called "skin trade." Although many factors constitute the reasons behind these conditions, one that is typically pointed

5. Quoted in Kevin Starr, *Americans and the California Dream, 1850–1915* (New York: Oxford University Press, 1973).
6. Ibid.

out is the high degree of tolerance by local agents of social control, a tolerance which has rightly been characterized as a politics of "hyperpluralism."

Two other signs of the pluralistic culture of the Bay Area are especially noteworthy. One institution that typically functions to preserve cultural tradition and to maintain uniform standards of social conduct is established religion. Another is ultraconservative politics. Both are notably weak in the Bay Area. With regard to religion, legend, at least, has it that the Bay Area has long been notably nonreligious. An observer writing in 1863, for example, claimed that 86 percent of all Californians were indifferent to religion. Another visitor, Samuel Bowles, editor of the Springfield *Republican*, who was more used to the sobriety of Massachusetts, was shocked to observe in 1865 that "even church-going San Franciscans went to dances and picnics and on Sunday outings recklessly dashed their carriages through the surf along Ocean Beach below the Cliff House." A more recent assessment of religious behavior is provided by a survey of the Bay Area conducted in 1972, which revealed that 18 percent of those sampled identified themselves as nonreligious. A similarly worded question put by Gallup to a national sample, by contrast, found only 4 percent who thus identified themselves and in all cities of one million or more only 5 percent did so. The absence of a conservative political structure can also be seen by comparing the Gallup poll, which found 14 percent (12 percent in cities of one million or more) who identified themselves as "very conservative" in contrast with the Bay Area study which found only 2 percent who described themselves in that way.

The Bay Area, then, appears to meet at least one of the conditions necessary for cultural innovation. Both historically and currently it manifests a wide spectrum of diverse cultures and life styles. Moreover, it seems to lack any particularly strong group—economic, political, or religious—capable of imposing universal cultural standards at the expense of diverse and novel ideas.

The second condition necessary for cultural innovation to occur is a set of beliefs that makes novel ideas and behavior legitimate. Not only must there be tolerance for innovations, there must also be some positive sanction for them, a frame of reference that makes experimentation both valued and meaningful. In the Bay Area this condition is fulfilled in part simply by the myths that have grown up surrounding the Gold Rush. Like "myths of origin" common to religions and nations, the Gold Rush myth plays an important part in the culture of the Bay Area. It portrays the Bay Area as a land of fortune and adventure and, most of all, as a land of loose and riotous living. Some truth, indeed, is contained in the myth. The Gold Rush established an unusual kind of settlement in the Bay Area, namely, one with virtually no women. In 1850 only 8 percent of California's population was female and in mining regions the proportion was only 2 percent. As a result there was hardly any home life of the type that brought stability to other new communities in the West and Midwest. Historians have described the accompanying turmoil; for example, Josiah Royce, writing in 1886, described San Francisco during its early days as a society "morally and socially tried as no other American community ever has been tried" and H. H. Bancroft, describing the same era, called it one of "moral, political, and financial night."

These unusual circumstances created an objective need for non-conventional social solutions, some of which undoubtedly influenced later stages of the Bay Area's development. But of much greater significance was the myth of origin that has survived in the culture of the Bay Area, a myth which undoubtedly helps to legitimate present-day experimentation with eccentric ideas and activities. Its continuing impact is still seen vividly in accounts of current deviance—radical movements, pornography, homosexuality, novel economic ventures—in the Bay Area which with rare exceptions make reference to the precedent established in the "Days of '49."

Myths have a habit of becoming self-perpetuating and self-fulfilling, and the myths that sanction experimentation and innovation in the Bay Area are no exception. In recent years the Bay Area has enjoyed national prominence (or notoriety as the case may be) for a number of "firsts." For example, it has claimed the first widespread student protest of recent years in the form of the Free Speech Movement at Berkeley in 1964, the first topless and bottomless nightclubs to be legally tolerated on a large scale, the home turf of the Black Panther Party and the Symbionese Liberation Army, and the first city to desegregate its schools totally (Berkeley). These facts and the myths surrounding them are widely known in the local culture and together they reinforce the myth of the Bay Area as a locus of experimentation, serving to legitimate further forms of cultural innovation.

A modicum of legitimacy and a pluralistic milieu are essential preconditions for cultural innovation, but for new ideas actually to develop there must be somebody with the resources to create and transmit them. In short, there must be leadership. Whether the Bay Area is unique in this respect is doubtful, although it is impossible to say for sure. Certainly the Bay Area has had a long tradition of bohemian leadership, dating back even before the founding of the actual Bohemian Club in 1872. In recent years the Bay Area without doubt has also been endowed with at least its share of high priests espousing alternative, counter-cultural ideas and life styles. Among the notables who have resided at least temporarily in the Bay Area during the past decade are Alan Watts, Ken Kesey, Eldridge Cleaver, Jack Kerouac, Theodore Roszak, and Buckminster Fuller. A host of groups and organizations devoted to the advocacy of alternative life styles are also widely in evidence. A recent guidebook, for example, lists over three hundred such groups in the Bay Area, with over half of them explicitly concerned with developing and communicating new forms of consciousness.

The last element suggested as a necessary ingredient for cultural innovation is some form of social strain sufficient to arouse disaffection with conventional values and to create a potential clientele for new ideas. Social strain, of course, can be of many varieties: economic hardship, disintegration of interpersonal ties, political disenfranchisement, disorienting cultural changes, and so on. Cultural and social innovations are influenced both by the type of social strain present and by its intensity.

Social strain is always relative both in comparison with what people are used to and with what they expect. Consequently, it is difficult to agree upon standard measures of strain that could be used to compare different geographic areas, even if the necessary data were available, which typically they are not. According to some indications, the Bay Area may be particularly subject to social strain in comparison with other metropolitan areas. High rates of suicide, alcoholism, divorce, and crime are typically considered manifestations of social strain, such as normlessness and social isolation. And on these measures, the Bay Area ranks among the highest in the country. Its suicide rate (highest of all metropolitan areas) is 22 per 100,000 whereas the national rate is 16, and its crime rate (also one of the highest in the country) is 5,329 per 100,000 persons whereas the national rate is only 2,741 and even in the ten largest metropolitan areas is only 3,843.

Another indication of at least *potential* social strain is a rapid growth rate. With the exception of Los Angeles, the Bay Area is the "newest" of America's ten largest metropolitan areas, experiencing much of its growth during World War II when shipping and defense industries attracted thousands of workers to the Bay Area, mostly young and mostly from the South and Midwest.[7] During that period, the Bay Area grew more rapidly than any of the other large urban areas (except Los Angeles) and much of its growth was experienced so rapidly that major urban problems were created. For example, between June 1941 and January 1943, the number of wage earners employed in Bay Area industrial plants increased by 150 percent and some cities, such as Richmond, grew fivefold. Since World War II the Bay Area has continued to grow rapidly and between 1960 and 1970 its growth rate (17.4 percent) was significantly higher than both the national average (13.3 percent) and the average rate for the ten largest metropolitan areas (also 13.3 percent).

With rapid growth come demands for new housing, more adequate civil services, and a need for new residents to be incorporated into the social life of the community. Of special importance in the Bay Area has been the latter, since many of its new residents have been black (between 1960 and 1970, for example, the black population of the Bay Area increased by 51 percent, compared with 23 percent nationally and 39 percent in other large cities). The amount of actual social strain experienced by a community because of rapid growth, of course, depends on its resources for coping with change. At minimum, however, the *potential* for social strain has been present in the Bay Area because of its high rate of growth and, consequently, the potential for people to be motivated to seek and to adopt new cultural ideas has also been present.

To suggest that social strain has been particularly severe in the Bay Area, however, would be misleading. On other indicators, strain seems relatively low. Its per capita income is one of the highest in the country; its rate of unemployment, although high (5 percent in 1970), is no higher than that of many other areas. Also when asked in early 1972 how satisfied they were with their community, a sample of Bay Area residents overwhelmingly (85 percent) indicated that they were satisfied.

Of the four conditions suggested as necessary prerequisites for

7. Mel Scott, *The San Francisco Bay Area: A Metropolis in Perspective* (Berkeley and Los Angeles: University of California Press, 1959).

cultural experimentation and innovation, in sum, the Bay Area seems to qualify distinctively on the first three. It is characterized by a high degree of tolerance for cultural diversity, it has a tradition that legitimates novel cultural and social experiments, and it has a significant body of leaders attempting to transmit new values and life styles. With regard to the fourth condition, social strain, the Bay Area also ranks high on some indicators. But there are few signs that strain is *particularly* pronounced in the Bay Area. Consequently, an overall assessment of the Bay Area as a locus of social and cultural experimentation would be that it is a fertile seedbed for novel developments, but that the extent to which such developments actually take root and spread will depend much on the nature of strains within the community. If these become severe, as they apparently did within many university communities during the late sixties, then cultural experimentation could assume major proportions.

While the Bay Area is similar to other large metropolitan areas in many respects, it seems to be relatively pronounced, therefore, on other, perhaps less readily comparable, characteristics which would appear to make it especially susceptible to social experiments and innovations, or at least to toleration of and attraction to such experiments. It was for these reasons that the Bay Area was chosen as a natural laboratory in which to study social experimentation, even though it was recognized that the Bay Area does not lend itself to generalizations about other parts of the country.

Methodological Notes

THE "DOMINANT MEANING SYSTEM" MEASURE

Logic. The purpose of this measure is somewhat different from that which is usually described in textbook treatments of index and scale construction. A word is necessary, therefore, about the logic underlying it.

Each of the meaning systems described in Chapter 3 is obviously composed of not just one idea but of a constellation of several ideas. The individualistic meaning system, for example, is a relatively unique constellation of assumptions about free will, about a natural order governing the universe, about the absence of social constraints, about the efficacy of hard work and moral discipline, and so forth. It is the *intersection* of all these ideas that becomes the defining characteristic of this meaning system, not any one of these ideas by itself. For a person to be described as individualistic, it is necessary for him to hold this *combination* of ideas. Holding only one of them is no indication of whether he is individualistic or not. Many people, for example, might believe in free will but not believe in the other assumptions that constitute the individualistic meaning system. To tap this meaning system, therefore, it is necessary to obtain information on a complex combination of ideas rather than on just a single idea.

Single survey questions are not particularly amenable to tapping such complex concepts. To avoid respondent confusion survey questions usually have to be relatively simple. They are typically designed to tap only one idea at a time so that it is clear what acceptance of an item means or what rejection means. The method used in the present instance to measure each meaning system, consequently, is to combine items that refer to the different ideas that together define each meaning system. Only if persons answer all of the relevant items appropriately are they judged to have a fairly high likelihood of actually holding the particular meaning system at issue.

The logic that informs more conventional index construction is different. It assumes that one unidimensional idea is being measured rather than a concept that is defined by the intersection of several ideas. Items combined to form such an index are all considered to indicate this one idea. Often the basis for assuming that they all point to some common idea is the fact that they are all highly related to one another empirically. Combining them into a single scale gives a "more-or-less" kind of measure. The more items a respondent accepts, the more strongly he is assumed to hold the idea at issue. Or, depending on the items involved, the idea is assumed to be held more extremely, more consistently, more centrally, or more saliently. The fewer the number of items that are accepted, the weaker (less extreme, less consistent, less central, less salient) the idea is assumed to be held. For example, if a respondent answers nineteen prejudice items affirmatively and only one negatively, he may be termed "highly prejudiced," while someone who answers only ten items affirmatively may be termed only "moderately prejudiced." This kind of language, and the logic behind it, does not apply in the present case. If there were six items available to tap the different ideas contained within the concept of individualism and a respondent answered four of them appropriately, it would not be correct to say that he was "moderately high" on individualism. Since he has not met all the conditions that define individualism, use of the term "individualistic" is not warranted in his case at all. However, it is necessary to take into account the possibilities of measurement errors in such a case.

If a person answered four out of six individualism items "correctly," there is the possibility that a mistake was simply made on the other two items (the respondent misunderstood the questions, for example). Had these errors not been made, the respondent might have been classified as individualistic. If a person answered none of the six items in the specified way, there is still a possibility that he actually holds an individualistic meaning system but failed to be classified properly because of measurement error. The probability of this person actually being individualistic is lower, however, than it is for the person who met all but two of the necessary conditions. The appropriate language to distinguish between these two respondents would be that there is only a "low" *likelihood* of the one being individualistic while there is perhaps a "moderately high" *likelihood* of the other being individualistic. It would be inappropriate simply to use more conventional scaling language and say that one scores low on individualism and the other moderately high, since neither one actually meets the requirements for being termed individualistic.

The possibility of measurement errors on questions concerning highly abstract understandings of life, it is worth noting, is probably somewhat greater than it might be on more specific issues. A question about an issue such as legalizing marijuana that had been in the news a lot might carry fairly uniform meanings for different respondents. Highly general assumptions about the nature of life, in contrast, are typically not a part of everyday discourse, even though people apparently give them a fair amount of thought. Standardized ways of articulating them are probably not as common, therefore, as with regard to matters involving more public kinds of discussion. Questions about such abstract matters may be subject to greater disparities of interpretation and, therefore, to greater measurement error.

A variety of alternative measures was developed and compared in the preliminary phases of analyzing the Bay Area data. Some of these measures combined virtually all the items available to measure each of the different meaning systems, while others were based on only a few of the items. Comparing these different versions showed that they were generally highly correlated with one another and that they were related to other variables in about the same ways. To the extent that measurement error is contained in the various items, combining more items together did not seem to produce substantial improvements in the validity of the measures. What the measures combining more items did, however, was to damage the "face validity" of the measures somewhat. That is, some of the items on hindsight were clearly not as appropriate for tapping the ideas derived from the historical material as others. Thus, the measures finally settled upon combine only those items that seem to have high face validity with respect to the way in which each meaning system was conceptualized. The measures are also ones which consist of relatively few items. This choice was made because the fewer numbers of items in a measure, the easier it is to bear in mind what the measure actually consists of and, therefore, the measure is less likely to become reified as the actual concept it was designed to approximate. Furthermore, since the study of meaning systems has largely been neglected in prior empirical research (except for research on religious beliefs), there seemed to be some merit in demonstrating that a whole battery of items is not necessarily required to tap such meaning systems. If this were not the case, it would undoubtedly be a deterrent to future studies in this area.

Factor analysis. That the items selected do tend to be predictive of empirically distinct phenomena is indicated by a factor analysis of the total 28 items included in the survey instrument as potential indicators of alternative meaning systems. Table B-1 presents the varimax factor pattern for these items.[1] Those items marked with an asterisk make up the submeasures for the four meaning systems. Looking at scores of .150 or greater (that is, scores most likely to be statistically significant on this size sample) and limiting attention to positive scores (since all items were designed to provide affirmative predictions of alternative meaning systems and no assumptions were made about negative associations) reveals that each of the four meaning systems is relatively distinct and is indicated by the items selected. Of the 11 qualifying scores obtained with regard to the items intended as theism measures, 7 are on a single factor, Factor I. Of the 9 qualifying scores involving individualism items, all but 2 are on Factors V and VI. Of the 5 qualifying scores on the social science items, all 5 are on Factors IV and VII. And of the 11 qualifying scores on the mysticism items, 7 are on Factor III and 10 are on either Factor III or Factor VIII. This suggests, as argued above, that (with the exception of theism) the meaning systems are not unidimensional. They are nonetheless relatively distinct.

Validity. That the four submeasures are capable of predicting items not included in the submeasures, that is, that they have external validity, is shown in Table B-2. An interesting indication of the validity of the mystical measure in particular is also available in the form of some story-type questions that describe people actually gaining new insights about life from dramatic peak experiences. These questions were not included in the Bay Area data itself, so were not available as items that could have been built into the mysticism measure. They were asked as part of a replication of the

1. Factor analysis results are from the program contained in the "Pickle" system, see Margaret Baker, *Pickle: The Berkeley Transposed File Statistical System* (Berkeley: Survey Research Center, 1973); number of factors produced is set by eigenvalues equal to 1; squared multiple correlation coefficients are substituted in the diagonal of the matrix prior to rotation.

Table B-1. VARIMAX FACTOR PATTERN OF 28 MEANING SYSTEM ITEMS

	I	II	III	IV	V	VI	VII	VIII	IX	X
Theism										
*Believe in God	.684	-.005	.046	-.129	.122	.024	-.219	-.023	-.016	-.122
*Influenced by God	.728	.008	.099	-.079	.012	-.072	-.032	.042	.056	-.052
*God causes suffering	.600	.120	.062	-.016	.148	.060	.069	-.097	-.029	.197
Devil causes suffering	.508	.096	-.049	.077	-.012	.098	.189	-.129	-.083	.040
Believe in afterlife	.603	-.027	-.071	-.056	-.059	.009	.088	.080	-.065	.149
Believe in creation	.652	-.023	-.054	-.068	.100	.023	-.201	-.159	-.099	-.006
Poverty caused by God	.447	.052	-.042	.016	.216	.169	-.063	-.066	-.034	-.146
Individualistic										
*Poverty caused by self	.014	.056	-.052	-.114	.340	.187	-.015	-.030	.042	-.003
*Work hard and equality	.197	.050	-.050	-.072	.590	.061	.079	-.012	-.043	-.144
*Suffering caused by self	.064	.025	.009	-.540	.151	.202	-.156	-.026	-.051	.148
Failure own fault	.037	.066	.030	-.026	.107	.451	-.033	-.079	-.017	.036
Blame self for failure	.076	.056	-.002	-.053	.016	.444	-.075	.063	.040	-.032
Influenced by willpower	-.078	.007	.043	-.029	-.020	.003	-.019	-.055	.381	-.004
Social Science										
*Childhood experiences	-.123	.056	.073	.665	-.090	.006	.059	.057	-.043	.123
*Suffering caused by society	-.035	-.590	.067	.531	-.051	.013	-.030	-.022	-.033	.018
*Evolution	-.494	.049	.048	.022	-.181	.116	.155	-.051	-.031	.095
Influenced by environment	-.082	-.030	-.064	.123	-.054	-.118	.393	-.003	-.029	.009
American way causes poverty	-.182	-.000	.075	.063	-.584	.049	.211	.058	.072	-.178
Suffering caused by class	-.056	-.723	-.022	.044	-.101	-.148	.024	-.047	-.057	.087

Table B-1 Continued.

Mysticism

*Experienced nature	-.085	.004	.447	.036	-.060	-.072	.031	.254	.118	.121
*Fantasy world good	-.022	-.000	.453	.071	-.071	.048	-.044	.025	.144	.089
*Influenced by new insights	-.088	-.024	.179	.056	-.055	.004	-.013	.437	-.084	-.002
Experienced harmony	-.028	-.027	.513	-.001	-.009	-.079	.110	.194	-.073	.081
Experienced sacred	.378	-.046	.411	-.100	-.057	-.048	.096	.016	-.279	.100
Learn from walks	.004	.011	.501	-.028	.067	.087	-.068	-.093	.062	-.159
Feel deeply	.038	-.005	.317	.049	-.098	.032	-.132	.020	-.068	-.109

Other

Selfishness causes suffering	.007	.816	-.024	.142	-.011	.066	-.028	-.102	-.045	.113
Science better than art	-.047	-.018	-.044	-.139	.025	-.142	-.029	-.042	-.175	-.153

Table B-2. **EXTERNAL VALIDITY OF THE FOUR
MEANING SYSTEM MEASURES***
(Total Weighted Sample)

	Likelihood of holding each meaning system is:				
External Validity	*Low*	*Medium Low*	*Medium High*	*High*	*Gamma*
Theism					
God created the first man and					
woman	20%	46%	80%	94%	.698
Number	(315)	(190)	(232)	(243)	
Individualism					
If someone does not succeed					
in life you can be pretty sure					
it's his own fault	28%	51%	57%	72%	.343
Number	(191)	(419)	(250)	(107)	
Social Science					
Social explanations for poverty	22%	37%	50%	67%	.414
Number	(111)	(304)	(346)	(197)	
Mysticism					
In harmony with universe and					
lasting effects on life	4%	6%	22%	45%	.453
Number	(76)	(257)	(384)	(256)	

*All relations significant at or beyond .05 level.

Bay Area survey among readers of *Psychology Today*. Since the mysticism measure was also contained in this data, the story-type questions can be used for purposes of validation. Forty thousand readers in all responded to this version of the questionnaire (reproduced in the December 1973 issue).[2] Of these, a random sample of 2,000 was chosen for analysis. These respondents are far from representative of any predefined population, but they do provide an external source of validation for the present measure.

2. For a report of the results of this poll, see Robert Wuthnow and Charles Y. Glock, "The Shifting Focus of Faith: A Survey Report," *Psychology Today* 8 (November 1974): 131–136.

One of the questions asked described an experience couched largely in Eastern religious language:

One day a Hindu boy named Shri Rama was walking through the hills outside of his home of Jodhpur. He came upon an opening in the rock face on a cliff. He describes what happened: "I slowly entered the opening. When my eyes got used to the dim light, I was startled to see an old man clad in a loin cloth. I was not scared at all, but was immediately overcome with a feeling of love and gratitude.

"The Holy Man looked directly at me and said in stern but kindly words: 'Shri Rama, look for eternity in the lotus petal. You will find the peace that passes all understanding.'

"Then the old man bowed and disappeared."

Table B-3 reports how respondents receiving different scores on the mysticism measure in the *Psychology Today* data answered this question. The mysticism measure is based on the same questions as in the Bay Area data except that the item about an experience of nature was replaced by the item about harmony with the universe since the first question was not asked. In interpreting the results of Table B-3, it is probably necessary to bear in mind that the *Psychology Today* respondents are a much more homogeneous sample in terms of such things as age, education, and interests than the Bay Area respondents. Therefore, most relations tend to show less variation than they do for the Bay Area sample. Nonetheless, it can be seen that the mysticism measure produces variation in the direction it would be presumed to. While 20 percent in the total *Psychology Today* sample say they like the story of Shri Rama because it makes them "feel good," this proportion is 38 percent for the "high" category but only 6 percent for the "low" category. The gamma for this relation is .299. The bottom half of the table reports whether or not respondents have had or would like to have such an experience. Twenty-seven percent of the total sample say they have either had an experience like the one described or would like to and feel they could sometime. This proportion varies from 52 percent in the "high" category to 14 percent in the "low" category (gamma = .363).

Another story read:

Pat told of spying a small green beetle on the porch steps one day. Pat said:

"I began to think about the beetle, where it was going, what it thought of me. Suddenly I felt very close to the beetle. It was just as important as I was. It overwhelmed me to be in the world with this beetle.

"Then the beetle smiled and said to me, 'How are you doing? It's such a nice day.' And the beetle began to glow and I felt warm all over. Never before have I felt so at peace with everything."

Table B-3. **SHRI RAMA'S EXPERIENCE BY MYSTICISM MEASURE**
(Psychology Today Respondents)

| | Likelihood of adhering to mystical meaning system is: | | | | |
	Low	Medium Low	Medium High	High	Total
Feelings about the story:*					
I like it because it makes me feel good	6%	10%	18%	38%	20%
I like it although I can't say why	17	16	19	18	18
It is mildly interesting	49	49	42	33	42
Somehow it makes me feel uncomfortable	4	5	5	2	4
It turns me off	25	20	15	9	15
Number	(84)	(502)	(967)	(412)	(1989)
Like to have such an experience:**					
I've had an experience like this	2%	2%	3%	12%	5%
I'd like to and feel I could sometime	12	12	21	40	22
I'd like to but doubt if I ever will	21	34	38	23	33
No	64	51	38	25	40
Number	(84)	(502)	(967)	(412)	(1989)

*gamma = .299, significant at or beyond .05 level.
**gamma = .363, significant at or beyond .05 level.

The answer categories for this story were the same. Again, the mysticism measure predicts responses fairly powerfully (see Table B-4).

The third story was designed to express a more traditional kind of religious experience:

Jim recounts this experience:

"I was working alone at the office late one night. I heard a soft knock

Table B-4. **PAT'S EXPERIENCE BY MYSTICISM MEASURE**
(*Psychology Today* Respondents)

	Likelihood of adhering to mystical meaning system is:				
	Low	Medium Low	Medium High	High	Total
Feelings about the story: *					
I like it because it makes me feel good	17%	22%	35%	55%	35%
I like it although I can't say why	11	14	13	10	13
It is mildly interesting	40	37	33	24	33
Somehow it makes me feel uncomfortable	4	5	4	2	4
It turns me off	29	23	14	9	16
Number	(84)	(502)	(967)	(412)	(1989)
Like to have such an experience: **					
I've had an experience like this	12%	13%	21%	44%	24%
I'd like to and feel I could sometime	12	18	26	27	24
I'd like to but doubt if I ever will	20	25	24	11	21
No	56	43	30	18	32
Number	(84)	(502)	(967)	(412)	(1989)

*gamma = .315, significant at or beyond .05 level.
**gamma = .358, significant at or beyond .05 level.

at the door and went to open it. I found myself face to face with a young man with the most radiant face I've ever seen. His eyes were so deep and peaceful. He had long flowing hair. I was tongue-tied. The man just gazed into my eyes. Finally he said: 'I bring you word from the Almighty. It is this: Love one another.' I suddenly felt all my problems melt away. I felt blessed and close to everything in the world."

The relations between the mysticism measure and the responses to this story are somewhat weaker than for the other two stories (gammas = .187 and .273), but again they are consistent and in the expected direction (see Table B-5).

Table B-5. **JIM'S EXPERIENCE BY MYSTICISM MEASURE**
(Psychology Today Respondents)

	Likelihood of adhering to mystical meaning system is:				
	Low	Medium Low	Medium High	High	Total
Feelings about the story:*					
I like it because it makes me feel good	18%	23%	27%	42%	29%
I like it although I can't say why	11	10	10	8	9
It is mildly interesting	26	29	32	25	30
Somehow it makes me feel uncomfortable	12	12	11	9	11
It turns me off	33	27	20	16	21
Number	(84)	(502)	(967)	(412)	(1989)
Like to have such an experience:**					
I've had an experience like this	2%	4%	5%	12%	6%
I'd like to and feel I could sometime	13	13	19	34	20
I'd like to but doubt if I ever will	27	33	34	24	31
No	57	50	42	31	42
Number	(84)	(502)	(967)	(412)	(1989)

*gamma = .187, significant at or beyond .05 level.
**gamma = .273, significant at or beyond .05 level.

The four submeasures were obviously constructed mostly on the basis of conceptual considerations rather than merely on empirical grounds. The intention was to combine items in such a way that each measure would tap a specific kind of meaning system more precisely than any separate item could do by itself. Items were selected not on the basis of how highly they were related empirically, but according to what their content added to the meaning of the measure. It is important, therefore, to see how the present measures differ from what they might have been if they had been constructed purely on empirical grounds.

As a way of examining the validity of the four submeasures, comparable measures were developed, based entirely on empirical considerations. First, all the items that had been placed in the survey instrument to tap each of the four meaning systems were grouped into their respective categories. Separate factor analyses of the items in each category were conducted, using the varimax rotation, to discover how highly each item related to the other items that had been designed to tap the same kind of meaning system. Then, additive scales were constructed in which each item contributed to the total scale an amount equal to its factor-score coefficient on each factor produced by the varimax rotation. (See Table B-6).[3]

Perfect relations between the two kinds of scales would not be expected; if it turned out that such were the case, it would have been pointless to be so selective about the particular items included in each measure. An absence of relations would not be expected either, however. All of the items in the empirically constructed scales were originally designed to be indicators of some aspect of one of the four meaning systems, although it was recognized that some items were more to the point than others. While the different versions of each scale should be somewhat different in what they measure precisely, they should, therefore, indicate *roughly* the same kind of meaning system and consequently be related. Table B-7 shows the relations between each of these new measures and its counterpart measure from Chapter 4.

These relations suggest that by developing the four measures using conceptual criteria, the resulting measures were not something

3. Factor-score coefficients produced by SPSS, see Norman H. Nie, Dale H. Bent, and C. Hadlai Hull, *SPSS: Statistical Package for the Social Sciences* (New York: McGraw-Hill Book Company, 1970), pp. 226–227; options used: PA2, maximum iterations = 99, varimax rotations with Kaiser normalization.

Table B-6. ITEMS IN FACTOR-SCORE COEFFICIENT SCALES

	Factor Score Coefficients		Mean	St. Dev.
Theism	I			
Suffering—devil	.107		2.607	.719
Suffering—disobey God	.196		2.187	.874
Influenced by God	.268		2.511	.942
Believe in God	.184		2.060	1.548
Creation	.230		1.767	.928
Afterlife	.150		3.520	1.700
Poverty—God	.120		2.457	1.142
Eigenvalue	3.609			
Proportion of variance	100%			
Individualism	I	II		
Suffering—naturally selfish	.034	.114	1.853	.802
Suffering—own fault	.091	.369	1.636	.668
Influenced by willpower	-.058	.244	1.885	.661
No succeed—own fault	.462	.006	2.501	.945
Work hard—do anything	.188	.096	2.004	.981
Fail—blame self	.213	.023	1.728	.806
Poor—don't work	.172	-.054	3.108	.910
Eigenvalues	1.892	1.050		
Proportion of variance	85%	15%		

Table B-6 Continued.

	Factor Score Coefficients			Mean	St. Dev.
	I	II	III		
Social Science					
Evolution	.027	-.065	.328	1.913	.959
Influenced by childhood	.020	-.002	.231	2.434	1.080
Ideas depend on income	.026	.051	.089	2.276	1.013
Poor—American way	.274	-.140	.161	2.392	1.097
Learn from psychology	-.055	.087	.207	1.957	.948
Poor—powerstructure	.546	-.152	-.076	2.346	.998
Influenced by powerstructure	-.034	.119	.208	2.742	.769
Influenced by way raised	-.044	.118	.049	1.960	.542
Suffering—social setup	.008	.367	.022	1.588	.727
Suffering—powerstructure	.211	.441	-.135	1.870	.783
Eigenvalues	2.182	1.350	1.151		
Proportion of variance	62%	21%	17%		
Mysticism					
	I	II			
Experienced the sacred	.252	.042		2.525	1.132
Experienced nature	.203	-.111		3.261	.862
Experienced harmony	.481	.063		2.350	1.102
Learn from the arts	.061	.369		1.874	.890
Influenced by new insights	-.071	.059		2.301	.764
Learn from the woods	.021	.447		1.993	.999

Table B-6 Continued.

	Factor Score Coefficients		Mean	St. Dev.
Mysticism Continued.				
Live in fantasy world	−.055	.074	2.266	1.027
Suffering—no inner peace	−.086	.022	1.530	.680
Eigenvalues	2.377	1.063		
Proportion of variance	82%	18%		

Table B-7. **VALIDATION OF MEANING SYSTEM SUBMEASURES USING FACTOR-SCORE COEFFICIENT SCALES***
(Total Weighted Sample)

	Low	Medium Low	Medium High	High	Gamma
Percent above mean on:					
	Theism Submeasure				
Theism Factor I	2%	26%	86%	99%	.971
Number	(271)	(175)	(217)	(224)	
	Individualism Submeasure				
Individualism Factor I	19%	47%	65%	86%	.588
Number	(184)	(408)	(247)	(107)	
Individualism Factor II	16%	56%	58%	69%	.432
Number	(184)	(408)	(247)	(107)	
	Social Science Submeasure				
Social Science Factor I	26%	44%	54%	73%	.413
Number	(102)	(284)	(326)	(193)	
Social Science Factor II	20%	42%	59%	82%	.555
Number	(102)	(284)	(326)	(193)	
Social Science Factor III	4%	32%	63%	91%	.777
Number	(102)	(284)	(326)	(193)	
	Mysticism Submeasure				
Mysticism Factor I	10%	22%	50%	82%	.707
Number	(73)	(251)	(384)	(251)	
Mysticism Factor II	16%	32%	56%	81%	.616
Number	(73)	(251)	(384)	(251)	

*All relations significant at or beyond .05 level.

entirely different from what would have resulted had purely mechanical scaling procedures been used. The items selected seem to be "valid" in the sense that they afford a powerful means of predicting responses to other questions having a similar focus. The original measures, nevertheless, have the advantage of being somewhat more precise in terms of their "face validity"; that is, they appear on the surface to contain the best items for tapping the kinds of assumptions that needed to be measured to reflect each meaning system as it was conceptualized in Chapter 3. In addition, the original measures also have the two advantages mentioned previously:

it is easier to remember what a high or a low score on each measure means since each item received equal weight. And since there are fewer items involved in each measure, replication or the construction of similar kinds of measures to study other meaning systems is shown to be less forbidding than if a large number of items was needed.

Interrelations. Are the four submeasures mutually exclusive or interrelated? In Chapter 3 the four meaning systems were described as alternative ways of constructing reality. But since all four have been (and apparently still are) part of American culture, there is no reason why individuals would necessarily be expected to hold one exclusive of all the others. Holding several meaning systems may be conducive to cognitive conflicts or dissonance in some ideal-typical sense, but the capacity for the human psyche to tolerate such dissonance (through compartmentalization, rationalization, etc.) has been shown to be rather remarkable.

An explicit effort was made to develop each of the four sub-measures in such a way that the relations between each pair could be examined empirically. Every item used to construct each measure could be answered in any way, no matter how the other items were answered; for example, no agree/disagree questions were used where "agree" was taken as a sign of one meaning system and "disagree" as a sign of another meaning system.

Table B-8. **INTERRELATIONS AMONG FOUR MEANING SYSTEM MEASURES*** (Total Weighted Sample)

	Theistic	Individualistic	Social Scientific	Mystical
Theistic	X	.222	−.403	−.105
Individualistic		X	−.303	−.130
Social Scientific			X	.286
Mystical				X

*Based on dichotomized versions of each measure, where scores of 2 or 3 = High; 0 or 1 = Low. Measure of association = gamma.

Table B-8 reports the gammas for all the possible two-way relations among the four submeasures. Obviously the four submeasures are not mutually exclusive. To accept one meaning system is not to reject all the others. The pattern is for the theistic and the individualistic meaning systems to go together and the social-scientific and mystical meaning systems to go together. Conversely, each of the first two

Table B-9. **HIGH SCORES ON SEPARATE MEANING SYSTEM MEASURES BY COMPOSITE MEASURE***
(Total Weighted Sample)

	Traditional	Theistic	Individualistic	Dominant meaning system: Transitional	Social	Mystical	Modern
Percent "high" on:							
Theism	60%	89%	0%	24%	0%	0%	0%
Individualism	60%	0%	64%	10%	0%	0%	0%
Social Science	0%	0%	0%	7%	74%	0%	61%
Mysticism	0%	0%	0%	25%	0%	80%	61%
Number	(43)	(145)	(80)	(250)	(139)	(127)	(118)

*All relations significant at or beyond .05 level.

tend to be negatively related to each of the last two. This pattern, it should be noted, seems to be consistent with the historical material presented in Chapter 3. If the theistic and the individualistic meaning systems are both more traditional to American culture, they might be expected to show a positive relation. By the same token, if the social-scientific and the mystical meaning systems are both of more recent vintage, they might also be expected to be found among somewhat the same kinds of people. And if the former two are in some measure being replaced by the latter two, the expectation would be for the two sets of measures to be negatively associated. But perhaps the most important feature about these relations is simply that they are no stronger than they are. The only relations that could be called strong are between theism and social science and between individualism and social science. These are negative relations, though, which indicates that these measures are at least tapping opposite kinds of meaning systems. In sum, the results of Table B-8 tend to confirm the results of the factor pattern shown in Table B-1, namely, that the four meaning systems appear to be relatively distinct.

Composite measure. The construction of the composite meaning system measure from the four submeasures is described in Chapter 4. Table B-9 summarizes the extent to which the composite measure reflects the information contained in the four submeasures. As can be seen, it categorizes people as it is intended to do.

Table B-10 shows further that the composite measure predicts well responses to items not contained within its component measures. In each case the category (or categories) expected to show the highest proportions does so. It is clear, however, that persons classified as holding one particular meaning system also accept some of the tenets of the other meaning systems. Furthermore, they do so with different likelihoods, depending on the items at issue. It can reasonably be objected, therefore, that the relations between any one meaning system and social experimentation may partly be due to the contaminating effects of other meaning systems. An examination of the *independent* effects of each meaning system is presented later in this appendix.

EXPERIMENTATION INDEXES

The five experimentation indexes, comprising the items listed in Table 8 in Chapter 4, were constructed to reduce the amount of

Table B-10. VALIDATING ITEMS BY COMPOSITE MEANING SYSTEM MEASURE* (Total Weighted Sample)

	Dominant meaning system:						
	Traditional	Theistic	Individualistic	Transitional	Social	Mystical	Modern
God created the first man and woman	93%	92%	57%	70%	32%	44%	20%
There is life after death, with rewards and punishments	50%	50%	8%	22%	4%	4%	2%
If someone does not succeed, it's his own fault	59%	48%	68%	55%	37%	48%	47%
The wealthy keep the poor poor	37%	49%	28%	57%	71%	61%	78%
Beliefs are influenced by income	60%	65%	61%	65%	80%	61%	70%
Experienced harmony with the universe	11%	19%	12%	19%	14%	37%	40%
Number	(43)	(145)	(80)	(250)	(139)	(127)	(118)

* All relations significant at or beyond .05 level.

Table B-11. **INTERRELATIONS AMONG POLITICAL EXPERIMENTATION ITEMS**
(Based on Weighted Sample, Whites Only)

	Demonstrated	Change gov't	Betty Wilson	Gammas: Radical or liberal	Pro-Communists	Anti-police	Social change
Demonstrated	X	.438	.613	.866	.758	.729	.447
Change gov't		X	.212	.453	.382	.299	.350
Betty Wilson			X	.629	.581	.566	.398
Radical or liberal				X	.720	.709	.553
Pro-Communists					X	.658	.490
Anti-police						X	.360
Social change							X

Average gamma = .534

random error always present in any single survey item and thereby to provide a more stable measure of each type of experimentation. The basis for combining the items into single indexes is chiefly that they are strongly associated with one another. As Table B-11 shows, the average gamma for the interrelations among the seven political experimentation items is .534. Tables B-12 through B-15 show similar interrelations among the other sets of items.

Table B-12. **INTERRELATIONS AMONG ECONOMIC EXPERIMENTATION ITEMS**

(Based on Weighted Sample, Whites Only)

	Gammas:			
	New tax laws	Guaranteed minimum wage	Women's rights	Affirmative action
New tax laws	X	.434	.299	.404
Guaranteed minimum wage		X	.354	.553
Women's rights			X	.398
Affirmative action				X
Average gamma = .407				

Table B-13. **INTERRELATIONS AMONG RELIGIOUS EXPERIMENTATION ITEMS**

(Based on Weighted Sample, Whites Only)

	Gammas:			
	Eastern groups	Low church attendance	Little prayer	Low value on church
Eastern groups	X	.326	.356	.424
Low church attendance		X	.947	.917
Little prayer			X	.855
Low value on church				X
Average gamma = .637				

Table B-14. **INTERRELATIONS AMONG FAMILY/SEXUAL
EXPERIMENTATION ITEMS**
(Based on Weighted Sample, Whites Only)

	Cohabitation	Gammas: Homosexuality	Communes
Cohabitation	X	.872	.731
Homosexuality		X	.536
Communes			X
Average gamma = .713			

Each index was constructed by assigning a point for each item responded to in the appropriate way, as indicated in Table 8 in Chapter 4. To simplify the presentation of tables, each index was then dichotomized. Cutting points were determined on empirical grounds (as in Table B-20 for the summary measure). In each case it turned out that the scores above the midpoint of the scale could be grouped together as could scores below the midpoint. An examination of missing data, "don't know," "undecided," and "other" responses (of which there were relatively few) showed that they could best be classified with nonexperimenters. The indexes were developed on the basis of whites only on the assumption that excluding nonwhites would enhance the homogeneity of the sample for validation purposes, but subsequent tests of the indexes on nonwhites revealed the same patterns.

It should be observed that the items included in the experimentation indexes all concern specific behavior (5 items), opinions toward specific issues (16 items), or relatively specific values or goals (7 items). None concern general understandings of the forces governing life as do the meaning system items. This theoretical distinction is crucial and is elaborated fully in Chapters 2 and 3. The meaning system items were designed to tap understandings of the *general forces* that shape life; the experimentation items concern *specific remedies* for coping with personal and social conditions.

It should also be noted that the only experimentation items discussed in Chapter 1 that are not included in these measures are those concerning Jesus People groups. These items appear to be more highly related to conventional than to nonconventional commitments.

Table B-15. INTERRELATIONS AMONG ALTERNATIVE LEISURE ITEMS (Based on Weighted Sample, Whites Only)

	Drug experience	Smoke dope	Encounter groups	Growth groups	Jim Smith	Inner self	Marijuana	Body awareness	Nature	Free time
				Gammas:						
Drug experience	X	.978	.557	.328	.332	.408	.881	.481	.448	.317
Smoke dope		X	.553	.246	.507	.368	.980	.637	.451	.455
Encounter groups			X	.272	.442	.584	.573	.546	.211	.216
Growth groups				X	.070	.180	.380	.153	.107	.078
Jim Smith					X	.236	.281	.295	.325	.170
Inner self						X	.348	.634	.539	.239
Marijuana							X	.374	.324	.256
Body awareness								X	.662	.391
Nature									X	.325
Free time										X

Average gamma = .326

The summary experimentation index was constructed chiefly for the multivariate analyses in Chapter 6. The five subindexes of experimentation are highly interrelated (see Table B-16). A factor analysis of the 28 items contained within the subindexes also suggests that a single dimension underlies these items (see Table B-17), indicating as suggested in Chapter 1 that the division of experimentation into subareas was somewhat arbitrary, although useful for expository purposes.[4] Rather than give each of the 28 items equal weight in the index or weight them according to factor-score coefficients, the summary index was constructed to give each of the five subareas of experimentation equal weight. A point was assigned for each kind of experimentation, yielding a scale ranging from 0 (low) to 5 (high). Table B-18 shows that the index strongly predicts responses to the subscales, and Table B-19 shows that it strongly predicts responses to each of the 28 original items. The face validity of the summary index was also established by having two independent judges determine which of a sample of 15 respondents should be called high experimenters (scores of 5) and which should be called nonexperimenters (scores of 0) by simply looking through the interview guides for these 15 respondents, having been told to use any definition of "social experimenter" they wanted. One judge agreed with the index in all 15 cases, the other agreed in 14 cases.

Table B-16. **INTERRELATIONS AMONG EXPERIMENTATION INDEXES** (Based on Weighted Sample, Whites Only)

			Gammas:		
	Politics	Economics	Religion	Family	Leisure
Politics	X	.701	.705	.806	.804
Economics		X	.244	.374	.452
Religion			X	.686	.618
Family				X	.771
Leisure					X
Average gamma = .616					

To facilitate the presentation of tables and the use of the Goodman analytic system, the summary experimentation index was dichotomized. Scores of 3 to 5 were designated high; scores of 0 to 2, low. The procedure for determining the proper cutting point is shown

4. Factor analysis program used, see Baker, *Pickle.*

Table B-17. **PRINCIPAL COMPONENT SCORES OF
EXPERIMENTATION ITEMS*** (Weighted Sample, Whites Only)

	Score on Factor I
Legalizing marijuana (L)	.711
Politically liberal or radical (P)	.677
Had a drug experience (L)	.652
Cohabitation (F)	.636
Freedom for homosexuals (F)	.623
Demonstrated (P)	.566
Like to smoke dope (L)	.544
Admire anti-Communist (−P)	−.526
Attracted to Eastern religion (R)	.508
Pray at least once a week (−R)	−.496
Give police more power (−P)	−.480
Tolerate a revolutionary (P)	.453
Value taking part in church (−R)	−.444
Been in encounter group (L)	.387
Favor special efforts to hire blacks (E)	.375
Like to live in commune (F)	.364
Value body awareness (L)	.333
Favor guaranteed annual income (E)	.323
Government needs major overhaul (P)	.312
Value inner awareness (L)	.304
Value women's liberation (E)	.302
Attend church weekly (−R)	−.298
Admire living in wilderness (L)	.284
Value living close to nature (L)	.270
Attracted to personal growth groups (L)	.264
Value social change (P)	.252
Tax the wealthy (E)	.244
Value lots of free time (L)	.236

Proportion of total commonality accounted for = .714

*Letters in parentheses indicate kind of experimentation: P = political, E = economic, R = religious, F = family, L = leisure.

Table B-18. **EXPERIMENTATION INDEXES BY SUMMARY INDEX**
(Weighted Sample, Whites Only)

| | Summary index excluding index for which relation is shown: | | | | | |
	Low 0	1	2	3	High 4	Gamma
Political	2%	7%	27%	50%	84%	.832
Number	(166)	(195)	(165)	(139)	(121)	
Economic	26%	30%	42%	45%	70%	.419
Number	(219)	(184)	(133)	(105)	(144)	
Religious	30%	37%	56%	72%	89%	.567
Number	(231)	(185)	(147)	(108)	(113)	
Family/sexual	15%	28%	51%	68%	96%	.711
Number	(191)	(217)	(145)	(126)	(105)	
Leisure	14%	30%	56%	73%	90%	.715
Number	(189)	(225)	(150)	(109)	(112)	

*All relations significant at or beyond .05 level.

Table B-19. **COMPONENT ITEMS BY SUMMARY EXPERIMENTATION INDEX*** (Weighted Sample, Whites Only)

| | Summary experimentation index | | | | | | |
	Low 0	1	2	3	4	High 5	Gamma
Politics							
Demonstrated	1%	3%	5%	17%	38%	60%	.807
Change government	30%	31%	48%	45%	61%	80%	.422
Betty Wilson	23%	36%	42%	58%	73%	90%	.567
Liberal	8%	4%	22%	44%	77%	95%	.833
Pro-Communists	19%	26%	26%	50%	71%	93%	.624
Anti-police	34%	50%	52%	75%	86%	98%	.595
Social change	6%	7%	11%	19%	26%	33%	.481

Table B-19 Continued.

	Summary experimentation index						
	Low 0	1	2	3	4	High 5	Gamma
Economics							
Tax wealth	14%	36%	40%	40%	43%	77%	.451
Guaranteed minimum wage	6%	22%	33%	34%	38%	69%	.542
Women's rights	24%	34%	54%	57%	56%	84%	.486
Affirmative action	3%	13%	12%	16%	27%	59%	.601
Religion							
Eastern groups	7%	15%	26%	40%	52%	75%	.656
Church not important	25%	55%	67%	79%	88%	98%	.685
Low church attendance	60%	81%	84%	89%	91%	99%	.550
Low prayer	8%	43%	51%	70%	79%	90%	.697
Family							
Cohabitation	8%	37%	66%	78%	98%	100%	.855
Homosexuality	10%	24%	47%	72%	90%	97%	.812
Communes	1%	6%	7%	16%	26%	34%	.630
Leisure							
Drug experience	3%	8%	14%	35%	60%	77%	.785
Smoke dope	0%	2%	2%	16%	24%	50%	.831
Encounter group	5%	7%	10%	31%	37%	45%	.601
Growth groups	14%	21%	38%	35%	49%	47%	.387
Jim Smith	30%	47%	59%	64%	65%	80%	.416
Inner self	42%	49%	55%	72%	71%	86%	.403
Marijuana	5%	19%	30%	63%	90%	98%	.846
Body awareness	40%	39%	62%	66%	75%	85%	.444
Beauty of nature	61%	61%	79%	78%	85%	92%	.387
Lots of free time	40%	56%	64%	73%	75%	79%	.386
Number	(162)	(185)	(133)	(114)	(90)	(101)	

*All relations significant at or beyond .05 level.

Table B-20. **DETERMINATION OF CUTTING POINT FOR EXPERIMENTATION INDEX*** (Weighted Sample, Whites Only)

		Summary Experimentation Index						
		Low 0	1	2	3	4	High 5	N
Politics	Lo	29%	33	22	12	4	0	(552)
	Hi	0%	2	6	19	30	44	(233)
Economics	Lo	35%	27	16	12	9	0	(468)
	Hi	0%	18	18	18	15	32	(316)
Religion	Lo	42%	30	17	8	3	0	(385)
	Hi	0%	17	17	21	19	25	(399)
Family	Lo	37%	36	16	9	1	0	(433)
	Hi	0%	8	18	21	24	29	(351)
Leisure	Lo	38%	37	16	7	2	0	(427)
	Hi	0%	7	19	24	22	28	(357)
	N	(162)	(185)	(133)	(114)	(90)	(101)	

*All relations significant at or beyond .05 level.

in Table B-20. The five component scales are used as independent variables, the summary index as the dependent variable. In all five parts of the table, scores of 0 and 1 on the summary index are associated with low scores on the component scales; scores of 3 to 5 are clearly associated with high scores. Scores of 2 are slightly associated with high scores in three instances, strongly associated with low scores in one, and associated with neither in the other. Since scores of 2 are ambiguous, they were judged to be better taken as a sign of low rather than of high experimentation to preserve more of the purity of the latter category.

INDEPENDENT EFFECTS OF EACH MEANING SYSTEM

The composite measure used to tap the various meaning systems, while having expository advantages, does not afford an accurate assessment of the *independent* effects of each of the four meaning systems. Does individualism, for example, actually discourage social experimentation, or do individualists only appear the way they do because they are relatively inclined toward theistic views? Do social-scientific orientations and mystical orientations function in similar ways just because the two are related, or does each produce effects apart from the other?

To show that each of the four meaning systems bears important relations with social experimentation and that these relations are not due simply to the effects of one of the other meaning systems, all that is necessary is to examine the relations between experimentation and the submeasures for each of the four meaning systems (from Chapter 4) *simultaneously.* Leo Goodman's log linear analytic system (discussed in Chapter 5) provides a useful tool for simultaneously examining the relations between several variables such as these.[5]

Table B-21. **NET EFFECTS OF EACH MEANING SYSTEM ON EACH KIND OF EXPERIMENTATION**
(Based on Total Weighted Sample)

	Ratios of the odds of being an experimenter for:			
Experimentation	*Low vs. High Theism*	*Low vs. High Individualism*	*High vs. Low Social Science*	*High vs. Low Mysticism*
Political	3.60	3.28	1.56	3.26
Economic	1.52	2.04	1.32*	1.21*
Family	4.16	1.66	1.87	3.15
Leisure	2.83	1.50	1.89	6.01
Religious	14.11	1.14*	1.60	1.72
Summary measure	7.41	2.32	1.88	4.77

*Net effect not significant at .05 level.

Table B-21 shows the net effects of each meaning system on each of the five kinds of experimentation and on the summary experimentation index, taking into account the effects of the other three

5. See Leo Goodman, "A Modified Multiple Regression Approach to the Analysis of Dichotomous Variables," *American Sociological Review* 37 (February 1972): 28–46.

meaning systems. Each of the meaning system measures is dichotomized to reduce the number of cells in the table from which the
present figures are calculated, scores of "low" and "medium low"
being redefined as "low" and scores of "high" and "medium high"
being redefined as "high." The figures in the table are ratios
between the odds of being an experimenter if one is low (or high)
on each meaning system to the odds of being an experimenter if one
is high (or low), taking into account the effects of the other three
meaning systems. The table shows, first, that in all but three
instances each meaning system bears a statistically significant relation
to each of the five kinds of experimentation and to the summary
index of experimentation.[6] The exceptions are that individualism
shows no significant relation to religious experimentation when
the other meaning systems are controlled, social science (ironically)
shows no significant relation to economic experimentation, and
mysticism shows no significant relation to economic experimentation.
Second, the table gives an indication of how strongly each meaning
system is related to each kind of experimentation independently of
the other meaning systems.[7] For instance, the odds of being a political
experimenter if one is *not* theistic are 3.6 times greater than if one
is theistic, the odds of being a political experimenter are also more
than three times as great if one scores low on individualism than if
one scores high. Being high on social science raises the chances of
being a political experimenter by about 60 percent. And being high
on the mystical meaning system triples the odds of being a political
experimenter. These are the *net* effects produced by each meaning
system apart from the effects of the other meaning systems. The
unexpected finding, of course, is that social science produces no
greater, although still significant, effects than it does. In general,
however, the effects are all quite strong.

6. A comparison of alternatives to the model {ABCD} {AE} {BE} {CE} {DE},
where A = theism, B = individualism, C = social science, D = mysticism, and
E = the experimentation variable at issue indicates that the term {CE}, when
E = economic experimentation, improves the "fit" of the model only at the .20
level of significance and the term {DE} improves it only at the .30 level. When
E = religious experimentation, the term {BE} improves the fit of the model only
at the .50 level. An examination of models including interaction effects, such
as {ABCD} {AE} {BE} {CDE}, shows no significant interactive terms except for
a small positive interaction between social science and mysticism on family
experimentation.
7. To facilitate comparability the odds-ratios are reported in such manner that each
exceeds unity.

Table B-21 also affords an opportunity to determine how much the *combined* effect of the four meaning systems is on experimentation. People who reject both the traditional meaning systems and accept both the modern meaning systems, for example, are over 60 times more likely to be political experimenters than those who accept both the traditional but reject both the modern meaning systems.[8] On this score, economic experimentation is least strongly related to these systems of meaning. The most purely modern types are only 3 times more likely than the most purely traditional types; still, this is not an insignificant difference. All the other kinds of experimentation are strongly related to the meaning systems when taken in combination. Religious experimentation is 44 times more likely among the most modern than among the most traditional. Family or sexual experimentation is 39 times more likely. And leisure experimentation is 46 times more likely. On the summary experimentation index, the most modern types are over 150 times more likely to be experimenters than the most traditional types.

8. These figures are obtained simply by multiplying the net odds-ratios for the four meaning systems.

APPENDIX C

Supplementary Tables

Table C-1. **COMPARISONS BETWEEN THE 1973 BAY AREA SAMPLE AND THE 1970 CENSUS FOR THE BAY AREA**

	Census	Sample
Sex:		
Male	48.2%	43.2%
Female	51.8	56.8
Age:		
16-19	9.1%	10.0%
20-24	12.5	9.7
25-34	19.4	22.9
35-44	16.2	17.2
45-54	17.0	14.5
55-59	7.0	6.3
60-64	5.8	5.6
65-74	7.9	9.2
75 and over	5.0	4.1
Education:		
Some grade school	10.2%	5.2%
Finished grade school	7.8	5.1
Some high school	15.9	10.9
Finished high school	32.7	29.4
Some college	16.6	22.1
College graduate	16.8	27.3

Table C-1 Continued.

	Census	Sample
Race		
White (including Spanish-American)	82.8%	85.2%
Black	10.6	8.4
Other	6.6	6.3
In labor force:		
Male (16 and over)	78%	79%
Female (16 and over)	45%	50%
Occupation:		
Professional	18.2%	23.5%
Managers	9.4	13.0
Sales	8.2	6.3
Clerical	23.0	17.3
Craftsmen	12.3	12.1
Operatives	11.6	6.6
Laborers	3.9	6.6
Farm	0.5	0.0
Service	11.5	12.4
Private household	1.3	0.9

Table C-2. **RESPONSE RATE BY GEOGRAPHICAL AREA**

	"Youth"		"Mature"	
	Percent	*Number*	*Percent*	*Number*
Berkeley	93	(43)	89	(19)
Oakland	82	(80)	70	(94)
Alameda	82	(91)	71	(96)
Richmond	83	(31)	74	(31)
Orinda	88	(51)	83	(37)
Pittsburgh	90	(20)	73	(15)
San Francisco—North	84	(53)	60	(75)
San Francisco—Mission	87	(32)	58	(36)
San Francisco—Sunset	89	(58)	67	(33)
San Francisco—Bayview	92	(13)	72	(11)
San Mateo	87	(135)	71	(122)
Marin	93	(32)	81	(43)
Dormitories	100	(10)	—	——
Total	87	(649)	71	(612)

Table C-3. THE SALIENCE OF ULTIMATE QUESTIONS (Total Weighted Sample)

Ultimate questions	Think about it a lot	Think about it some	Used to think about it, don't now	Never thought about it, but it's important	Never thought about it, not important	(Number)
				For each ultimate question, percent who say they:		
How you can find real happiness in life	39%	35	12	10	4	(1,000)
What the purpose of life is	30%	40	11	13	6	(1,000)
How you came to be the way you are	32%	32	12	12	12	(1,000)
The existence of God	43%	30	16	6	6	(1,000)
How the world came into being	19%	38	21	10	11	(1,000)
Why there is suffering in the world	38%	45	7	6	3	(1,000)
What happens after death	20%	38	15	7	20	(1,000)

Table C-4. EXPERIMENTATION ITEMS BY MEANING SYSTEMS* (Total Weighted Sample)

	Dominant meaning system:						
	Traditional	Theistic	Individual	Transitional	Social	Mystic	Modern
Been in demonstration	1%	5%	4%	11%	23%	31%	37%
Tolerate revolutionary	15%	31%	39%	51%	63%	68%	67%
Overhaul government	26%	36%	35%	50%	51%	54%	67%
Dislike anti-Communist	25%	37%	17%	36%	61%	60%	64%
Oppose police power	30%	48%	33%	59%	75%	73%	89%
Radical or liberal	15%	15%	18%	23%	47%	50%	62%
Value social change	0%	7%	7%	11%	23%	25%	21%
Affirmative action	5%	16%	10%	15%	29%	25%	30%
Women—equal rights	25%	38%	27%	45%	54%	53%	64%
New tax laws	26%	32%	34%	38%	47%	38%	50%
Guaranteed wage	15%	30%	28%	31%	42%	35%	50%
Eastern religions	6%	12%	18%	26%	32%	53%	51%
Value church little	41%	28%	64%	56%	79%	77%	90%
Don't attend church regularly	84%	56%	85%	76%	88%	89%	97%
Don't pray regularly	24%	15%	54%	36%	76%	59%	81%
Favor cohabitation	25%	20%	41%	50%	79%	75%	82%
Freedom for homosexuals	8%	16%	30%	40%	61%	69%	78%
Like to live in commune	1%	8%	3%	12%	18%	18%	25%
"High" on drugs	6%	14%	8%	18%	39%	41%	55%

Table C-4 Continued.

				Dominant meaning system:			
	Traditional	Theistic	Individual	Transitional	Social	Mystic	Modern
Smoke dope	0%	3%	4%	9%	15%	22%	32%
Legalize marijuana	8%	20%	13%	33%	58%	61%	77%
Value inner self	44%	54%	34%	63%	55%	77%	75%
Value body awareness	44%	55%	45%	57%	54%	69%	72%
Value nature	53%	51%	60%	71%	74%	87%	82%
Value free time	40%	52%	56%	63%	63%	68%	70%
Admire wilderness life	47%	43%	45%	55%	47%	62%	75%
Been in encounter group	8%	5%	12%	14%	20%	32%	31%
Like growth groups	16%	14%	19%	32%	36%	39%	42%
Number	(43)	(145)	(80)	(250)	(139)	(127)	(118)

*All relations significant at or beyond the .05 level.

Table C-5. SUMMARY EXPERIMENTATION INDEX BY MEANING SYSTEMS BY AGE, SEX, AND RACE*
(Total Weighted Sample)

				Dominant meaning system:			
	Traditional	Theistic	Individualistic	Transitional	Social	Mystical	Modern
Age:							
16-30	**	21%	39%	42%	71%	78%	81%
Number	(5)	(35)	(13)	(73)	(69)	(61)	(58)
Over 30	0%	4%	16%	17%	44%	54%	64%
Number	(39)	(110)	(66)	(178)	(70)	(66)	(60)
Sex:							
Female	0%	6%	20%	18%	61%	53%	65%
Number	(30)	(85)	(44)	(143)	(70)	(68)	(61)
Male	4%	12%	20%	33%	55%	79%	80%
Number	(13)	(60)	(36)	(107)	(69)	(59)	(58)
Race:							
Nonwhite	**	8%	36%	28%	49%	61%	67%
Number	(6)	(54)	(12)	(45)	(23)	(23)	(20)
White	2%	9%	17%	24%	60%	66%	74%
Number	(37)	(91)	(67)	(205)	(116)	(105)	(98)

* All relations significant at the .05 level.
** Too few cases for stable percentages.

Table C-6. EDUCATION BY MEANING SYSTEMS BY OCCUPATION AND INCOME* (Total Weighted Sample)

	Dominant meaning system:						
	Traditional	Theistic	Individualistic	Transitional	Social	Mystical	Modern
Percent college graduates:							
White collar	30%	33%	47%	50%	70%	62%	70%
Number	(20)	(46)	(34)	(101)	(60)	(69)	(70)
Blue collar	0%	20%	10%	21%	22%	37%	39%
Number	(11)	(55)	(29)	(65)	(37)	(27)	(28)
Percent college graduates:							
$10,000 or more	17%	22%	32%	38%	51%	55%	75%
Number	(24)	(55)	(38)	(125)	(70)	(60)	(56)
Less than $10,000	16%	23%	18%	32%	52%	50%	51%
Number	(19)	(84)	(38)	(117)	(65)	(66)	(59)

* All relations significant at or beyond the .05 level.

Table C-7. **GOODMAN MODELS FOR EXPERIMENTATION BY MEANING SYSTEMS BY MARGINALITY BY AGE**

Models tested		Likelihood ratio X^2	Degrees of freedom	P
*H_1	{ACD} {AB} {BC} {BD}	59.29	71	.836
H_2	{ACD} {AB} {BD}	87.45	76	.174
H_3	{ACD} {AB} {BC}	66.00	72	.681
H_4	{ACD} {BC} {BD}	238.20	77	.000
H_5	{ACD} {ABD} {BC}	57.21	65	.745
H_6	{ACD} {ABC} {BD}	29.50	41	.907
H_7	{ACD} {BCD} {AB}	55.50	66	.819
H_8	{ACD} {ABC} {ABD}	26.00	35	.864
H_9	{ACD} {ABD} {BCD}	53.11	60	.726
H_{10}	{ACD} {ABC} {BCD}	26.85	36	.864

*Model chosen.

A = Dominant Meaning System Typology (7 categories).
B = Summary Social Experimentation Index (2 categories).
C = Marginality Index (6 categories).
D = Age (2 categories).

Table C-8. **GOODMAN MODELS FOR EXPERIMENTATION BY MEANING SYSTEMS BY COGNITIVE SOPHISTICATION BY AGE**

Models tested		Likelihood ratio X^2	Degrees of freedom	P
H_1	{ACD} {AB} {BC} {BD}	61.73	58	.344
H_2	{ACD} {AB} {BD}	90.31	62	.011
H_3	{ACD} {AB} {BC}	91.06	59	.005
H_4	{ACD} {BC} {BD}	214.55	64	.000
H_5	{ACD} {ABD} {BC}	58.25	52	.256
H_6	{ACD} {ABC} {BD}	38.05	34	.290
*H_7	{ACD} {BCD} {AB}	50.59	54	.614
H_8	{ACD} {ABC} {ABD}	33.37	28	.223
H_9	{ACD} {ABD} {BCD}	45.96	48	.564
H_{10}	{ACD} {ABC} {BCD}	26.94	30	.613

*Model chosen ($H_1 - H_7 = 11.14$, df = 4, p = .02).

A = Dominant Meaning System Typology (7 categories).
B = Summary Social Experimentation Index (2 categories).
C = Cognitive Sophistication Index (5 categories).
D = Age (2 categories).

Table C-9. **ODDS-RATIOS FOR MODEL H_7, TABLE C-8**
(Based on Total Unweighted Sample)

	Cognitive Sophistication Index				
	Low 0	1	2	3	High 4
Experimentation (odds-ratios):					
Controlling for age	1.0	.9	1.9	3.2	5.3
Controlling for age and meaning systems					
Age 16-30	1.0	1.8	3.6	6.1	6.4
Over 30	1.0	.3	.5	.7	1.4

Table C-10. **GOODMAN MODELS FOR EXPERIMENTATION BY MEANING SYSTEMS BY LIBERAL BACKGROUND BY AGE**

Models tested		Likelihood ratio X^2	Degrees of freedom	P
*H_1	{ACD} {AB} {BC} {BD}	42.78	45	.571
H_2	{ACD} {AB} {BD}	73.15	48	.011
H_3	{ACD} {AB} {BC}	96.22	46	.000
H_4	{ACD} {BC} {BD}	226.68	51	.000
H_5	{ACD} {ABD} {BC}	40.25	39	.415
H_6	{ACD} {ABC} {BD}	19.36	27	.836
H_7	{ACD} {BCD} {AB}	37.52	42	.617
H_8	{ACD} {ABC} {ABD}	16.27	21	.758
H_9	{ACD} {ABD} {BCD}	34.68	36	.540
H_{10}	{ACD} {ABC} {BCD}	14.95	24	.918

*Model chosen.

A = Dominant Meaning System Typology (7 categories).
B = Summary Social Experimentation Index (2 categories).
C = Liberal Background Index (4 categories).
D = Age (2 categories).

Table C-11. PATH MODEL OF MAJOR VARIABLES (Based on Total Weighted Sample)

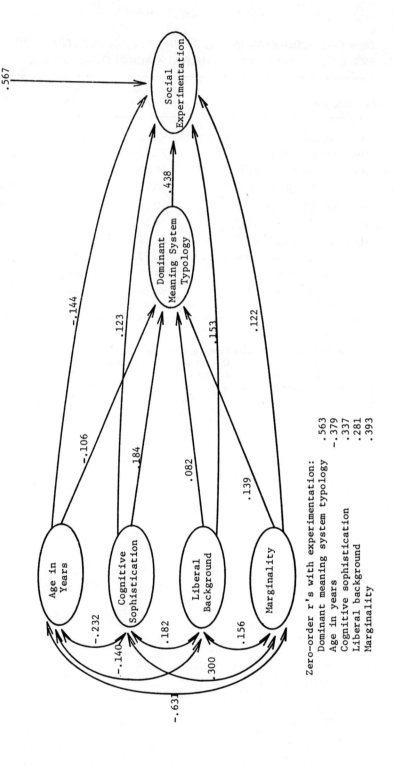

Zero-order r's with experimentation:
Dominant meaning system typology   .563
Age in years   -.379
Cognitive sophistication   .337
Liberal background   .281
Marginality   .393

APPENDIX D

Interview Schedule

Serial # (__ ____ __)
(1-4)
5/
6-7/01

1. First, I'd like to talk to you about some things that effect us in our everyday lives. Please tell me how much each one of these has been on your mind lately.

	A lot	A fair amount	Hardly at all	
How about your health? Has that been on your mind a lot, a fair amount, or hardly at all lately.	1	2	3	8/
How about events in the news? (Have they been on your mind a lot, a fair amount, or hardly at all lately?)	1	2	3	9/
What about money matters?.	1	2	3	10/

2A. Do you find yourself thinking much these days about your plans for the future?

                              Yes. 1   11/
                              No . . . .(SKIP TO 3). . . . 2

B. *IF YES:* Do you think about this quite a lot, a fair amount, or only a little?

                              A lot. 1   12/
                              A fair amount. 2
                              Only a little. 3

3. Have you ever found yourself thinking much about meaning in life?

                              Yes. 1   13/
                              No . . . .(SKIP TO 5). . . . 2

4A. How meaningful are you finding life now -- is it very meaningful to you, fairly meaningful, or not meaningful at all?

                              Very meaningful. 1   14/
                              Fairly meaningful. 2
                              Not meaningful .(SKIP TO D). 3

269

B. What are a few of the things that give your life meaning? *PROBE:* What is it about (each thing mentioned) that gives your life meaning? Anything else?

C. Could you tell me briefly what you think the meaning of your life is? *(IF RESPONDENT SAYS SUCH THINGS AS "HAPPINESS," "OTHER PEOPLE," "LOVE," ETC., ASK:* What do you mean by that? *OR:* Could you give me an example?*)*

D. Are there any things you can think of that would make your life more meaningful?

5. | Booklet Page 1 | I'm going to read you some questions about life, and I'd like you to use the answers on Page 1 to tell me how much thinking you do about each one.

The first question is: How you can find real happiness in life. Do you think about it a lot; do you think about it some; did you used to think about it but don't now; have you never thought about it although you think it is important; or have you never thought about it and it just isn't important to you?

	A lot	Some	Used to, not now	Never, but imp.	Never, not imp.	
How you can find real happiness in life.	1	2	3	4	5	15/
How much do you think about what the purpose of life is?.	1	2	3	4	5	
How much do you think about how you came to be the way you are?	1	2	3	4	5	
How much do you think about the existence of God?.	1	2	3	4	5	
What about how the world came into being?	1	2	3	4	5	
What about why there is suffering in the world?. .	1	2	3	4	5	
How much do you think about what happens after death?	1	2	3	4	5	21/

6A. Are there any other questions about life that you have spent time thinking about?

Yes 1   22/

No . . . . (SKIP TO 7A). . . . 2

B. *IF YES:* What are they?

7A. |Booklet| Which of the statements printed here comes closest to
|Page 2| expressing your view about answering the question,
"What is the purpose of life?"

I don't think the question can be answered and it doesn't
bother me that it can't. . . . .(SKIP TO 8).   1   23/

I don't think that the question can be answered, but I
wish there were an answer. . . .(SKIP TO 8).   2

I somehow believe that there must be an answer, although
I don't know what it is. . . . .(SKIP TO 8).   3

I have an answer which satisfies me. . .(ASK B).   4

B. Could you tell me what that answer is?

8. |Booklet| I'm going to read you some reasons people have given to
|Page 3| explain why there is suffering in the world. Please say
whether you think each one is a major reason for suffering, a minor
reason for suffering, or not a reason at all. The first reason is:
Suffering is the work of the devil. Is this a major reason for
suffering, a minor reason, or not a reason for suffering at all?

	Major reason	Minor reason	Not a reason at all	
Suffering is the work of the devil	1	2	3	24/
Suffering is caused by social arrangements that make people greedy for riches and power .	1	2	3	
Suffering comes about because people are just naturally selfish	1	2	3	
People at the top keep those at the bottom from getting their share	1	2	3	
Suffering comes about because people don't obey God	1	2	3	
It's because science hasn't found out yet what causes suffering.	1	2	3	
People are being punished for what they did in a previous life	1	2	3	
People usually bring suffering on themselves .	1	2	3	
People suffer because they haven't learned how to find inner peace.	1	2	3	32/

9. Here are some ways of learning about life and the forces governing it.
Please say how much you think you could learn from each one.

	A lot	A fair amount	Only a little	Nothing	
First, how much do you think you could learn about life from religious teachings -- a lot, a fair amount, only a little, or nothing?	1	2	3	4	33/
How much do you think you could learn about life from poetry, art, or music -- a lot, a fair amount, only a little, or nothing?	1	2	3	4	

How much from psychology?	1	2	3	4
How much from talking with friends? . .	1	2	3	4
How much from taking walks in the woods?.	1	2	3	4	37/

10A. | Booklet Page 4 | Using the answers at the bottom of the page, would you please tell me how much you think your life is influenced by each of these things listed here. *READ EACH ITEM.*

	Determines almost entirely	Has a strong influence	Has a small influence	Has no influence at all	
(1) The way you were brought up.	1	2	3	4	38/
(2) God or some other supernatural force. . .	1	2	3	4	
(3) Luck.	1	2	3	4	
(4) The characteristics you were born with. . .	1	2	3	4	
(5) What people in power decide.	1	2	3	4	
(6) Your own will power . .	1	2	3	4	
(7) New insights about yourself.	1	2	3	4	44/

11.   People who believe in astrology claim that the stars, the planets, and our birthdays have a lot to do with our destiny in life. What do you think about this -- are you a firm believer in astrology, are you somewhat doubtful, are you very doubtful, or are you a firm disbeliever?

        Firm believer 1   47/
        Somewhat doubtful 2
        Very doubtful 3
        Firm disbeliever. 4

  B.   Now, please go back over the list and choose the <u>one</u> thing that you think has the <u>most influence</u> on your life.

        Greatest influence # /___/   45-46/
        Can't choose between two or more /___/
        None of the above /___/

12.   How much do you know about astrology -- a lot, a fair amount, or only a little?

        A lot 1   48/
        A fair amount 2
        Only a little 3

13A. Do you happen to know what a horoscope is?

        Yes 1   49/
        No. . . . . . .(SKIP TO 14A). . 2

B. *IF YES:* How interested are you in your horoscopes -- quite interested, fairly interested, slightly interested, or not interested at all?

Quite interested.	1	50/
Fairly interested	2	
Slightly interested	3	
Not interested at all	4	

14A. Do you know your sign?

Yes	1	51/
No. . . . . . .(SKIP TO 15A). .	2	

B. *IF YES:* What is it?

Aquarius.	01	52-53/
Aries	02	
Cancer.	03	
Capricorn	04	
Gemini.	05	
Leo	06	
Libra	07	
Pisces.	08	
Sagittarius	09	
Scorpio	10	
Taurus.	11	
Virgo	12	

15A. Have you ever heard of extra sensory perception -- ESP?

Yes	1	54/
No. . . . . . .(SKIP TO 16) . .	2	

B. *IF YES:* What is your view of ESP -- would you say you are sure it exists, think it probably exists, think it probably doesn't exist, or are you sure it doesn't exist?

Sure it exists.	1	55/
Think it probably exists. . . .	2	
Think it probably doesn't exist . . . .(SKIP TO E). . .	3	
Sure it doesn't exist . . . .(SKIP TO E). . .	4	

C. Have you ever had an experience which you thought might be an example of extra sensory perception?

Yes	1	56/
No. . . . . . .(SKIP TO E). . .	2	

D.   Could you briefly describe your experience?

15E.   Do you know anyone (else) who claims to be, or whom you feel to be capable of extra sensory perception?

Yes 1   57/

No. . . . . . .(SKIP TO 16) . . 2

F.   We are interested in making a special study of people who have had ESP experiences. If you think that the person or people you know would be interested in being included in such a study, please give me their names and addresses.

16.   One of the beliefs of spiritualism is that it is possible to communicate with the dead. Do you think it is definitely possible, probably possible, probably not possible, or definitely not possible to communicate with the dead?

Definitely possible 1   58/

Probably possible 2

Probably not possible 3

Definitely not possible 4

17. | Booklet Page 5 | As I read each of the statements to you, please tell me whether you strongly agree, somewhat agree, somewhat disagree, or strongly disagree. You can just give me the number of your answer.

	Strongly Agree	Somewhat Agree	Somewhat Disagree	Strongly Disagree	Can't say	
Most of life is decided for us rather than by us.	1	2	3	4	5	59/
Songs and stories tell us more about life than science does.	1	2	3	4	5	
If someone does not succeed in life, you can be pretty sure it's his own fault	1	2	3	4	5	
Some people are born lucky and others are born unlucky.	1	2	3	4	5	
A person's ideas and beliefs are greatly influenced by how much income he has	1	2	3	4	5	
If one works hard enough, he can do anything he wants to. .	1	2	3	4	5	
I am superstitious about a lot of little things.	1	2	3	4	5	

```
I believe forgotten
childhood experiences
have an effect on me. .     1        2        3       4        5

Whenever I fail, I have
no one to blame but
myself. . . . . . . .      1        2        3       4        5

It is good to live in
a fantasy world every
now and then. . . . .      1        2        3       4        5        68/
```

The next questions are about religious beliefs, activities and groups.

18. | Booklet | Which of these statements comes closest to expressing your
     | Page 6 | belief about God?

I don't believe in God . . . . (SKIP TO 22). 1   69/

I don't believe or disbelieve in God, I don't think
it is possible to know if there is a God . (SKIP TO 22). 2

I am uncertain but lean toward not believing in
God. . . . . (SKIP TO 22). 3

I am uncertain but lean toward believing in God. 4

I definitely believe in God. 5

I am uncomfortable about the word 'God' but I do
believe in something "more" or "beyond". (SKIP TO 20). . 6

None of the above expresses my views . . (SKIP TO 21). . 7

19. *IF "DEFINITELY BELIEVE IN GOD" OR "AM UNCERTAIN BUT LEAN TOWARD
    BELIEVING IN GOD":*

> A. Do you picture God as having a human form?
>
>   Yes . . . . . . (SKIP TO C) . . 1   70/
>
>   No. 2
>
> B. How do you picture God?
>
> C. Which of these two statements comes closest to your view of
>   God's influence on your life?
>
>   God has left each of us completely free to decide
>   our life 1   71/
>
>   Our lives are completely decided by God. 2
>
>   Other: *(SPECIFY)* _____ 3
>
> _____
>
> D. Do you feel that God influences history?
>
>   Yes 1   72/
>
>   No. 2
>
> E. Do you feel that God answers prayers?
>
>   Yes 1   73/
>
>   No. 2
>
>   *(SKIP TO 22)*   74/9

20. *IF "UNCOMFORTABLE ABOUT THE WORD 'GOD' BUT...":* If possible, please
    say what you think "something more" is like.

                    (SKIP TO 22)

21. *IF "NONE OF THE ABOVE...":* What do you believe about God?

                                            (___ _____ ___)
                                                  (1-4)

                                                        5/
            ASK EVERYONE   6-7/02

22. | *Booklet* | As I read each of these statements to you, please tell me
    | *Page 7* | whether you mostly agree or mostly disagree. First......

	Mostly agree	Mostly disagree	Undecided	
Man evolved from lower animals	1	2	3	8/
God created the first man and woman. .	1	2	3	9/
We do not know for sure how human life began	1	2	3	10/
The story of Adam and Eve tells important truths about life.	1	2	3	11/

23. | *Booklet* | Would you please read along with me and tell me which of
    | *Page 8* | the statements comes closest to your views on life after
    | | death? *READ ALL STATEMENTS.*

    I don't believe that there is a life after death 1   12/

    I am unsure whether or not there is life after death . . 2

    I believe that there must be something beyond death,
    but I have no idea what it may be like 3

    There is life after death, but no punishment 4

    There is life after death, with rewards for some
    people and punishment for others 5

    The notion of Reincarnation expresses my view of
    what happens to people when they die 6

    Other *(SPECIFY):* _____ 7

    _____

    _____

24A. Do you take part in the activities of any church, synagogue, or
     other religious group?

                    Yes 1   13/
                    No. . . . . . .(SKIP TO 25) . . 2

24B. <u>IF YES:</u> What is its name? *(PROBE FOR FULL NAME: e.g. Holy Name Episcopal Church of Oakland)*

C. | Booklet Page 9 | Using the answers on Page 9, how often, if at all, do you attend church or synagogue meetings?

Never 1   14/

Several times a year or less. . 2

About once a month. 3

Several times a month 4

About once a week 5

Several times a week. 6

Every day 7

25. | Booklet Page 9 | Using the answers on Page 9, how often, if at all, do you pray?

Never 1   15/

Several times a year or less. . 2

About once a month. 3

Several times a month 4

About once a week 5

Several times a week. 6

Every day 7

26A. | Booklet Page 10 | The next question is about meditation. Which of these statements on Page 10 best describes you?

I practice meditation using definite techniques such as sitting or breathing or thinking in special ways. . . 1   16/

I don't use any definite meditation techniques, but I do spend quiet times meditating about my life. . . . . (SKIP TO 27A). . . 2

I really don't do any kind of meditation . (SKIP TO 27A) 3

Other *(SPECIFY):* _____ 4

_____

IF "PRACTICE MEDITATION USING DEFINITE TECHNIQUES":

B. How often do you practice meditation -- almost every day, at least once a week, several times a month, or several times a year?

Almost every day. 1   17/

At least once a week. 2

Several times a month 3

Several times a year. 4

C. Do you usually do any of these things while meditating?

	Yes	No	
Try to clear your mind of all thoughts	1	2	18/
Try to communicate with God.	1	2	
Use a mantra	1	2	
Take drugs	1	2	
Use breathing techniques	1	2	
Try to tap into unlimited energy	1	2	23/

27A. | Booklet | One of the purposes of our study is to find out how
       | Page 11 | interested people are in new religious and semi-religious
groups that have appeared in the last few years. Please follow
along as I read the names of the groups listed here and use the
answers to tell me if you know nothing, know a little, or know a
lot about each one.

		PART A		
	Know Nothing	Know a Little	Know a lot	
a. Transcendental Meditation	1↓	2→	3→	24/
b. Hare Krishna.	1↓	2→	3→	25/
c. Scientology	1↓	2→	3→	
d. Zen	1↓	2→	3→	
e. Synanon	1↓	2→	3→	
f. Campus Crusade.	1↓	2→	3→	
g. Christian World Liberation Front. . . .	1↓	2→	3→	
h. Jews for Jesus.	1↓	2→	3→	
i. Children of God	1↓	2→	3→	
j. Yoga groups	1↓	2→	3→	
k. Satanism.	1↓	2→	3→	
l. Erhard Seminars Training (EST).	1↓	2→	3→	
m. Groups that speak in tongues.	1↓	2→	3→	36/

FOR R's WHO ANSWER 2 OR 3 TO PART A, ASK "B" AND "C".

B: Are you strongly attracted by the group, mildly attracted, turned
    off by the group, or have you no feelings either way?
C: Have you ever taken part in any of these groups?

	PART B		Nothing Either Way	PART C		
Strongly Attracted	Mildly Attracted	Turned Off		Yes	No	
a. . . . 1	2	3	4	1	2	37-38/
b. . . . 1	2	3	4	1	2	39-40/
c. . . . 1	2	3	4	1	2	41-42/
d. . . . 1	2	3	4	1	2	43-44/
e. . . . 1	2	3	4	1	2	45-46/
f. . . . 1	2	3	4	1	2	47-48/
g. . . . 1	2	3	4	1	2	49-50/
h. . . . 1	2	3	4	1	2	51-52/
i. . . . 1	2	3	4	1	2	53-54/
j. . . . 1	2	3	4	1	2	55-56/
k. . . . 1	2	3	4	1	2	57-58/
l. . . . 1	2	3	4	1	2	59-60/
m. . . . 1	2	3	4	1	2	61-62/

ASK EVERYONE

28A. Have you ever taken part in any other groups similar to these?

Yes 1   63/

No . . . .(SKIP TO 29) . . 2

B. *IF YES:* Which ones?

Next are several questions about experiences you may have had.

29A. Booklet Page 12   Please answer the next question by choosing one of the answers on Page 12. During your lifetime, have you ever had the feeling that you were in close contact with something holy or sacred?

No, and I really don't care whether I ever do . . . .(SKIP TO 30A). 1   64/

No, but I would like to. . . . .(SKIP TO 30A). 2

Yes, but it has not had a deep and lasting influence on my life . . . . . .(SKIP TO 30A). 3

Yes, and it has had a lasting influence on my life. . . . .(ASK B). 4

B. When was the last time you had such an experience -- within the last year, one to five years ago, six to ten years ago, or more than ten years ago?

Within the last year. 1   65/

One to five years ago 2

Six to ten years ago. 3

More than ten years ago 4

30A. Have you ever experienced the beauty of nature in a deeply moving
      way? Please choose one of the answers on Page 12.

No, and I really don't care whether I ever
do . . . . (SKIP TO 31A). 1   66/

No, but I would like to. . . (SKIP TO 31A). 2

Yes, but it has not had a deep and lasting
influence on my life . . . . (SKIP TO 31A). 3

Yes, and it has had a lasting influence on
my life. . . . . (ASK B). 4

   B. When was the last time you had such an experience -- within the last
       year, one to five years ago, six to ten years ago, or more than ten
       years ago?

Within the last year. 1   67/

One to five years ago 2

Six to ten years ago. 3

More than ten years ago . . . 4

31A. How about the feeling that you were in harmony with the universe, have
      you ever experienced that? Please choose one of the answers on Page 12.

No, and I really don't care whether I ever
do . . . . (SKIP TO 32A). 1   68/

No, but I would like to. . . (SKIP TO 32A). 2

Yes, but it has not had a deep and lasting
influence on my life . . . . (SKIP TO 32A). 3

Yes, and it has had a lasting influence on
my life. . . . . (ASK B). 4

   B. When was the last time you had such an experience -- within the last
       year, one to five years ago, six to ten years ago, or more than ten
       years ago?

Within the last year 1   69/

One to five years ago. 2

Six to ten years ago 3

More than ten years ago. . . . 4

32A. Have you ever experienced being 'high' on drugs? Use the answers on
      Page 12 again.

No, and I really don't care whether I ever
do . . . . (SKIP TO 33) 1   70/

No, but I would like to. . . (SKIP TO 33) 2

Yes, but it has not had a deep and lasting
influence on my life . . . . (SKIP TO 33) 3

Yes, and it has had a lasting influence on
my life. . . . . (ASK B, C, & D). 4

B. How many such experiences have you had -- one, several, or many?

One 1   71/

Several 2

Many. 3

C. When was the last time you had such an experience -- within the last
year, one to five years ago, six to ten years ago, or more than ten
years ago?

Within the last year. 1   72/

One to five years ago 2

Six to ten years ago. 3

More than ten years ago 4

D. All in all, how good or bad would you say your experience with drugs
has been? Would you say that it has been more good than bad or that
it has been more bad than good?

More good than bad. 1   73/

More bad than good. 2

$$(\underline{\quad} \ \frac{\quad}{(1-4)} \ \underline{\quad})$$

5/

6-7/03

33. | *Booklet* | Feeling lonely bothers people sometimes. Please use the
     | *Page 13* | answers provided on Page 13 to say whether loneliness is
     something that is bothering you or has ever bothered you. You can
     just give me the number of your answer if you wish.

It has been bothering me a lot lately 1   8/

It has been bothering me a little lately. 2

It has bothered me in the past, but it hasn't recently. 3

It has never bothered me. 4

34. Now, I'll read some other problems people have mentioned. Please
use the same answers to say whether each is something that is
bothering you or has ever bothered you.

	Bothered a lot lately	Bothered a little lately	Bothered in past, not now	Never bothered	
Money problems.	1	2	3	4	9/
Problems with your physical health	1	2	3	4	
Problems with your work or work plans. . . .	1	2	3	4	
Problems with your sex life.	1	2	3	4	
Wondering about the meaning and purpose of life	1	2	3	4	
The death of a loved one	1	2	3	4	14/

Next are some questions about your values and preferences.

35. Since one can't do everything in life, each person has to decide what is important and what is not so important. Please look at these cards *HAND 'VALUES' DECK TO RESPONDENT.*

A. I'd like you to sort the cards into four piles -- one for things that are of great importance to you, another for things of fair importance, another for those of little importance, and one for those of no importance at all to you. *GIVE FACE CARDS TO "R".*

B. *COLLECT 'NONE' PILE.* Now could you tell me which three seem most important of all to you? *RECORD BELOW.*

		Importance is:				
		Great	Fair	Little	None	
(1)	Having a lot of friends	1	2	3	4	15/
(2)	Living up to strict moral standards	1	2	3	4	
(3)	Having children	1	2	3	4	
(4)	Living close to nature.	1	2	3	4	
(5)	Having job security	1	2	3	4	
(6)	Having a lot of free time	1	2	3	4	
(7)	Becoming famous	1	2	3	4	
(8)	Having a beautiful home, a new car and other nice things	1	2	3	4	22/
(9)	Learning to be aware of your body .	1	2	3	4	
(10)	Spending a lot of time getting to know your inner self	1	2	3	4	
(11)	Having a high paying job.	1	2	3	4	
(12)	Following God's will.	1	2	3	4	
(13)	Helping solve social problems such as poverty and air pollution .	1	2	3	4	
(14)	Giving your time to help people who are in need	1	2	3	4	
(15)	Helping women to get equal rights .	1	2	3	4	
(16)	Working for major changes in our society	1	2	3	4	
(17)	Taking part in church or synagogue	1	2	3	4	31/

Three most important of all are: # /☐/ 32-33/

                                                                            # /☐/ 34-35/

COLLECT CARDS USING FACE CARDS TO KEEP THEM SORTED.   # /☐/ 36-37/
AFTER INTERVIEW RECORD ANSWERS IN SPACES ABOVE AND
SHUFFLE CARDS.

36.   In general, how do you feel about 'communes' in which a number of
      people live together and share the work -- do you dislike the whole
      idea, do you think communes are OK for others but not for you, or
      would you like to try living in a commune for a while?

                              Dislike the whole idea.   1   38/

                              OK for others, not for me . . .   2

                              Would like to try living in
                                a commune for a while   3

                              NOW LIVING IN A COMMUNE   4

The next questions deal with your feelings about our country and some of
the problems it faces.

37.   First, what things about our country do you think are most in need
      of change? *IF NECESSARY:* If you think of a number of things, please
      mention the three you are most concerned about.

38A. | *Booklet* | One of the problems in the country is the fact that so
      | *Page 14* | many people are still poor. On Page 14 are some different
      ideas people have used to explain why we have poverty in America.
      As I read each one, please say how much you agree or disagree by
      using the answers at the bottom of the page.

	Agree Strongly	Agree Somewhat	Disagree Somewhat	Disagree Strongly	Can't Say	
(1) The poor are poor because the wealthy and powerful keep them poor.	1	2	3	4	5	39/
(2) God gave people different abilities so that the work of the world will get done	1	2	3	4	5	
(3) The poor simply aren't willing to work hard.	1	2	3	4	5	
(4) Poor people are born without the talents to get ahead	1	2	3	4	5	
(5) The poor are poor because the American way of life doesn't give all people an equal chance	1	2	3	4	5	
(6) The poor don't teach their children how to get ahead	1	2	3	4	5	44/

B. *IF RESPONDENT STRONGLY AGREES WITH MORE THAN ONE OR IF STRONGLY
AGREES WITH NONE BUT AGREES SOMEWHAT WITH MORE THAN ONE, ASK:*
Of the reasons you said you (strongly) agreed with, which do you
think is the most important reason? *(READ TIED ITEMS)*

Most important reason is #____   45/

39. | Booklet | Which of the three statements here comes closest to your
     | Page 15 | view of what the country should do about poverty. Would
you say that....*READ EACH STATEMENT.*

Since the poor will always be with us, not much can
be done except through private charity   1   46/

The country could and should do a lot more to provide
jobs for poor people who want to work.   2

More jobs should be provided and the country should
also guarantee a minimum income for everyone   3

NONE OF THESE: What do you think should be done?. . . .   4

---

40. Would you say that you mostly favor, or mostly oppose each of the
following?

	Mostly Favor	Mostly Oppose	Undecided	
Do you mostly favor or oppose giving the police more power	1	2	3	47/
Do you mostly favor or oppose spending more money exploring outer space.	1	2	3	
How about new laws and taxes making it impossible for anyone to become extremely wealthy	1	2	3	
Legalizing the use of marijuana	1	2	3	
An unmarried couple living together	1	2	3	
More freedom for homosexuals.	1	2	3	52/

41. Americans are in some disagreement about how well our form of
government can handle the problems facing us. To deal with our
problems best, do you think we need a completely different form
of government, a major overhaul, only minor changes, or do you
think our form of government is fine as is?

Completely different system . .   1   53/

Major overhaul.   2

Minor changes   3

Fine as is.   4

42. How do you feel about the role science has played in the world --
do you think:

Science has done a lot more good than harm for the world.   1   54/

Science has done a lot of good but caused a lot of
harm along with it, or that.   2

Science has probably done more harm than good.   3

Next are some 'story-type' questions. In these questions you are faced with some difficult situations and asked to make a choice in each. As in real life, none of the choices may seem very good to you, but please try to say what you would do if you <u>had</u> to choose one. You may just read these questions to yourself and show your answer by circling the appropriate number.

TURN PAGE AND HAND SCHEDULE TO RESPONDENT.

43. Imagine two candidates, Smith and Jones, are running against each other for a seat in the state government. In the state there are a lot of black people, but only a few of them have been hired for state jobs.

    JONES says the state should make special efforts to hire blacks until they get their rightful share of jobs.

    SMITH says the state should pay no attention to color and hire people who are best fitted for the job whether they are black or white.

    You may not be completely happy with either Jones' or Smith's point of view, but they are the only choice you have in the voting booth. How would you vote? Jones or Smith?

Jones	1 55/
Smith	2

44. In another political race, Adams is running against Brown. Their state has been growing rapidly and experts say there will soon be a shortage of electrical power.

    ADAMS is in favor of building a new atomic plant and argues that it won't hurt the environment any.

    BROWN argues that we could do without a new power plant and that we should start conserving our natural resources.

    Which candidate would you vote for?

Adams	1 56/
Brown	2

45. Imagine now that there are two stores on the same street selling phonograph records.

    CASTLE RECORDS is a large chain store which is operated for profit and sells records for $3.

    PALACE RECORDS is owned by local citizens and whatever money that store makes is contributed to a local health clinic and other charities. Palace sells records for $3.57.

    If you were going to buy a record, which store do you think you would buy from? Castle Records or Palace Records?

Castle Records.	1 57/
Palace Records.	2

GO ON TO NEXT PAGE

46. Jim Smith was a talented young scientist doing research on cancer;
    then he moved away to the Alaskan wilderness with some of his friends
    and made plans to spend his life there living off the land. Without
    knowing anything else about him, do you think that Jim is someone you
    would probably admire or probably would not admire?

    Probably would admire him . . . 1   58/

    Probably would not admire him . 2

47. Betty Wilson thinks of herself as a 'revolutionary.' She is working
    to overthrow the U.S. government, but she has not broken any laws.
    Which of these answers best expresses your feelings about her?

    She should be arrested immediately 1   59/

    The FBI should tap her telephone to get evidence
    against her 2

    The police should keep their eye on her. 3

    She should be treated like anyone else since she
    hasn't broken any laws. 4

    Personally, I'm in favor of what she's trying to
    do, even if she does break a few laws 5

    None of these. 6

48. Although it's hard to say what you will actually do in certain
    situations, do the following things sound like something you
    <u>feel you might do</u> or something you <u>definitely wouldn't do</u>?

	Feel you might do	Definitely wouldn't do	Honestly don't know	
Tell somebody off if they tried to crowd in front of you while waiting in line.	1	2	3	60/
Say you were sick when you really weren't in order to get an extra day off.	1	2	3	
Approve of a parent slapping his child for getting mad and screaming.	1	2	3	
Admire someone who was trying to stop Communism from spreading in the U.S..	1	2	3	
Buy a radio or TV from someone who had stolen it and was selling it cheap	1	2	3	
Try out some herbs that were said to make you feel healthier	1	2	3	65/

PLEASE HAND QUESTIONNAIRE BACK TO INTERVIEWER NOW.   66/9

Serial # (___ ___ ___ ___)
(1-4)

5/

6-7/04

Next are some questions about your interests and your background.

49. | Booklet | Please use the answers provided on Page 16 to say how much
    | Page 16 | you like to do each of the following things. Just tell me
                   the number.

	A lot	Some	A little	Not at all	Have never done this	
Read books or magazines.	1	2	3	4	5	8/
Go to concerts, plays or other cultural events.	1	2	3	4	5	
Watch sports events.	1	2	3	4	5	
Keep up to date on national news .	1	2	3	4	5	
Work on hobbies.	1	2 .	3	4	5	
Go to movies	1	2	3	4	5	
Smoke dope	1	2	3	4	5	14/

50.   About how many hours a week do you usually spend watching TV?   *CHECK
      THE ANSWER THAT COMES CLOSEST.*

                                        1 to 5 hours. 1   15/
                                        6 to 10 hours 2
                                        11 to 15 hours. 3
                                        16 to 20 hours. 4
                                        21 to 30 hours. 5
                                        More than 30 hours. 6
                                        Rarely or never 7

51A. Have you ever tried organic foods?

                                        Yes 1   16/
                                        No. . . . . . .(SKIP TO 52A). . 2

  B. *IF YES:* Are organic foods a major part of your diet, a minor part,
               or not a regular part?

                                        Major part. 1   17/
                                        Minor part. 2
                                        Not a regular part. 3

52A. Have you ever taken part in an encounter group or similar kind of
      training, such as sensory awareness, sensitivity training, a "T"
      group, or growth group?

                                        Yes 1   18/
                                        No. . . . . . .(SKIP TO 53) . . 2

B. *IF YES:* What kind of groups were they? *OBTAIN BRIEF DESCRIPTION. IF SEVERAL, PROBE FOR THREE MOST IMPORTANT.*

First group: _____

_____

Second group: _____

_____

Third group: _____

_____

C. How many times have you taken part -- once, several times, or many times?

Once. 1   19/

Several times 2

Many times. 3

D. How helpful or harmful do you feel it has been for you -- very helpful, slightly helpful, slightly harmful, or very harmful?

Very helpful. 1   20/

Slightly helpful. 2

Slightly harmful. 3

Very harmful. 4

E. We are doing a special study of people who have been in encounter groups. Would you be interested in talking further with someone about your experiences?

Yes 1   21/

No. 2

ASK EVERYONE

---

53. How many friends do you have at the present time that you feel really close to?

RECORD NUMBER HERE. . . . . (___)   22/
IF MORE THAN 7, WRITE 7

54. The next question is another one that you may fill out yourself.
TURN THE PAGE AND HAND SCHEDULE TO RESPONDENT.

This question concerns various talents and characteristics. Please indicate whether you think you have a lot, a fair amount, only a little, or none at all by circling the appropriate number next to each item.

	A lot	Fair amount	Only a Little	None at all	
Leadership ability	1	2	3	4	23/
Musical ability.	1	2	3	4	
Artistic ability	1	2	3	4	
Ability to make friends easily	1	2	3	4	
Ability to organize things well. . . .	1	2	3	4	
Ability to feel things deeply. ·	1	2	3	4	
Ability to make things with your hands	1	2	3	4	
Self confidence.	1	2	3	4	
Intelligence	1	2	3	4	
The gift of gab.	1	2	3	4	
Good looks	1	2	3	4	
Creativity	1	2	3	4	34/

PLEASE HAND QUESTIONNAIRE BACK TO INTERVIEWER NOW.

55. | Booklet Page 17 | Suppose that the line drawn on Page 17 shows the range of political opinion in our country. Where would you say you stand politically on most issues?

Radical		Liberal		Moderate		Conservative		Very Conservative	
X------X------X------X------X------X------X------X------X									
1	2	3	4	5	6	7	8	9	35-36/

56. Have you ever been involved in any of these political activities?

	Yes	No	
Writing a letter to a public official.	1	2	37/
Attending political meetings, speeches or rallies. . . .	1	2	38/
Taking part in demonstrations or marches, not just watching.	1	2	39/

57. Are you currently attending school either full time or part time?

Full time 1   40/
Part time 2
Not attending 3

58A. What was the last year of regular school you attended?

Some grade school (0-7). . . . . . (SKIP TO 59A) 1   41/

Finished grade school (8). . . . . (SKIP TO 59A) 2

Some high school (1-3) . . . . . . (SKIP TO 59A) 3

Finished high school (4) . . . . . (SKIP TO 59A) 4

Some college (1-3) . . . . (SKIP TO C) 5

Finished college (4) 6

Attended graduate school or professional
school after college (5+). 7

B. How would you rank the college from which you graduated -- above
average, about average, or below average?

Above average 1   42/

About average 2

Below average 3

C. | Booklet | Which one of these comes closest to your college major?
   | Page 18 | *(IF MORE THAN ONE MAJOR, CHECK ONE CONSIDERED MOST IMPORTANT.)*

Agriculture	01	Library Science	26 43-44/
Anthropology.	02	Linguistics	27
Architecture.	03	Mathematics	28
Art	04	Military Science.	29
Astronomy	05	Music	30
Biology	06	Nursing	31
Botany.	07	Nutrition	32
Business Administration . . .	08	Philosophy.	33
Chemistry	09	Physics	34
Computer Science.	10	Physiology.	35
Communication	11	Political Science	36
Dramatic Art.	12	Pre-Medicine.	37
Economics	13	Psychology.	38
Education	14	Public Health	39
Engineering	15	Religion.	40
English	16	Social work	41
Environmental Design.	17	Sociology	42
Fine Arts	18	Statistics.	43
Foreign Language.	19	Zoology	44
Forestry.	20	Other	45
Genetics.	21		
Geography	22	*SPECIFY:* _____	
History	23		
Humanities.	24	_____	
Journalism.	25		

ASK EVERYONE

59A. Do you plan to take any further formal education?

Yes 1   45/

No. . . . . . .(SKIP TO 60A). . 2

B. _IF YES:_ How much formal education do you expect to end up having?
(*MARK CLOSEST ANSWER*)

Some grade school (0-7) 1   46/

Finish grade school (8) 2

Some high school (1-3). 3

Finish high school (4). 4

Some college (1-3). 5

Finish college (4). 6

Attend graduate school or
professional school after
college (5+). 7

60A. Are you now married, widowed, separated, divorced, or never married?

Married 1   47/

Widowed 2

Separated 3

Divorced. 4

Never married . . (SKIP TO 61A) 5

B. _IF MARRIED, WIDOWED, SEPARATED, OR DIVORCED, ASK:_ How many years
has it been since you were (last) married (widowed, separated,
divorced)?

Years: (_ _ _)   48-49/

61A. Are you presently working full time, working part time, looking for
work, (going to school), (keeping house), or something else? *CODE
FIRST APPEARING ITEM.*

Working full time. 1   50/

Working part time. 2

Looking for work or laid off . . . (SKIP TO 62). 3

Retired. . . . . (SKIP TO 62). 4

Going to school, . .
    school vacation   5
                          } SKIP TO 63A {
Unable to work . . .   IF MARRIED;   6
                              IF NOT
Keeping house. . . .   SKIP TO 65   7

Something else 8

    SPECIFY: _____

B. How long have you been employed at your present job?

Less than six months. 1   51/

Six months to one year. 2

Two to three years. 3

Four to five years. 4

More than five years. 5

62. What is (was) your (last) occupation? *WRITE SPECIFIC DESCRIPTION AND MARK CLOSEST CATEGORY BELOW.*

PROFESSIONAL, TECHNICAL AND SIMILAR WORKERS: teachers, editors, dentists, clergymen, professors, instructors, doctors, lawyers, nurses, architects, librarians, social workers, accountants, funeral directors, photographers, dancers, optometrists, aviators, surveyors, chiropractors, athletes, etc. 01   52-53/

PROPRIETORS, MANAGERS AND OFFICIALS: public officials, credit managers, buyers, officers, floor managers, merchants, railroad conductors, etc. 02

SALES WORKERS: salesmen, insurance and real estate agents and brokers, stock and bond salesmen, newsboys, demonstrators, etc. 03

CLERICAL AND RELATED WORKERS: Bookkeepers, stenographers, cashiers, mail carriers, shipping clerks, secretaries, ticket agents, telephone operators, office machine operators, etc. 04

CRAFTSMEN, FOREMEN AND RELATED WORKERS: Tinsmiths, bakers, masons, carpenters, shoemakers, electricians, inspectors, cement workers, jewelers, machinists, painters, etc. 05

OPERATIVES AND RELATED WORKERS: Chauffers, delivery men, laundry workers, apprentices, meat cutters, semi-skilled and unskilled employees in manufacturing establishments (bakers, tobacco, textiles, etc.), wholesale and retail workers, mine laborers, motormen, etc. 06

SERVICE WORKERS, EXCEPT PRIVATE HOUSEHOLD WORKERS: Firemen, policemen, barbers, beauticians, janitors, porters, waiters, ushers, practical nurses, etc. 07

LABORERS: Garage laborers, car washers, stevedores, lumbermen, teamsters, gardeners, unskilled helpers in construction, manufacturing, etc. 08

PRIVATE HOUSEHOLD WORKERS: Servants, launderers, employed housekeepers, etc. 09

FARMERS, FARM MANAGERS 10

ARMED FORCES 11

OTHER: What? _____ . 12

> **MARRIED MAN OR WOMAN**

63A. Is your (husband/wife) presently working full time, working part time, looking for work, (going to school), (keeping house), or something else? *CODE FIRST APPEARING ITEM.*

         Working full time. 1   54/

         Working part time. 2

         Looking for work or laid off . . . (SKIP TO 64). 3

         Retired. . . . . (SKIP TO 64). 4

         Going to school, school vacation . (SKIP TO 65). 5

         Unable to work . . . . (SKIP TO 65). 6

         Keeping house. . . . . (SKIP TO 65). 7

         Something else . . . . (SKIP TO 65). 8

         SPECIFY: _____

63B. How long has (he/she) been employed at (his/her) present job?

Less than six months. 1   55/

Six months to one year. 2

Two to three years. 3

Four to five years. 4

More than five years. 5

64. What is (was) his/her (last) occupation? *WRITE SPECIFIC DESCRIPTION AND MARK CLOSEST CATEGORY BELOW.*

_____

_____

PROFESSIONAL, TECHNICAL AND SIMILAR WORKERS: Teachers, editors, dentists, clergymen, professors, instructors, doctors, lawyers, nurses, architects, librarians, social workers, accountants, funeral directors, photographers, dancers, optometrists, aviators, surveyors, chiropractors, athletes, etc.. 01   56-57/

PROPRIETORS, MANAGERS AND OFFICIALS: public officials, credit managers, buyers, officers, floor managers, merchants, railroad conductors, etc. 02

SALES WORKERS: salesmen, insurance and real estate agents and brokers, stock and bond salesmen, newsboys, demonstrators, etc. 03

CLERICAL AND RELATED WORKERS: Bookkeepers, stenographers, cashiers, mail carriers, shipping clerks, secretaries, ticket agents, telephone operators, office machine operators, etc. 04

CRAFTSMEN, FOREMEN AND RELATED WORKERS: Tinsmiths, bakers, masons, carpenters, shoemakers, electricians, inspectors, cement workers, jewelers, machinists, painters, etc.. 05

OPERATIVES AND RELATED WORKERS: Chauffers, delivery men, laundry workers, apprentices, meat cutters, semi-skilled and unskilled employees in manufacturing establishments (bakers, tobacco, textiles, etc.), wholesale and retail workers, mine laborers, motormen, etc.. 06

SERVICE WORKERS, EXCEPT PRIVATE HOUSEHOLD WORKERS: Firemen, policemen, barbers, beauticians, janitors, porters, waiters, ushers, practical nurses, etc.. 07

LABORERS: Garage laborers, car washers, stevedores, lumbermen, teamsters, gardeners, unskilled helpers in construction, manufacturing, etc. 08

PRIVATE HOUSEHOLD WORKERS: Servants, launderers, employed housekeepers, etc.. 09

FARMERS, FARM MANAGERS. 10

ARMED FORCES. 11

OTHER: What? _____ 12

$\boxed{\text{ASK EVERYONE}}$

65. $\boxed{\begin{array}{c}\textit{Booklet}\\\textit{Page 19}\end{array}}$ Which figure on Page 19 comes closest to your present yearly family income? (Include spouse's income, if any; or, if still living with parents, include only your own income.) Just give me the number.

Less than $3,000.	01	58-59/
Between $3,000 and $5,000 . . .	02	
Between $5,000 and $7,500 . . .	03	
Between $7,500 and $10,000. . .	04	
Between $10,000 and $15,000 . .	05	
Between $15,000 and $20,000 . .	06	
Between $20,000 and $25,000 . .	07	
Between $25,000 and $30,000 . .	08	
Between $30,000 and $40,000 . .	09	
More than $40,000	10	

66. How many children, if any, do you have? *(INCLUDE NATURAL, ADOPTED AND STEPCHILDREN).*

(___ ___)   60-61/

67. *IF ANY CHILDREN:* What is the age of your oldest child?

Years (___ ___)   62-63/

68. How often within the past two years have you changed addresses? *(MARK CLOSEST ANSWER.)*

None.	1	64/
Once.	2	
Twice	3	
Three times	4	
Four times.	5	
Five times or more.	6	

69. How often did you attend church or synagogue most of the time up to age 15 -- nearly every week, approximately once a month, several times a year, or hardly ever?

Nearly every week	1	65/
Approximately once a month. . .	2	
Several times a year.	3	
Hardly ever	4	
Don't remember.	5	

70. Were you raised on a farm, in a small town, or in a city (most of the time up to age 15)?

On a farm	1	66/
Small town.	2	
City.	3	

67/9

$$(\underline{} \; \frac{}{(1-4)} \; \underline{})$$

5/

6-7/05

71. From which country or countries did most of your ancestors come?

	Item mentioned	Item not mentioned	
Africa	1	2	8/
China (Hong Kong).	1	2	
England.	1	2	
France	1	2	
Germany.	1	2	
Ireland.	1	2	
Italy.	1	2	
Japan.	1	2	
Mexico	1	2	
Poland	1	2	
Russia	1	2	
Scandanavian Countries	1	2	
Scotland	1	2	
Other *SPECIFY:* _____	1	2	21/

72A. | Booklet Page 20 | On Page 20, which of the descriptions best expresses your present religious preference? *CODE IN COLUMN 1 BELOW.*

  B. *IF PROTESTANT:* Which denomination is that? *CODE IN COLUMN 1 ON NEXT PAGE.*

73A. Which best describes your <u>mother's</u> religious preference? (Most of the time while you were growing up) *CODE IN COLUMN 2 BELOW.*

  B. *IF MOTHER IS PROTESTANT:* What denomination did she belong to? *CODE IN COLUMN 2 ON NEXT PAGE.*

74A. Which best describes your <u>father's</u> religious preference? (Most of the time while you were growing up? *CODE IN COLUMN 3 BELOW.*

  B. *IF FATHER IS PROTESTANT:* What denomination did he belong to? *CODE IN COLUMN 3 ON NEXT PAGE.*

	1 Resp.	2 Mother	3 Father
No religious beliefs	01	01	01
Agnostic	02	02	02
Atheist.	03	03	03
Humanist	04	04	04
Protestant . . . . (ASK B)	05	05	05
Roman Catholic	06	06	06

```
Jewish . . . . . . . . . . . . . . . . . . . . .    07      07      07

Eastern Orthodox . . . . . . . . . . . . . . . .    08      08      08

Mormon . . . . . . . . . . . . . . . . . . . . .    09      09      09

Buddhist: (FOR R:  Which branch?) . . . . . . . .   10      10      10
_____

Hindu: (FOR R:  Which branch?) . . . . . . . . .    11      11      11
_____

Islam:  (FOR R:  Which branch?) . . . . . . . . .   12      12      12
_____

Mysticism:  (FOR R:  What kind?) . . . . . . . .    13      13      13
_____

Other:  (FOR R:  SPECIFY) . . . . . . . . . . .     14      14      14
_____

Don't know . . . . . . . . . . . . . . . . . . .    15      15      15

                                        22-23/  24-25/  26-27/
```

ANSWER CATEGORIES FOR PROTESTANTS

	1 Resp.	2 Mother	3 Father
Baptist			
American Baptist	01	01	01
Southern Baptist	02	02	02
Other Baptist.	03	03	03
Christian Church (Disciples of Christ)	04	04	04
Community Churches	05	05	05
Episcopalian (except with modifiers)	06	06	06
Lutheran			
American Lutheran Church	07	07	07
Lutheran Church of America	08	08	08
Missouri Synod Lutheran.	09	09	09
Other Lutheran	10	10	10
Methodist (except with modifiers).	11	11	11
Presbyterian			
Presbyterian U.S..	12	12	12
United Presbyterian.	13	13	13
Other Presbyterian	14	14	14
Protestant Sects (e.g. Nazarene, Holiness, Pentacostal, Assembly of God, Church of Christ, Salvation Army, Plymouth Brethren, 7th Day Adventist, etc.).	15	15	15
Quakers/Friends.	16	16	16
Unitarian-Universalist	17	17	17

United Church of Christ

Congregational (originally).	18	18	18
Evangelical & Reformed (originally). .	19	19	19
Don't know which	20	20	20

Protestant unspecified 21   21   21

Other Protestant 22   22   22

       SPECIFY: _____

       28-29/ 30-31/ 32-33/

75. How much formal education did your mother have? *MARK NEAREST ANSWER.*

    Some grade school 1   34/

    Finished grade school 2

    Some high school. 3

    Finished high school. 4

    Some college. 5

    Finished college. 6

    Attended graduate school or
    professional school after
    college 7

    Don't know. 8

76. How much formal education did your father have? *MARK NEAREST ANSWER.*

    Some grade school 1   35/

    Finished grade school 2

    Some high school. 3

    Finished high school. 4

    Some college. 5

    Finished college. 6

    Attended graduate school or
    professional school after
    college 7

    Don't know. 8

77. | Booklet Page 21 | What was your parents' political position most of the time while you were growing up?

MOTHER:

							Very
Radical		Liberal		Moderate	Conservative		Conservative

X------X------X------X------X------X------X------X------X
1   2   3   4   5   6   7   8   9   36-37/

          Don't know ☐

FATHER:

							Very
Radical		Liberal		Moderate	Conservative		Conservative

X------X------X------X------X------X------X------X------X
1   2   3   4   5   6   7   8   9   38-39/

          Don't know ☐

78. Are your (natural) mother and father still living?

Both parents living	1	40/
Mother deceased	2	
Father deceased	3	
Both parents deceased	4	

79. *IF MOTHER LIVING:* All things considered, how close is your relationship with your mother now -- Quite close, pretty close, not very close, or not close at all?

Quite close	1	41/
Pretty close.	2	
Not very close.	3	
Not close at all.	4	

80. *IF FATHER LIVING:* Is your relationship with your father quite close, pretty close, not very close, or not close at all?

Quite close	1	42/
Pretty close.	2	
Not very close.	3	
Not close at all.	4	

81. What was your date of birth?

MONTH: 1 2 3 4 5 6 7 8 9 10 11 12   43-44/

DAY: 1 2 3 4 5 6 7 8 9 10 11 12   45-46/

        13 14 15 16 17 18 19 20 21 22 23 24

        25 26 27 28 29 30 31

YEAR: Year: (_1_ ___ ___ ___)   47-49/

82. Is there a telephone in this (house/apartment)?

Yes . . . .(SKIP TO b). .	1	50/
No. . . . .(ASK a). . . .	2	

a. *IF NO PHONE IN HOUSE/APARTMENT:* Is there a telephone (in this building) on which you can be called?

Yes . . . .(ASK b). . . .	1	51/
No. . . . .(SKIP TO 83) .	2	

b. *IF CAN BE REACHED ON ANY PHONE:* May I have the number?

___ ___ ___ - ___ ___ ___ ___

83. Finally, we've covered many topics in this interview, but we often find we haven't covered important things some people want to talk about. Is there anything you'd like to add that wasn't covered or do you have any suggestions of things we should add or omit next time?

☐ Nothing to add

PROBE: Any other suggestions?

> ### DO NOT ASK -- INTERVIEWER OBSERVATIONS

1. Respondent's sex: Female. 1   52/

   Male. 2

2. Respondent's ethnicity: White or Anglo. 1   53/

   Mexican-American. 2

   Other Spanish-American. 3

   Black 4

   Chinese, Japanese, Korean . . . 5

   Other: *(SPECIFY:* _____ 6

   _____ *)*

3. What language was the interview conducted in?

   English 1   54/

   Spanish 2

   Other: *(SPECIFY:* _____ 3

   _____ *)*

4. Did the respondent have any difficulty <u>hearing</u> the questions?

   Yes, great difficulty 1   55/

   Yes, some difficulty. 2

   No, none at all 3

5. Did the respondent have any difficulty <u>reading</u> the booklet or cards?

   Yes, could not or did not read at all. 1   56/

   Yes, read with great difficulty. 2

   Yes, read with some difficulty 3

   No, none at all. 4

6. Did the respondent have any difficulty <u>understanding</u> the questions?

   Yes, great difficulty 1   57/

   Yes, some difficulty. 2

   No, none at all 3

> DO NOT ASK -- INTERVIEWER OBSERVATIONS

7. What was the respondent's initial attitude about being interviewed?

Very interested or enthusiastic .	1	58/
Somewhat interested	2	
Indifferent	3	
Somewhat reluctant.	4	
Very reluctant.	5	

8. What was the respondent's attitude during the interview?

Friendly and eager, volunteered information.	1	59/
Cooperative but not particularly eager	2	
Indifferent or bored	3	
Often irritated or hostile -- seemed anxious to get interview over with.	4	

9. At what points of the interview did the respondent seem irritated, bored or less interested. Identify problem areas by question or page numbers.

(___) No problems
at any point

Problems with: _____

_____

_____

10A. Was anyone else present during the interview?

Yes, for most of the interview . . . (ANSWER b).	1	60/
Yes, for some of the interview . . . (ANSWER c).	2	
Yes, but only for a minute or two. . (SKIP TO 11).	3	
No, not at any time. . . . . (SKIP TO 11).	4	

B. *IF OTHERS PRESENT FOR MORE THAN A MINUTE OR TWO:* Who else was present?

	Yes	No or DNA	
Husband or wife.	1	2	61/
Other adult household member (18+)	1	2	
Teenager (13 to 18).	1	2	
Child or infant (under 13)	1	2	
Friend, visitor, other *(SPECIFY:* _____)	1	2	65/

11. Did the respondent have any obvious physical disabilities or impairments, such as loss of limb, paralysis, facial disfigurement, serious speech problems, palsy, or the like?

No.	1	66/
Yes	2	

```
DO NOT ASK -- INTERVIEWER OBSERVATIONS
```

12. How tall was the respondent?

Unusually tall. 1   67/

Taller than average 2

About average 3

Shorter than average. 4

Unusually short 5

13. How did the respondent's weight appear compared with normal for his or her height and age?

Very much overweight. 1   68/

Somewhat overweight 2

About right for age and height. 3

Somewhat underweight. 4

Very much underweight 5

14. How would you rate the respondent's physical attractiveness compared to others of his or her age?

Far above average (striking). . 1   69/

Somewhat above average. 2

About average 3

Somewhat below average. 4

Far below average 5

15. How would you rate the respondent's IQ?

Far above average 1   70/

Somewhat above average. 2

About average 3

Somewhat below average. 4

Far below average 5

16. Other comment about interview or respondent -- Please write out below.

EDITORS' COMMENTS
---

1. On the open-ended questions about meaning, what kind of answers did the respondent give?

    Detailed and interesting. . . . 1   71/

    Detailed but not especially interesting 2

    Didn't have much to say 3

    Didn't answer 4

2. Are there any interesting comments written in?

    Yes 1   72/

    No. 2

                                         73/9

NAME INDEX

SUBJECT INDEX

Affluence, 203–204
Alienation, 204. *See also* Political disenchantment
Atheism. *See* Nonreligion

Belief in God: decline in, 84; in Bay Area, 85–86. *See also* Theism
Body awareness, 53

Campus Crusade for Christ, 34, 35, 36
Capitalism, 204–205
Children of God, 34, 35, 36
Christian World Liberation Front (CWLF), 34, 35, 36
Churches: losing influence, 38, 41; attendance, 39, 40, 41n; attendance by age, 39; attendance by education levels, 39–40; membership, 39n; construction of new buildings, 40; interest in, 40; interdenominational switching, 83–84; and new religions, 201
Cognitive sophistication: and meaning systems, 165–168; and social experimentation, 179–184
Cohabitation. *See* Marriage, trial marriage
Commercialization, 205–207
Communes, 24, 43–44, 197, 209, 210
Community, 212
Consciousness, 60–65; definition of, 60. *See also* Reality construction
Counter-Culture, 1, 11; interpretations of, 12; types of experimentation, 12. *See also* Social experimentation
Cultural change, 3, 190–191, 195–196; direction of, 171–172; rate of, 172. *See also* Diversification
Cultural pluralism, 217, 219

Demonstrations: among students, 13–15; in Bay Area, 14–15; among Berke-

ley students, 15–16; attitudes of public toward, 17–18
Deviance, 202–203
Diversification: and institutional differentiation, 197–198; and pluralism, 197n; in religion, 198; and creativity, 200–201; and disintegration, 201; cultural legitimacy of, 202; and the economy, 204–205. *See also* Social order
Drug use: marijuana, 50; LSD, 50; legalization, 50–51; in Bay Area, 51; in California, 51n

Ecology, 55
Economic experimentation. *See* Social experimentation
Encounter groups, 51–53, 209, 210
Erhard Seminars Training (EST), 52, 53
Everyday reality: here and now, 65–66; time, 66; space, 66; pragmatic concerns, 66–67; routine, 67; spheres of relevance, 67–68; boundaries, 68; efficiency, 68; mystery excluded, 69; and ultimacy, 69; and meaning, 70

Family styles. *See* Communes; Marriage; Social experimentation
Festivals of misrule, 208, 209–210

Glossalalia. *See* Speaking in tongues

Happy-Healthy-Holy Organization (3HO), 31, 211
Hare Krishna, 32, 33, 207, 211
Homosexuality, 45–46, 219
Human potential movement, 52. *See also* Encounter groups

Individualism: defined, 4, 98; origins, 98; and laws of nature, 100–101; im-

307

Southern Methodist Univ.   br
HN 79.C22S338
The consciousness reformation /

3 2177 00912 1029

DATE DUE

AP 2 6